Gladstone, Gordon and the Sudan Wars

GLADSTONE, GORDON AND THE SUDAN WARS

The bat   tion in

Fergus Nicoll

Pen & Sword
MILITARY

First published in Great Britain in 2013 by
Pen & Sword Military
an imprint of
Pen & Sword Books Ltd
47 Church Street
Barnsley
South Yorkshire
S70 2AS

ISBN 978 1 78159 182 6

A CIP catalogue record for this book is available from the British Library

Typeset in Palatino and Gentium by
Phoenix Typesetting, Auldgirth, Dumfriesshire

Printed and bound in England by
CPI Group (UK) Ltd, Croydon, CR0 4YY

Pen & Sword Books Ltd incorporates the Imprints of Pen & Sword Aviation,
Pen & Sword Maritime, Pen & Sword Military, Wharncliffe Local History, Pen
and Sword Select, Pen and Sword Military Classics, Leo Cooper, Remember
When, Seaforth Publishing and Frontline Publishing.

For a complete list of Pen & Sword titles please contact
PEN & SWORD BOOKS LIMITED
47 Church Street, Barnsley, South Yorkshire, S70 2AS, England
E-mail: enquiries@pen-and-sword.co.uk
Website: www.pen-and-sword.co.uk

Contents

List of Illustrations

Author's Note

This book had its origins in my research for a PhD in the history faculty at the University of Reading. It develops what I have felt to be 'missing links' in my earlier work on Sudan during the nineteenth century, inasmuch as I have focused on the Sudanese side of the conflict rather than the ideological, political and military debates within the British establishment over the morality and practicality of intervention in Africa. Parts of my Introduction and what forms Chapter 8 appeared in the *Journal of Imperial and Commonwealth History*, while other parts of Chapter 8 were published in *Sudan Studies*, the journal of the Sudan Studies Society of the United Kingdom. I am grateful to the editors of both for their permission to reproduce these sections.

For Sudanese and Egyptian names, in an attempt at clarity and consistency, I transliterate as precisely as possible from the Arabic. Thus the name of the Mahdī is given as Muḥammad Aḥmad rather than Mahomet Achmet, for example, or ʿUthmān Diqna instead of Osman Digna. This applies to place names too: al-ʿUbeiḍ not El Obeid; Sawākīn not Suakin, let alone the contemporary 'Suakim'; and Wādī-Ḥalfāʾ instead of Wady Halfa or any of its many variants. In a few, more widely recognised cases, not least because so many crop up so frequently in news coverage of today's conflicts in Sudan, I have allowed non-academic convention to prevail. Thus, for example, I use Berber not 'Barbar', Darfur not 'Dār-Fūr', Dongola not 'al-Danqalā', Khartoum not 'al-Kharṭūm', Kordofan not 'Kurdufān' and Omdurman not 'Umm-Durmān'.

In many of the primary, hand-written sources, emphasised words are frequently underlined. This has been rendered here in italics. Particularly strong emotions, especially in the correspondence and journals of both General Gordon and Queen Victoria, are conveyed in double or even triple underlining. These I have represented in capitals and underlined capitals respectively. Thus, for example, the monarch's third-person injunction to Gladstone: 'The Queen *trusts* Lord Wolseley's plan WILL be considered, and our *whole position remembered*'.

Acknowledgements

I would like to thank the following for their assistance in the completion of this book: Rashīda ʿAbd-al-Karīm, Dr Jonathan Bell, Prof. John Darwin, Rupert Harding, Prof. Yūsuf Fāḍl Ḥassan, Roger Hearing, Jane Hogan, Prof. Richard Hoyle, Walīd Khalafallah, Rabāḥ al-Sādiq al-Mahdī, Kamāl ʿAbd-al-Karīm Mīrghanī, Jaqueline Mitchell, Prof. Philip Murphy, Dr Feisal Muḥammad Mūsa, Flora Nicoll, James Nicoll, Dr Kate Nicoll, Qāsim ʿUthmān Nūr, ʿUthmān Jaʿfar al-Nuṣairi, George Pagoulatos, Thanassis Pagoulatos, Selma al-Rāyah, Dr David Stack, Prof. Peter Woodward and ʿAbbās al-Zein.

Dramatis Personae

British

Ellis Ashmead-Bartlett	Conservative MP
Sir Samuel Baker	Nile explorer; interventionist agitator
Gen. Valentine Baker	Commandant of Police in Cairo
Sir Evelyn Baring*	British Agent and Consul-General in Cairo
Wilfrid Scawen Blunt	Poet and anti-interventionist agitator
Demetrius Boulger	Writer; friend of Gordon's
Capt. John Brocklehurst	Household Cavalry officer; friend of Gordon's
Col. William Butler	Officer in command of Wolseley's riverboats
Duke of Cambridge	Commander-in-Chief of the British Army
Lord Carlingford	Lord President of the Council
Joseph Chamberlain	President of the Board of Trade
Hugh Childers	Chancellor of the Exchequer
Lord Randolph Churchill	Conservative MP
Acting Maj.-Gen. Sir Andrew Clarke	Inspector-General of Fortifications
Lt.-Col. Henry de Coëtlogon	Acting Governor-General of Sudan
Lord Derby	Colonial Secretary
Sir Charles Dilke	President of the Local Government Board
John Dodson**	Chancellor of the Duchy of Lancaster
Lord Dufferin	Special Commissioner in Cairo

* Later Lord Cromer
** Later Lord Monk Bretton.

Lord Fitzmaurice	Under-Secretary at the Foreign Office
William Gladstone	Prime Minister
Maj.-Gen. Charles Gordon	Governor-General of Sudan; Gladstone's agent
Sir Henry Gordon	Gordon's brother and executor
Gen. Gerald Graham	Commander of British forces in Red Sea Hills
Lord Granville	Foreign Secretary
Lt.-Col. J. Donald Hamill-Stewart	Intelligence officer and ADC to Gordon
Edward Hamilton	Gladstone's private secretary
Sir William Harcourt	Home Secretary
Lord Hartington	Secretary of State for War
Adm. Sir William Hewett	Governor of Sawākīn
Acting Gen. William Hicks	Commander, Egyptian forces in Sudan
Lord Kimberley	Secretary of State for India
Baron Samuel de Kusel	Controller-General of Egyptian Customs
Sir Edward Malet	British Agent in Cairo
Charles Moberly Bell	Cairo correspondent of *The Times*
Comm. Lynedoch Moncrieff	Royal Navy officer; British Consul at Sawākīn
Lord Northbrook	First Lord of the Admiralty
Sir Stafford Northcote	Leader of the Opposition in the Commons
Sir Henry Ponsonby	Queen Victoria's private secretary
Frank Power	Correspondent for *The Times,* British Consul at Khartoum
Lord Ripon	Viceroy of India
Lord Salisbury	Leader of the Opposition in the Lords
Lord Selborne	Lord Chancellor
Lord Spencer	Lord Lieutenant of Ireland
Henry Moreton Stanley	Administrator of the Congo
William Stead	Editor of the *Pall Mall Gazette*
Gen. Sir Frederick Stephenson	Commander, British army of occupation in Egypt
Sir Ralph Thompson	Permanent Under-Secretary at the War Office
Sir Charles Wilson	Military Attaché to the British Agency in Cairo

Lord Wolseley	Commander, Gordon Relief Expedition
Gen. Sir Evelyn Wood	Commander, Egyptian Army
Augustus Wylde	Sawākīn merchant

Ottoman/Egyptian

Sultan Abdülhamit II	Ruler of the Ottoman Empire
Colonel Aḥmad ʿArābi	Leader of anti-Ottoman rebellion
Ḥassan Fahmī	Egyptian ambassador to London
Gen. ʿAbd-al-Qādir Ḥilmi	Governor-General of Sudan
Gen. Muḥammad ʿAlī Ḥussein	Senior officer in Khartoum garrison
Khedive Ismāʿīl	Ruler of Egypt
Ḥussein Khalīfa	Governor of Berber
Baron Karl de Malortie	German resident in Cairo
Constantine Musurus	Ottoman Ambassador to London
Nūbār Nubārian	Prime Minister of Egypt
Muḥammad Sharīf	Prime Minister of Egypt
Rudolf Slatin	Governor of Darfur; imprisoned by the Mahdī
Khedive Ṭawfīq	Ruler of Egypt; successor to Ismāʿīl
Muṣṭafa Yāwar	Governor of Dongola

Sudanese

Khalīfa ʿAbdullāhi	Successor of the Mahdī
Muḥammad al-Tayyib wad al-Baṣīr	Mahdist general in the Jazīra region
Sheikh Maḥmūd Mūsa	Leader of the Hadendawa in the Red Sea Hills
Muḥammad Aḥmad ibn ʿAbdallah	The Mahdī
ʿUthmān Abū-Bakr Diqna	Mahdist general in the Red Sea Hills
al-Zubeir Raḥma Manṣūr	Slave-trader; Gordon's candidate for Governor-General of Sudan
Sheikh Muḥammad Badr al-ʿUbeiḍ	Mahdist general on the Blue Nile
Muḥammad ʿAbdallah Khojali	Mahdist general in the Berber district

'A true and equitable judgement'

My Lords, and Gentlemen . . . When you assembled in October last I informed you that an Expedition was advancing up the Valley of the Nile for the relief of Khartoum. Three months later, with a deep sorrow, which was shared by all my people, I learnt that the Expedition had arrived too late, and that the heroic General Gordon and his companions had fallen. An endeavour, which was ineffectual, was made to reach Khartoum by constructing a railway from Suakin to Berber. My troops were ultimately withdrawn from the whole of the Eastern Soudan except Suakin.

Queen Victoria addressing Parliament, 14 August 1885[1]

This is a story about imperial intervention in Africa, its advocates and its opponents. It describes a determined and often single-handed campaign by William Gladstone, waged over several years, *not* to become embroiled in Sudan. It gives the lie to the assumption prevailing today that the British occupation of Khartoum at the end of the nineteenth century was either inevitable or the product of an easy, uniform imperialist consensus in Britain – and establishes that Gladstone responded with integrity and consistency to a foreign policy problem that presented a serious challenge to his frequently declared values of imperial retrenchment. The drama in Sudan exemplified all the main moral, practical and ideological arguments about imperial expansion in general and the imminent 'scramble for Africa' in particular – and by the time it was over, it had inflicted profound personal damage on a reputation for statesmanship built up over decades.

What became a brief but full-blown political and military crisis for the British was, for the Sudanese, the culmination of a spiritual, social and military uprising. It began on 29 June 1881, when Muḥammad Aḥmad ibn ʿAbdallah, a charismatic Islamic leader, launched a jihad against Sudan's Egyptian colonial masters.[2] He had already developed a considerable following through preaching missions south-east along the Blue Nile, west into Kordofan and north as far as Berber, but

1

it was Muḥammad Aḥmad's self-declared status as the *Mahdī* – a long-expected figure, pre-destined to restore true Islam to the world at the End of Times – that made him a danger not just to the colonial authorities in Khartoum, but to Egypt itself and the existing authorities in kingdoms and colonies with substantial Muslim populations as far away as British India.[3]

The fact that the 'Sudan Question' was even a topic of discussion in London stemmed directly from Gladstone's September 1882 invasion of Egypt. Ostensibly an Ottoman province (*vilayet*), Egypt was in effect a wholly autonomous if incompetently run nation, whose colonial reach had spread since the early 1820s into all corners of what we now call Sudan.[4] So responsibility for Egypt dictated responsibility for Sudan. Britain's invasion, led by General Sir Garnet Wolseley, was applauded by Conservatives and other advocates of imperialist assertion, who argued that the 'provocations' of the Egyptian nationalist movement led by a renegade officer, Colonel Aḥmad ʿArābi, created a 'condition of anarchy' that compelled Britain to intervene.[5] To dissatisfied Liberals and their Radical partners, however, the invasion was a hypocritical misadventure on Gladstone's part; a fundamental betrayal of his declared belief in non-interference abroad.

Gladstone's response to the Sudan crisis, then, was a crucial measure of his sincerity. He had four strategic options. He could accept continued Egyptian colonial rule in Sudan, notionally on behalf of Cairo's own Ottoman master at Constantinople. This occupation would be maintained with tacit British oversight, at least as long as the British domination of Egypt itself continued. A second option was a substitute occupation, most likely by the Ottoman Sultan (without Egypt as an intermediary) or by another European power. Alternatively, Gladstone could authorise a British military occupation of the northern portion of the Sudan territories, including Sawākīn on the Red Sea coast and the Nile passage as far as Khartoum itself. This option precluded retention of either Equatoria and Bahr al-Ghazāl to the south, or Kordofan and Darfur in the west. The fourth option was politically the most ruthless: complete abandonment of Sudan to the Mahdī. Would commercial pragmatism and the largely military logic of Britain's continued possession of Egypt proper prevail over ideological values? Such a position would surely mean it was impossible to accept a hostile autonomous Islamic power on Egypt's southern frontier. Or would Gladstone refute the charges of hypocrisy by reclaiming the moral high ground so damagingly lost in the Egyptian occupation and let the Sudanese go their own way?

This narrative sets out for the first time the phase-by-phase evolution of a Sudan policy that could be summed up as 'minimum engagement, zero responsibility'. It was, at a personal level, consistently rooted in an absolute commitment to non-intervention, though on more than one occasion the Prime Minister had positively to claw his way back to this premise. Policy evolution was rapid, often reactive and sometimes downright uncontrolled. It passed through several significant phases: some with Gladstone in assertive mode, others when he was forced into a more defensive posture.

His initial approach was a blanket refusal to engage with the Sudan issue at all. This was followed by a decision to compel the government of occupied Egypt to withdraw from its southern colony. To supervise the evacuation, Major-General Charles Gordon was appointed, first merely as a Sawākīn-based advisor, then as Khartoum-based executive officer. During his early months in the Sudanese capital, a partial but substantial evacuation of Egyptian personnel was achieved, via Berber and Dongola. The next important phase saw active British military intervention on the Red Sea coast in a succession of engagements, the names of which still resonate in individual regimental histories. Back in Khartoum, the evacuation was forcibly terminated by the Mahdī's encirclement and siege of the city. Later in the summer the 'Gordon Relief Expedition' was despatched; the original, more feasible Sawākīn-Berber desert route, using a force under General Sir Frederick Stephenson, was scrapped in favour of the far longer Nile route, under Wolseley. The dilatory progress of the expeditionary force led to its failure, while the Mahdī's capture of Khartoum, during which Gordon was killed, obviated any further British military initiatives in the interior. So the final phase of Gladstone's turbulent policy was marked by Wolseley's retreat, acrimony at Westminster and the abandonment of Sudan.

Most of the phases described in this cursory summary of events resulted from Gladstone's unilateral executive decisions, in a climate where the public debate on policy was restricted by the suppression of important diplomatic correspondence and dissenting political opinion. Other developments were precipitated by a lack of consensus within the cabinet, by the parliamentary opposition, by hostile elements in the British Army or simply by the increasingly intransigent actions and political initiatives of Gordon, whose mission to Khartoum Gladstone had reluctantly sanctioned.

Gladstone's steely determination not to be dragged off course, not to be dragged from Egypt into Sudan, was tested on numerous occasions. More than once, pressure from influential aristocratic lobby groups compelled the Prime Minister to make policy adjustments that jeopardised his declared aim of absolute non-intervention. The most conspicuous of these occasions, in the early part of 1884, was the deployment of British military personnel on the ground in eastern Sudan, a presence that prompted the first calls for a 'relief expedition' for Khartoum. Setting a pattern that would be followed throughout the summer and autumn, Gladstone fell back on a dogged passive resistance, using his political wiles to resist the lobby campaigning for Gordon's rescue from Khartoum and his executive authority to withdraw the bulk of the eastern force, thus neutering the threat posed by his own agent to his own policy.

The demonization of Gladstone

In the bitter political aftermath of the fall of Khartoum to the Mahdī and the death of General Gordon on 26 January 1885, and in several decades of imbalanced and lastingly prejudicial writing on the subject, Gladstone suffered severely in comparison to his late antagonist. The juxtaposition of 'Gordon the Hero' and 'Gladstone the Villain' is a central leitmotif of both contemporary reportage on the crisis and most subsequent histories of the period. Despite the fact that the Prime Minister had both achieved his strategic aim and reasserted the core ideological values of retrenchment with which he had begun his second administration, he was, by the end of 1885, a gravely tarnished figure whose loss of credibility prompted desertions by political allies and made him vulnerable to Conservative machinations that exploited the name of Gordon and contributed directly to electoral defeat.

In the brutal language of the partisan press, echoed in many personal accounts and journals of the day, the G.O.M., 'Grand Old Man', became simply M.O.G., the 'Murderer of Gordon', reproached for his perceived 'sacrifice' or 'abandonment' of a British Christian hero to the mercy of savages in the interests of a distastefully craven policy. Gladstone himself, standing on dignity and strategic vindication, made few public attempts to defend his conduct. As early as 19 April 1884, however, he instructed that documents relating to the Gordon mission be 'kept apart for reference in case of dispute'.[6] A private letter written to Lord Granville,' his Foreign Secretary during the crisis, neatly sums up the points that he might have fairly marshalled in his own defence.

> Gordon ought, at a very early date, to have come away [from Khartoum] of his own motion. He really remained in defiance of the whole mind and spirit of our instructions. To remain beleaguered in Khartoum was only the proof of his failure. It was his absolute duty to withdraw if he could, and I have never heard his power to do so disputed. For us to have complied with his demands was madness and crime.[8]

Those last, powerful words give a clear sense of Gladstone's own, usually veiled, opinion of both his former agent and his determination to maintain course on policy. The declaration that even a temporary departure from that policy had amounted to insanity and criminal wrong-doing are particularly striking. Still, such protests, even had they been voiced by the dignified Gladstone, would have carried little weight against the vilification expressed by Queen Victoria herself. Blaming the government for 'refusing to send the expedition till it was too late', the monarch sent strong telegrams to Gladstone, Granville and Lord Hartington at the War Office to say how 'dreadfully shocked' she was at the news. Her decision not to use the customary cipher was an ostentatious and discourteous signal of her displeasure.[9] Victoria was not so vindictive, however, that she withheld the offer of an earldom when Gladstone's administration subsequently fell. But the crisis had left Gladstone weary to the bone and he declined the offer, both because his personal wealth was 'not adequate to sustain so great an honour' and because, anxious to retire from politics, he was reluctant to face further obligations in the House of Lords, 'until my dying day chained to the oar of a life of conflict & contention'.[10]

Fully five years after the fall of Khartoum, Gladstone wrote to a former cabinet colleague that 'in the Gordon case we all, and I rather prominently, must continue to suffer in silence. Gordon was a hero . . . It was unfortunate that he should claim the hero's privilege by turning upside down and inside out every idea and intention with which he had left England, and for which he had obtained our approval.'[11] The same year, Gladstone replied to an American interviewer seeking opinion on the disastrous 1884-5 mission:

> I feel myself precluded from supplying any material or entering upon any communications for the purpose of self-defence against the charges which are freely made and I believe widely accepted against myself and against the cabinet of 1880-5 in connection with General Gordon. It would be felt in this country, by friends I think in many cases as well as adversaries, that General Gordon's much-lamented death ought to secure him, as far as we are concerned, against the counter-argument which we should have to present on his language and proceedings. . . . I do not doubt that a true and equitable judgement will eventually prevail.[12]

More than 130 years later, however, Gladstone still struggles to get a fair hearing, let alone the benefit of the doubt, on the central questions of integrity and consistency in policy. Instead, most significant histories of the period have been premised on assumptions of Machiavellianism, irresponsibility, inconsistency, vacillation or downright insincerity, all summed up in the catch-all phrase 'policy of drift'.[13] In the vilification of Gladstone by academics, the arguments presented by Ronald Robinson and John Gallagher have perhaps attracted the widest following. Their analysis of the Egyptian imbroglio and the consequent involvement in Sudan is in most respects unimpeachable. Where they lack fairness, however, is in their treatment of Gladstone as an individual, standing aside from and, in self-defined moral terms, above his cabinet colleagues. On his complex personality, they set out their stall with startlingly intemperate language:

> Of all British statesmen it is Gladstone whose character is the most convoluted. . . . The ambiguities which bedeck his speeches and letters, the prolixity, the lurches into the conditional mood and the qualifying clause – these marked the intricacy of his nature. He could chop logic with the most sparkling of the High Churchmen, yet frame budgets with the grimmest of the utilitarians. He had learning without taste, eloquence without style, sweetness without light; he could toss moral judgements into the affairs of state, and yet conduct politics as one of the fine arts. . . . The vehemence, the scalding volcanic objurgations which poured up from the craters of his personality were calculated to attract some temperaments and repel others.[14]

These personality defects, in an argument that many other writers have followed, rarely translate into a political style that is anything other than scheming, inconsistent, even, if only by implication, hypocritical. Gladstone is acknowledged to have protested 'impotently' in cabinet against precipitate unilateral military action in Egypt – insisting in writing to Granville on 'the exhaustion of every effort to procure collective or joint [i.e. Anglo-French] action' – but at no point is credited with restraint.[15] Nor are these analysts any fairer in respect of the motives discovered for involvement in Sudan: ignorance, incompetence, an endless ideological flexibility and/or an inability to stand up to cabinet rivals are preferred over a simple, dogged, indeed lofty, insistence on retrenchment.

Of course, Gladstone has had his champions. One important analysis describes Gladstone, in the aftermath of the fall of Khartoum, as handling an 'appalling overseas situation . . . with astonishing force and judgement unclouded by emotion. He showed himself, once again, able in the most serious crisis to work harder than anyone else and to produce correct and agreed solutions at exactly the right moment.'[16] In taking this determination and, above all, consistency as its premise, the following account offers a new treatment of Gladstone as the architect and prime motive factor in Sudan policy: a highly personal, ideologically-informed and absolutist policy of non-intervention, stemming directly from his bruising experience in Egypt. Confirmation comes from a wide variety of sources, including cabinet minutes, confidential journals, official documents and the sometimes grudging recognition accorded by ministerial colleagues.

It might seem perverse to claim that Gordon's death and the failure of the expedition to pluck him from Khartoum amounted to a victory of any kind for the Prime Minister. After all, it was in the name of his government that both general and relief expedition were deployed and Gladstone's most immediately contemporary biographer was hardly exaggerating in describing 1885 as 'the severest epoch' of his life.[17] Yet from the perspective of Gladstone's earliest, absolutist formulation of Sudan policy, both the appointment of Gordon and the deployment of British military personnel had been anomalies, indeed cardinal errors, against which he had fought with every parliamentary device available to him.

So what political adversaries described as a 'policy of drift and shirking' followed by a 'reckless, helter-skelter . . . scuttling out of Soudan' was, in fact, a resolute but covert policy of passive resistance – and it had succeeded.[18] By the end of the final phase of policy evolution, Gladstone had achieved his initial stated objective: minimum engagement in and zero responsibility for Egypt's erstwhile colony. Indeed, weathering the short-term outrage, renewed appeals for retributive action and Hartington's bid for the Liberal Party leadership, Gladstone was politically strong enough to reassert his original policy determination, hold the cabinet intact and order the complete abandonment of Sudan to the Mahdī.

The apotheosis of Gordon

If Gladstone was vilified, even long after his own lifetime, the posthumous treatment of Gordon has been extraordinary, prolonged and almost uniformly uncritical. His manifest flaws included the reversal or fudging of almost every stated position, practical and ideological, on the Sudanese rebellion. He was wilfully disobedient and contemptuous of his superiors, both civil and military. He gravely misread the Mahdī's military capacity, tribal following and spiritual status. Despite all this and despite the fact that he had nearly dragged his nation into a costly and attritional military intervention that he himself opposed, Gordon swiftly became a figure of awe and reverence. There were a few dissenting voices. From within the Socialist movement, for example, Annie Besant wrote that Gordon's death was 'but the natural outcome of his fanatical imprudence and self-will'; once his true character was laid bare, she believed, the 'glamor-mist which enwraps him' would dissolve away – precisely the point Gladstone made but refused to pursue even in defence of his own reputation.[19]

Most early British studies of the Sudan wars took the figure of Gordon as their emotional core, acclaimed equally (and equally tendentiously) as imperial icon and double victim, of both political betrayal and non-Christian savagery. This prevailing tone of uncritical hero-worship was typified by the hagiography of Elizabeth Rundle Charles, in which 'that heroic Christian soldier and single-hearted English gentleman' is revealed in his lonely outpost, 'more and more forsaken, more and more alone . . . yet still commanding, and as far as possible inspiring, helpless multitudes, and with the shield of his own brave heart and right arm defending a whole city'.[20] This trend was maintained in the Victorian periodicals, which featured probing but partisan commentaries on the foreign affairs crises of the moment, their tone underpinned by a routine assumption that the Briton's overseas mission was to civilize the savage.[21]

In reassessing Gordon's role, this book seeks to present a more objective critical appraisal of an officer whose status can be accurately described not, as many have done, as 'the ultimate soldier of empire', but as the quintessential mercenary. In an unusually episodic career, the periods in which Gordon wore conventional British uniform, at home or abroad, were largely periods of stagnation and under-achievement, while the years of hyperactivity and fame (in China and once previously in Sudan) were those in which he was on secondment to a foreign power.[22] This is not to suggest that Gordon was disinterested. Even from a distance, he maintained his interest in Sudanese affairs. A letter of 2 September 1883 from self-imposed exile in the Holy Land contained a prescient insight into the debate over Gladstone's Sudan policy, even as it was first being defined:

> Her Majesty's Government, right or wrong, will not take a decided step in re Egypt and the Soudan; they drift, but at the same time cannot avoid the onus of being the real power in Egypt, with the corresponding advantage of being so. . . . Also, Her Majesty's Government cannot possibly avoid the

responsibility for the state of affairs in the Soudan, where a wretched war drags on in a ruined country at a cost of half a million per annum at least.[23]

Nor does this account disparage Gordon's skills as an engineer, draftsman, military strategist and leader of men. He certainly achieved remarkable success, at least until the Mahdî's final closure of the siege circle around Khartoum, in arranging for civilians and Egyptian soldiers judged *hors de combat* to be evacuated from the city – an area in which he is conventionally described as having failed or never even tried. But important questions about Gordon's mental stability should have been addressed much more firmly by the cabinet before making their choice for the Sudan mission. It certainly did not take long for senior government officials, not all of them involved in Gordon's hurried despatch, to acknowledge that someone had blundered. Crucially, though, these observations were made off the record or after the event.

Shortly after Gordon's departure, Lord Northbrook, the First Lord of the Admiralty, wrote to his friend Lord Ripon in India to express the private opinion that Gordon was 'an extraordinary mixture of common sense and flightiness almost approaching insanity'.[24] At the end of the same month, Sir Charles Dilke, also in cabinet as President of the Local Government Board, recorded a series of typically eccentric telegrams from Gordon before concluding: 'We were evidently dealing with a wild man under the influence of that climate of Central Africa which acts even upon the sanest men like strong drink'.[25] And Gladstone's own right-hand man, principal private secretary Edward Hamilton, described Gordon in his diary as 'a half cracked fatalist' and 'a man who is not wholly sane and who perpetually contradicts himself'.[26]

Any valid analysis of Gordon's character must, of course, be set in the context of the mission or, to be more precise, the worsening 'mission creep', in which the parameters of his employment evolved even more rapidly than the policy that led to that employment. With Gladstone struggling to retain control, Gordon became a primary agent of change, though not as much change as he would have liked. His psychological instability led to a series of erratic and inconsistent proposals and initiatives, many of which ran counter to his pledged intention of adhering to the policy of evacuation.

What was most remarkable was the degree to which Gordon's eccentric actions or rapidly changing opinions escaped any serious censure in the public domain. Those pursuing their own agendas in London and Cairo cherry-picked from among the general's range of views on any given strategic position, finding one that matched most closely those that they themselves advanced. The mere fact that it could be represented as Gordon's view meant that it could be, as Todd Willy has observed, 'employed actively as a reinforcement of the communicator's position, regardless of the communicator's political, religious, social, or educational background or predisposition'.[27]

No-one ventured, in public at least, to suggest that Gordon had changed his mind, let alone that he was wrong. While hard-line socialists like Annie Besant and William Morris condemned Gordon for his part, even as a stalking-horse for more blatant imperialists, in the subjugation of Africans, few politicians or parties at Westminster saw criticism of the general as a viable vote-winning tactic: not in 1884, not after the fall of Khartoum in the spring of 1885, nor even, most critically for Gladstone, after the publication of Gordon's journals.

Legacy and future policy

Gladstone may have achieved, in ideological terms, a policy victory, but it was, politically, a pyrrhic victory. After surviving the brutal political recriminations triggered at Westminster and beyond by the fall of Khartoum, Gladstone was laid low by a posthumous blow from his old antagonist. For it was the publication of Gordon's Khartoum journal on 26 June 1885, exactly five months after the general's demise, that triggered fatal erosion in support.[28] This happened mainly because the journal was systematically and effectively used as a political weapon by the Conservatives in elections later that year. The journal was the first and arguably the most lethal shot in a war of words over the Sudan legacy that has lasted more than a century. It sold in extraordinary numbers, it was reviewed everywhere and it was read from palace to public house. And it proved to be a rare example of a single book that could kill a political career.

The often distressingly manic nature of Gordon's ink-blotched scrawl, which so troubled Gladstone and other government officials during an intense two-month debate over the pros and cons of publication, again appears to have escaped the public's attention, let alone condemnation. The journal certainly did nothing to counter a rapid mythologizing trend and its emotional power created a posthumous memoir that, given the uncritical public response to Gordon's personal myth, was hard to gainsay in person. As the protagonist of one contemporary novel notes, reading one of Gordon's diatribes against Gladstone, 'I should be very sorry to have such a man leave such a letter on record against me'.[29]

Those whom Gordon had traduced or misunderstood were compelled to set the record straight in writing. Indeed, many of the prime movers in the evolution of British Sudan policy left us closely argued versions of events, impeccably sourced in contemporaneous documentation, not least Gordon's own often wildly inconsistent letters and telegrams. Cross-referencing these important sources helps us pin-point events both political and military with accuracy and lay bare misrepresentations. As third-person accounts began to proliferate, however, an unashamedly partisan tone developed, in which sentimentalism and hero-worship, especially for Gordon, were set against a contemptuous denigration for both Gladstone and the Sudanese themselves.

This trend persisted well into the twentieth century, informing a significant proportion of a wildly proliferating genre known, sometimes pejoratively, as the 'Gordon Literature'. Indeed, one article written as long ago as 1963 calculated that the biography under review was already the 323rd known book on Gordon.[30]

There was variety as well as longevity in the Gordon brand: words like 'mission', 'apotheosis' and 'martyr' pervade the genre, with disobedience, mania and failure being no bar to lasting memory.

For Britain's relationship with Sudan itself, the seeds of future policy were sown with Gordon's death. The lasting impact of Gladstone's personality and ideology can be seen in the changing balance of domestic and foreign priorities in British politics; the assertion of a neo-imperialist military agenda by those who believed that the Sudan mission had been left unfinished; the place of Egypt and then Sudan in the larger arena of international colonial rivalry. Beyond these political considerations, however, there was also room for a more human emotion, felt especially keenly by British officers involved in both the failed Rescue Expedition and the inconclusive Red Sea Hills campaigns: vengeance.

The elections of 1885 and 1886, culminating in Gladstone's defeat and the formation of a Conservative government under Lord Salisbury, marked the end of an immensely turbulent period. The Sudan wars of 1884-5 played a crucial part in shaping late Victorian attitudes to Empire and to Africa: after a trough of despondency that permeated salon society in the wake of Lord Wolseley's igno-minious retreat from Sudan, a gloom fed by the works of poets and essayists who lamented Britain's role as the world's aggressor, imperialism was to return with a vengeance. 'With the victory of the Conservatives in 1886,' noted Bertrand Russell caustically, 'from that year until the end of the century the passion for empire continually grew, taking forms which were sometimes criminal, often ridiculous, and always disgusting.'[31]

Ideas of vengeance for Gordon were directly fed by the vivid published accounts of the Sudan wars by articulate British officers, well aware of the lucra-tive market in tales from the battlegrounds of empire. Impartiality was never on the agenda. Several accounts scored commercial success within the first few years of Gordon's death, proving that a diet of romance, swash-buckling and self-aggrandisement, occasionally leavened with useful eye-witness evidence and contemporaneous documentation, had abiding appeal. They also perpetuated the skewed Gordon/Gladstone discourse and gave considerable momentum to a trend predicted with great accuracy by the Arabophile poet Wilfrid Scawen Blunt, who warned Gordon in March 1884 in a personal letter that, were the general to be killed during the Khartoum mission, his death would mean 'the certainty of a cry for vengeance for England and an excuse for those who seek no better than a war of conquest'.[32]

Still more influential were the highly coloured eyewitness accounts by European captives of the Mahdī and his successor, the Khalīfa ʿAbdullāhi. The *raison d'être* for the publication of this material in English was often specific to British politics in the early 1890s: primarily its value in mobilising press and public opinion behind a renewed military campaign to 'avenge Gordon'. Two memoirs published in 1892 and 1896, by Fr Josef Ohrwalder and Rudolf Slatin, erstwhile Governor of Darfur, were particularly successful in catching and building the mood of outrage over Gordon's fate that persisted years after his demise.[33] Setting new norms in denigrating and demonizing the enemy, they established a pejorative stereotype of the Sudanese. Both were published under the aegis of British military intelligence in Cairo.[34]

Gordon's lasting perception as the quintessential Victorian icon touches on Britain's own self-perception as an imperial power. In fact, the publication of the journals represented a high point in both imperialist sentiment and in the percolation of Empire into British culture and society. This is all the more extraordinary because this peak of enthusiasm was achieved despite the fact that the term 'Empire' only obtained in its loosest context. It was an exaggeration at any time before 1898 to call Khartoum, as did Maria Trench in the full flush of emotion after Gordon's death, 'our country's furthest outpost'.[35] Indeed, few who used such expressions of identification, then or since, have seen any irony in taking Gordon – an officer whose appointment in Khartoum was designed purely to *extract* Britain from any further political, military or even moral commitment to 'Sudan' or the Sudanese – as the primary emotional point of connection between the people of Victorian Britain and the 'Sudan Question'.

CHAPTER 1

Non-interventionism: policy and practice

Between the two parties . . . there is a perfect agreement that England has a mighty mission in the world; but there is a discord as fundamental upon the question [of] what that mission is. With the one party, her first care is held to be the care of her own children within her own shores, the redress of wrongs, the supply of needs, the improvement of lives and institutions. Against this homespun doctrine, the present [Conservative] Government appears to set up territorial aggrandisement, large establishments, and the accumulation of a multitude of fictitious interests abroad, as if our real interests were not enough.

William Gladstone, *The Nineteenth Century*, September 1878[1]

Gladstone's determination to have nothing to do with Egypt's Sudanese misadventures can be traced back to the earliest days of his second administration and his frequent avowal of aspirations to what might today be called an 'ethical foreign policy'. The wily veteran MP for Edinburghshire had come out of retirement to resume his leadership of the Liberal Party in the wake of clear victory in the 1880 general election.[2] Following a campaign labelled by *The Times* as the 'hottest political struggle ever known in this country', Gladstone returned to Downing Street for his second term as Prime Minister.[3]

From the start, it was clear that the Prime Minister intended to use his majority to reassert domestic priorities, while foreign affairs were comprehensively reassessed. The assumption that retrenchment abroad was the only morally acceptable policy went to the heart of Gladstone's political identity as an ideological heir of Richard Cobden, the Radical-Liberal statesman and peace campaigner.[4] R.C. Mowat has given us a useful description of what that meant in effect.

The true Cobdenite was a pacifist and an anti-imperialist. He was opposed to annexations, and as regards the existing colonies he favoured their evolution as rapidly as possible towards autonomy, if not outright independence. . . . Concern for the welfare of the masses was the starting-point of this creed: war on monopolies of all kinds was its means of fulfilment, whether these were protected by tariffs or land laws. The strictest economy in public expenditure was matched by a pacifist approach in foreign affairs.[5]

Setting himself in stark opposition to what he described as Disraeli's morally bankrupt and endlessly greedy imperialism, Gladstone had aired his own views on foreign policy in a series of articles and campaign speeches. The right of 'Eastern' nations to self-determination would, he argued, be undermined by any quasi-imperial assumption of responsibility, let alone administrative control, by Britain. On 27 November 1879, in the third of a series of constituency addresses that became known as the 'Midlothian Speeches', Gladstone outlined six 'right principles of foreign policy': good government at home; the preservation of peace; cultivation and maintenance of the 'concert of Europe'; avoiding unnecessary foreign commitments; acknowledging the equal rights of all nations; and sympathy for both freedom and order.[6] It was that fourth point of argument that resonated most powerfully when the questions of Egypt and Sudan subsequently came up for discussion.

You should avoid needless and entangling engagements. You may boast about them; you may brag about them. . . . But what does all this come to, gentlemen? It comes to this, that you are increasing your engagements without increasing your strength; and if you increase engagements without increasing strength, you diminish strength, you abolish strength; you really reduce the empire and do not increase it. You render it less capable of performing its duties; you render it an inheritance less precious to hand on to future generations.[7]

The previous September, Gladstone – at the time not just out of government but technically retired – had contributed a long article to one of the most important political periodicals of the day, *The Nineteenth Century*. In 'England's Mission', he denounced the imperialist policies of the Conservatives. 'At no time,' he thundered, 'have they failed to maintain . . . that the further enlargement of the bounds of the Empire is the noblest achievement, to which statesmanship can aspire', adding that 'they have appealed, under the prostituted name of patriotism, to exaggerated fears, to imaginary interests, and to the acquisitiveness of a race which has surpassed every other known to history in the faculty of appropriating to itself vast spaces of the earth.'[8]

More specifically in relation to Egypt, Gladstone had also written in 1877 that the annexation or occupation of Egypt – a point of contemporary debate because of the recent purchase of Khedive Ismāʿīl's Suez Canal shares – would be 'the almost certain egg of a great African Empire that will grow and grow', loading Britain with unwelcome attendant responsibilities.[9] Put most simply in one 1883 analysis of contemporary colonies and dependencies, Gladstonian foreign policy 'discourage[d] any increase of territory in tropical countries already occupied by native races'.[10]

In the 1880 election, these reiterated views won the approval of the electorate, even if Gladstone's stated principle of acting 'in concert' with other European powers appeared unrealistic, if not naïve, in the face of the rival ambitions of Count Otto von Bismarck's Germany, France under the Third Republic and the still expansionist Portuguese. But while foreign policy was clearly, as one modern historian has put it, 'singularly out of phase with developments elsewhere', the Prime Minister was not alone in his thinking.[11]

It is striking that in *Expansion of England*, widely praised as one of the most important and influential foreign policy analyses of the late Victorian era, the Cambridge professor Sir John Seeley asserted unequivocally that the age of imperial expansion was over.[12] One Gladstone biographer described it as an 'immensely influential prophetical text'.[13] No less a personage than the Headmaster of Marlborough commended it for the 'very rousing effect [it had] upon his boys'.[14] But instead of correctly predicting the imminent and more intense phase of European jostling for global empire, especially the highly competitive 'scramble for Africa', Seeley's central – and already outdated – conviction was that contemporary territorial ambitions on the part of the French, say, were manifest folly.

Seeley made a clear distinction between the colonies in Canada and Australia, a white-majority 'Greater Britain', and the imperial anomaly that was British India. The former, he argued, was 'a real enlargement of the English State; it carries across the seas not merely the English race, but the authority of the English Government. We call it for want of a better word an Empire . . . But yet it is wholly unlike the great Empires of the Old World, Persian or Macedonian or Roman or Turkish, because it is not in the main founded on conquest.'[15] In the Raj, precisely because it *was* built on military conquest, power became 'precarious and artificial', while public opinion at home looked in 'blank indignation and despair' upon a fundamentally un-English bureaucracy, a millstone round the British neck that threatened to 'lock up an army which the nation may grievously need for other purposes or even for defence'.[16]

Thus, as Britain's rivals prepared in earnest to seize the greatest possible amount of land in Africa, the Pacific and East Asia, Gladstone struggled to match ideological theory with geopolitical reality in territories such as South Africa, Afghanistan and Egypt. Still, as Charles Gordon was himself to write in September 1884, 'Any one who, 2 ½ years ago, had said that the Gladstone Ministry would not only go to Egypt and, not content with one expedition to Soudan . . . would go in for *two expeditions*! would have been scouted as a mad man'.[17] Indeed, the irony of Gladstone's wholly unexpected interventions in north-east Africa was lost on few late-nineteenth-century analysts. 'Of all our Empire-builders *malgré eux*,' wrote Henry Traill, 'there has been none to compare in readiness and reluctancy to Mr Gladstone':

> Alike by victory [i.e. Egypt in 1882] and by defeat [Sudan in 1884-5], Mr Gladstone was fated to enlarge the borders of that Imperial power for which he was always anxious to apologise, and to increase the burden of those Imperial responsibilities which he always contemplated with dismay. . . . His resolution to advance and his determination to retreat were equally fruitful in results which he cordially detested, and contributed equally to a policy which he had spent his life in denouncing.[18]

Gladstone's critics, especially those within his own coalition of Liberals and Radicals, were horrified at the Egyptian adventure, insisting, despite his protestations to the contrary, that the conquest of the weaker nation by Britain's powerful army amounted to the execution of an imperialist policy, even if it technically stopped short of colonial annexation. Blunt believed simply that the Prime Minister suffered from a personal/political schizophrenia. 'His public life,' Blunt wrote, 'was to a large extent a fraud . . . if he had a new distasteful policy to pursue his first objective was to persuade himself into a belief that it was really congenial to him, and at this he worked until he had made himself his own convert.'[19] More recently, John Newsinger has noted the stark fact that 'every government Gladstone had been a member of had invaded somewhere and he had always managed to find some way of justifying this to his conscience'.[20]

Certainly the invasion prompted a long and bitter debate with Gladstone's fellow Cobdenite, John Bright, who agreed that 'he seems to have the power of convincing himself that what to me seems a glaring wrong is evidently right, and though he regrets that a crowd of men should be killed, he regards it as almost an occurrence which is not to be condemned, as if it was one of the incidents of a policy out of which he hopes for a better order of things.'[21] Writing to Bright in the aftermath of the bombardment of Alexandria, Gladstone expressed his regret for what he insisted had been a 'solemn and painful' necessity.[22] But Bright's parting response was damning: such weasel words were 'the stock arguments of the Jingo school . . . the words of Palmerston throughout his mischievous career'.[23]

At the level of day-to-day party politics, Gladstone's loyal secretary, Edward Hamilton, noted the frustration of the Conservatives that his master had 'adopted their policies and taken leaves out of their books which he cut up to pieces so when he was in opposition'.[24] But it was one of Wolseley's staff officers, Colonel William Butler, who, in the aftermath of the battle at al-Ṭall al-Kabīr ('the big hill') that decided British ownership of Egypt, evoked the 'piles of Egyptian dead' as the most vivid proof that the 'Midlothian spirit' was dead.

Which, he mused rhetorically, was the 'bad, revolting star in this Egyptian business . . . the Egyptian peasant in revolt against his plunderers, or an English Liberal Government in revolt against Liberalism?'[25]

Some modern historians are willing to give Gladstone greater credit for integrity over Egypt. John Darwin, who recognises the occupation as 'the single most important forward movement made by Britain in the age of partition which set in after 1880', identifies the vote for war credits as a 'defeat' for Gladstone and describes the 'false prospectus' that persuaded influential ministers to back the suppression of the 'Arābi uprising and made Egypt 'an exposed salient on the rim of Europe, a great hostage to diplomatic fortune'.[26] But an anti-Gladstone consensus persists: foreign intervention stilled dissent within the Liberal party, stole the Conservatives' clothes and upheld British economic interests in Egypt – not least the Prime Minister's own substantial investments.[27] 'That,' notes Newsinger sarcastically, 'was what the British state was for, after all.'[28]

Egypt was certainly pacified in the wake of the invasion. Political, economic, military and legislative reforms in Cairo were taken quickly in hand, under the guiding hand of British civil officials and army officers. Constantly professing this central mission – the education of Egyptians in self-government and fiscal responsibility, coupled with maintaining the security of citizens and foreign nationals alike – became for Gladstone the only way of mitigating the accusations of Tory-style imperialism. But the invasion would have a profound and lasting impact on international geopolitics. And there were reputations to be made, too. As Martin Daly has observed, 'Egypt . . . offered a stage to ambitious soldiers and administrators who, in other circumstances, might have had only supporting roles in the imperial drama: Cromer, Kitchener, Gordon, and their understudies'.[29]

Britain and Sudan: refusal to engage

By sanctioning the invasion, in violation of the non-interventionism principle, Gladstone had no room to manoeuvre when it came to the consequent problem of Sudan. The fact that he strenuously refused to declare a formal protectorate over Egypt in no way concealed the reality: once force had been used to realise the occupation, responsibility for Egypt and for Egypt's wider affairs lay squarely with Britain. The Prime Minister was thus faced with a syllogism: it was right to become involved in the politics and economy of Egypt, if necessary by invasion; Sudan is an integral part of the 'Egyptian Question', both by administrative occupation and geographical proximity; therefore it must be right to become involved in the politics and economy of Sudan, if necessary by invasion.

The early formulation of what was to become an uncompromising Sudan policy stemmed from ignorance and an equally profound lack of interest, making it all the easier to determine that Britain should have no role in what were seen as events peripheral to the main business in Egypt. Nothing else could explain the extraordinarily naïve question put by Gladstone to Granville as late as December 1883: 'It is wholly impossible that this Mahdi who has no quarrel with us (unless as Christians) might be disposed to accept us as mediators? I speak very doubtingly for we know neither his disposition nor his power.'[30] The same month, responding to the Prime Minister's confession that he knew next to nothing about the land between the Egyptian frontier and Khartoum – 'its military position, & the power of easy defence; its civil position, & the power of easy steady government' – Granville replied sympathetically, joking that he could not even spell the town Wādī-Ḥalfā' correctly.[31]

But if Gladstone misunderstood the scope and depth of motivation behind the Mahdī's uprising, he was far from alone in this failing. Few policy-makers in London had ever seen the countries they dealt with and the driving issues were 'apprehended intellectually from reports and recommendations on paper'.[32] As to Sudan itself, discussion involved fewer than a dozen men – members of the aristocracy, graduates from Oxford and Cambridge and old boys from Eton and Harrow – within a foreign policy clique that had no interest in portraying it as a 'problem', let alone a 'crisis'. It is certain that this clique suppressed documentation that would usually have been made available at least to MPs and thence, by virtue of parliamentary debate, the wider electorate and press. So the clique limited awareness of the true state of affairs in both Egypt and Sudan, in turn severely restricting the capacity of the public to contribute to the argument.

In practical terms, public indifference and parliamentary ignorance established the clique's monopoly of foreign policy. The Foreign Secretary was influential and largely autonomous, his information coming from a small number of trusted representatives in foreign capitals via personal and usually encrypted correspondence. Those same hand-picked men then implemented the orders transmitted back to them by the same confidential means. This narrow channel of information and instruction often effectively obviated consultation even with cabinet colleagues, let alone parliamentary opposition, leaving Granville free to view any policy or action implemented by his department as a matter of 'exclusively executive concern'.[33]

Even cabinet debate was restricted. There are just two references to the troubles in Sudan in official cabinet minutes during the final months of 1882. On 15 September, in the immediate aftermath of al-Ṭall al-Kabīr, a preliminary briefing paper on the 'Settlement of Egypt' projected the 'organisation of a force under the Khedive . . . as far as is requisite to defend the territory especially in the direction of the Soudan'.[34] Six weeks later, cabinet discussions on reforming the Egyptian army noted only: 'Southern Army separate, paid from Soudan revenues'.[35]

Nor is there any correspondence between Gladstone and Granville during this crucial period.[36] This evident cut-out occurred despite the explicit revelation by Egyptian officials to their British conquerors, soon after al-Ṭall al-Kabīr, of the precarious state of their southern colony and the limits of their own military capacity to respond. Cairo may even have hoped for assistance. After all, had not the British intervention been informed by a desire to act 'in support of the authority of His Highness the Khedive as established by the Firmans[37] of the Sultan and existing international engagements', an authority that, as all Egyptians took for granted, extended into Cairo's Sudanese holdings?[38]

The point man at this early stage was Sir Edward Malet,[39] who dutifully relayed to London a desperate appeal from the Governor-General in Khartoum, ʿAbd-al-Qādir Ḥilmi. Originally from Homs in the Ottoman province of Syria, General ʿAbd-al-Qādir's main achievement was the construction of improved earthworks around Khartoum, which subsequently helped Gordon defend the city through 320 days of siege.[40] He now requested an urgent infusion of 10,000 troops to contain the Mahdī's rebellion.[41] This appeal was effectively negated when Malet despatched a follow-up message two days later, offering the personal interpretation that 'though the situation appears to be serious, the danger to Khartoum itself is hardly so imminent as was at first supposed'.[42]

This pronouncement rang true because it was endorsed by the occasional news report percolating out of Sudan. The *Daily News*, for example, concluded that 'the much talked of Mahdi, who has been baptized the False Prophet, does not, after all, appear to be making quite so much headway . . . The capital of Kordofan [al-ʿUbeiḍ, then still under siege] still seems to prove a tough morsel. Khartoum appears to have been allowed what ought to be ample time for putting itself into a state of defence, and well-informed persons even deny that the Western and Southern Soudan have been in any unusual commotion at all'.[43]

Such reportage made it all the easier for London to decline any suggestion of direct British military involvement and led to the first formulation of policy. As early as 28 October, just six weeks after al-Ṭall al-Kabīr, Malet conveyed to the Foreign Office a request from the Egyptian government for 'English officers' to accompany a relief force for Sudan.[44] This proposal got short shrift from Granville.

> Her Majesty's Government are not prepared to undertake any expedition into the Soudan, but they will be glad to receive full reports from your Excellency as to the condition of affairs in the Soudan, the amount of danger resulting from the insurrection to Egypt Proper, and the nature and extent of the measures which, in your opinion, and in those of Sir E. Malet, of the Commander-in-Chief of Her Majesty's forces [General Sir Evelyn Wood], and of the Egyptian authorities, should be taken against such dangers.[45]

According to General Wood, the British high command in Cairo were still discussing a range of options by which a force of 2,300 Egyptian infantry and cavalry under British officers could be sent to Sudan to assist the retreating garrisons well into 1884. 'The English officers are very eager to take their Egyptian soldiers into action,' Wood reported, 'but when I put this question –

"Are you confident of ensuring the success bearing in mind we do not object to any risk of your lives, but we must not risk a disaster?" they all including their brigadier answered "No – we are not confident, and however anxious we are to have a fight, we should like to have a backing of English soldiers at hand".'[46]

Back in London, the name 'Sudan' scarcely featured on the agenda of Westminster's politicians, mirroring a wider lack of interest in a distant, value-less and irrelevant territory. The year after the invasion of Egypt, during a long parliamentary session that stretched from 15 February to 25 August 1883, only two opposition questions and ministerial replies of any substance were uttered with regard to the territory south of Wādī-Ḥalfā'.

On 17 July, the Earl of Fife rose in the House of Lords to ask about the state of the slave trade in what he called 'Upper Egypt'. Noting the vigorous conduct of the trade through the western Sudanese region of Darfur, via the town of al-ʿUbeiḍ and up into Egypt proper, the Conservative peer suggested that, since 'the Oriental mind was peculiarly obtuse to unpalatable facts and suggestions ... power and authority must be placed in the hands of some resolute European, backed by that civilizing influence which it was surely now our bounden duty to exert'.[47] Replying for the government, Granville noted mildly and without apparent interest that 'the state of disorganization in which the Soudan is now is most unfavourable for any active measure on this subject'.[48]

This evasive understatement was typical of Granville, a man described by Queen Victoria as 'a very weak reed to lean upon' and by his cabinet colleague Lord Kimberley as 'a complete failure at the F.O.'.[49] It was true that at this time, Colonel William Hicks, a British veteran of Indian Army service hired by the Egyptian Khedive and promoted to the rank of Major-General, was still based in Khartoum as head of the Egyptian army of occupation. With successful interim military operations underway, the disastrous dénouement to Hicks's mission at Sheikān two months later was utterly unforeseen.

But by then the Mahdī had seized al-ʿUbeiḍ, an important central garrison and second largest town in the territory, and was directing operations from this new base. South of Khartoum, the Jazīra region was aflame, Sinnār on the Blue Nile was under siege and Egyptian garrisons in Bahr al-Ghazāl, Darfar and Equatoria provinces were all under sustained attack by the Mahdī's forces. Still, Granville noted that two British Consuls had been appointed: Commander Lynedoch Moncrieff of the Royal Navy for the Red Sea port town of Sawākīn and Frank Power, a young reporter sending exclusives to *The Times*, for Khartoum itself. Granville's conclusion was vague and without commitment: 'I believe they will be able to give valuable assistance to the endeavours which the government are most anxious to make in regard to these matters'.[50]

The only prior, much more specific reference to the Mahdī's uprising served at least to reveal explicitly the Gladstone government's attitude to the Sudan territories. Lord Eustace Cecil, Conservative MP for West Essex, asked whether there was 'any reason to believe the alarming reports of the progress of the rebellion in the Soudan and the imminent danger of Khartoum'. Replying for the government, Lord Edmond Fitzmaurice, Under-Secretary at the Foreign Office, confirmed that 'Her Majesty's Government have received information that Obeid and, it is believed, Bara have fallen into the hands of the rebels, but that there is no reason to apprehend danger to Khartoum'. His next sentence clearly spelt out current policy: 'The suppression of the rebellion in the Soudan is a matter which has been left entirely to the Egyptian Government . . . and neither Lord Dufferin[51] nor Sir Edward Malet has been concerned in any of the arrangements made'.[52]

Press coverage was similarly meagre. Since the declaration of Muḥammad Aḥmad as the Mahdī at Jazīra Aba on 29 June 1881, only sporadic reports had reached the British public of his steady military progress and growing influence. There had been a mere glimpse of the insurgents' first confrontation with the occupation authorities in the pages of *The Times*, which noted that 120 Egyptian soldiers were killed in an 'affray' between 'the population and the military, caused by the preaching of a "false prophet"'.[53] The subsequent destruction of the Egyptian force sent from the White Nile garrison at Fashoda on 8 December 1881, the flailing attempts by Cairo to instigate a competent military defence of its colony and the Mahdī's capture of al-ʿUbeiḍ were documented, but in brief.[54]

Policy under pressure

There appears to be no reason to doubt Gladstone's immediate intention to withdraw from Egypt. On 7 April 1883, Dufferin reported to Granville that he had told anxious European residents in Alexandria that 'the idea of a permanent military occupation of Egypt by Great Britain would certainly not be entertained'.[55] By 9 October, Malet's replacement as Agent and Consul-General, Sir Evelyn Baring, consulted the commander of the army of occupation in Egypt before recommending to London that the British force be reduced from around 6,700 men to 3,000 and concentrated at Alexandria. This deployment would be 'amply sufficient . . . to maintain the honour of Her Majesty's arms against any force that . . . it may have to encounter'.[56] At the end of the month, Granville directed Hartington at the War Office to implement Baring's recommendations.[57] The decision, as Gladstone noted in a private letter to Lord Rosebery, 'narrowed the scope of the Egyptian problem', although there still remained the question of 'how to plant solidly western & beneficient institutions in the soil of a Mahomedan community?'[58]

What appeared to be an imminent pull-out caused consternation in some quarters, not least because it correctly implied absolute disinterest in the war already well underway in Sudan. Inasmuch as there was a 'Sudan policy', it amounted to a bland refusal to be drawn in. Writing to Malet as late as 8 August 1883, Granville noted that, while cabinet ministers were 'glad to receive information as to the progress of the campaign [led by Hicks], it is their policy to abstain as much as possible from interference with the action of the Egyptian

Government in that quarter'.[59] And beyond that assertion, neither the cabinet nor the British authorities in Cairo expressed any interest in dealing with the issue on any specific terms.

Even when the Egyptian cabinet created a new 'special bureau for the superintendence of the affairs of the Soudan' in early April 1883, under an official identified only as Ibrāhīm Bey, British officials paid little attention beyond the suggestion that Cairo 'abandon Darfour and perhaps part of Kordofan, and be content with maintaining her jurisdiction in the Provinces of Khartoum and Senaar'.[60] 'By this modest policy,' Dufferin suggested, 'if Ibrahim Bey succeeded in endowing Dongola, Khartoum, and Senaar with a just, humane, and beneficient administration, there could be no doubt [that] the ultimate recovery of so much of the abandoned territories as it might be desirable to re-annex would be easily effected at a later period.'[61] It was not until much later that Gladstone reproved Dufferin for going beyond policy by offering 'the opinion of an intelligent friend, though not of a responsible Government': 'Lord Dufferin did not speak on our behalf,' he insisted, 'but the rejection [by Cairo] of that opinion . . . is a clear proof of the importance which they attached to the holding of the Soudan.'[62]

A few prominent individuals began to criticise government policy. The veteran Nile explorer, Sir Samuel Baker, many of whose expeditions had been carried out under the aegis of the Khedive, argued in public for a powerful joint Anglo-Egyptian counter-strike against the Mahdī, embracing indigenous tribal leaders in a pincer attack on Khartoum. 'The Soudan and Egypt cannot be separated,' he argued, '[but] how are the necessary changes and reforms in the Soudan to be carried out? First of all, it has to be reconquered. After that it must be reorganised. It must then be governed upon Liberal principles. Who is to do all this? Much as I deplore the necessity, I believe the task must be undertaken by Great Britain.'[63]

Queen Victoria agreed. A great admirer of imperial force projection and a better analyst of European competition than many of her ministers, she was equally dismayed by the planned retreat from Egypt. Her frank opinion, conveyed in a letter to Granville on 22 October 1883, was that Gladstone did not 'have the honour and power of his country strongly at heart' and that 'the interests of Egypt as well as of this country' militated against a total withdrawal:

> The Egyptians cannot govern themselves, that *everyone says* who is not inclined to yield to the cry of *non-interference* in *everything*. . . . We have not allowed precious British blood to be shed [during the 1882 invasion] only to see Egypt fall into the hands of France and Italy.[64]

Following Gladstone's personal letter clarifying the scale of the planned force reduction, Victoria telegraphed reluctant consent, on the condition that the last 3,000 troops 'remain indefinitely in Egypt and no promise of definite withdrawal or further reduction is made in Parliament'.[65] In the context of Sudan, Victoria took a dim view of her government's refusal to engage. A full year earlier, she had ordered her private secretary, Sir Henry Ponsonby, to convey her anxieties about the strength of the Mahdī's uprising to Lord Granville: 'The Queen is very anxious about Egypt and fears you do not sufficiently recognise the importance of at once acting against the rebels in the Soudan. We should give every assistance to the Egyptian Government to crush at once this rising. Or else we must send British troops. Have you consulted Wolseley?'[66]

The first appearance of Gordon

The most important early example of the foreign policy clique suppressing information about the Sudan debate centred on the troubled personality of General Gordon, a figure of national celebrity but problematic personal behaviour.[67] Though he achieved the rank of Major-General by the age of forty-nine, his successes were all in foreign uniform. His campaigns to suppress the Taiping rebellion in China during the 1860s, which won him both fame and the nickname 'Chinese Gordon', must still be reckoned his most remarkable mercenary exploits, although Chinese accounts of the period have cast Gordon's achievements in a more sceptical light, suggesting that 'Gordon's role in the events and even his "mystical" qualities were, if not complete fabrications, certainly over-exaggerated'.[68] During two spells in Sudan in the late 1870s,[69] Gordon won further renown for spearheading a tireless but largely unsuccessful drive to end the equatorial slave trade.[70] But this venture, too, was under a foreign flag, that of the Khedive of Egypt.

The *Morning Post* summed it up neatly in late 1883: Gordon's career had been 'eccentric, insofar as it has been strikingly unlike the majority. At intervals he has blazed out into world-wide notice . . . and again, after his work has been distinguished, as suddenly disappeared, so that only a few know whether he has retired.'[71] Certainly his recent record was one of serial under-achievement, a 'period of agitated indecision'.[72] Following his return from Khartoum in May 1880, emaciated and exhausted, he had lasted just days as Private Secretary to Lord Ripon, Viceroy of India. Admirers like Seton Churchill believed that the appointment had been doomed from the moment of Ripon and Gordon's departure from England.

> The P. & O. steamer that conveyed the Viceregal party had on board two kings, the greater man being, so to speak, the uncrowned one. . . . To make matters worse, the ship was compelled to pass through the very territory where Gordon's name was best known, and he was most beloved, and thus the Suez Canal voyage was a kind of royal progress. Unfortunately the homage paid was to the subordinate, the uncrowned king, and not to him who held the higher position.[73]

The inauspicious experience in India was but the beginning of a long period of drift. Gordon stayed less than a year in the backwater posting of Mauritius as 'Officer Commanding Royal Artillery' before, inexplicably promoted to Major-General, spending four months as 'Commandant General Colonial Forces, Cape of Good Hope' in South Africa. Charged with resolving the 'Basuto Problem', Gordon instead inflamed political tensions to such a degree that, accepting his resignation, the Premier of the Cape Colony, Thomas Scanlen, was moved to write: 'I regret to record my conviction that your continuance in the position you occupy would not be conducive to the public interest'.[74] Many aspects of the South Africa debacle bear remarkable similarities to Gordon's 1884-5 Sudan appointment: he was selected for his 'proved ability, firmness, and energy' but was cautioned that his 'proceeding to the Cape had solely to do with advising upon the position of affairs . . . and had no reference to the command of the Cape forces'.[75]

Such personality clashes were far from rare in Gordon's career; nor did they just occur with figures in authority. After Cecil Rhodes rejected two invitations to work with Gordon in Sudan, the latter responded, tetchily and hypocritically, 'I have never met a man so strong for his own opinion; you think your views are always right'.[76] Dr Georg Schweinfurth, a German botanist and anthropologist who knew Gordon in Equatoria, testified that 'at times he is condescending, affable, and cordial; but at other times, is rough, crusty, and unapproachable. His plans are changed even during their execution, and his actions only proceed in a straight line when carried along by his enthusiasm.'[77] Such imprecations would soon, once Gordon was deployed in Khartoum, seem mild indeed. Even King Leopold, who had been trying to recruit Gordon for service on the Congo River since 1880, described the general as 'most indiscreet' and a 'stiff-necked' eccentric.[78]

Indeed, of England's contemporary imperial heroes, only Florence Nightingale and Wolseley appear to have succumbed to Gordon's charm. On meeting him in 1880, Nightingale had been dismayed at his aimlessness and tried to help him find a job worthy of his military talent, courage and care for the welfare of the oppressed.[79] As for Wolseley, a decorated war hero, conqueror of Egypt and newly elevated peer of the realm, his behaviour towards Gordon was nothing short of a star-struck admirer.[80] He was convinced that political differences alienated Gordon from figures like Lord Northbrook at the Admiralty and Baring in Cairo. 'They dislike Gordon,' Wolseley wrote, 'and never lose an opportunity to *dénigrer* his worth: they call him mad because he does not worship the party gods whom Gladstone & Co. have set up.'[81]

The clique in London first caught sight of Gordon on 28 October 1882, when Malet in Cairo saw fit to forward to London a memorandum from Sir Charles Wilson, military attaché to the British Agency, suggesting that Gordon be sent back to Sudan, where he would be able to 'reduce the country to order in a few months'.[82] This specific nomination of Gordon followed an earlier, more general proposal from Wilson, that 'it would be advisable to send two English officers to the Soudan to report on the state of the country and the steps which will be necessary to insure its pacification'.[83] The important difference between the two is that while the general recommendation was made public, the specific proposal of Gordon was not: a clear instance of control by the foreign policy clique.

Wilson's was but the first of a rapid series of interventions, all invoking the name of Gordon. Sir Harry Verney was a veteran Liberal MP, who may have reflected, in part, the admiration for Gordon felt by his own sister-in-law, Florence Nightingale. On 17 November 1882, Verney wrote to Granville to champion Gordon's return to Sudan, not only arguing that he had 'always exercised a very remarkable influence over wild, uncontrollable, uncivilized peoples' but warning him that Gordon was about to depart for the Middle East on a prolonged period of leave 'unless work was offered him by the Government'.[84]

The following day, Dufferin mused aloud in a cable from Cairo that a solution to the Sudan problem might be found not in merely despatching an investigator to report on the scale of the Mahdī's rebellion and the capacity of the Khartoum administration to respond, as Wilson had initially suggested, but in installing a competent expatriate administrator in Khartoum instead. 'It is probable,' he wrote, 'that if only some person like Colonel [sic] Gordon could be found to undertake its administration fairly good government might be maintained there, without drawing upon Egypt either for men or money'.[85] Written just ten days after arriving in Cairo, Dufferin's observations on Sudan formed part of his first 'General Report' into the 'reorganization of the Egyptian army, and the establishment of liberal institutions in the country'. So it is clear that he, like the Egyptians themselves, assumed that 'the Soudan and Darfour' were part of Egypt.

The fourth and final call for Gordon came on 24 December, when Queen Victoria herself authorised Ponsonby to convey similar opinions, adding that a partnership between Gordon and Sir Samuel Baker 'might settle the revolt in two months'.[86] Granville evidently took these interventions seriously enough to become personally involved, while taking care to screen Gladstone from the ongoing discussions. This is remarkable, given their political partnership of more than a quarter-century: an alliance of the 'feline' and the 'bookish', as Tony Little has put it, reflected in a correspondence of 'inevitable intimacy, directness and confidence'.[87]

But Granville was not hard to persuade that sending Gordon was an undesirable option. Correctly, his first point of contact with respect to Gordon's desirability or otherwise to the Egyptian cabinet, was Malet in Cairo. The response was swift: Cairo did not want Gordon and would only appoint him if forced to do so by London.[88] Having suppressed Wilson's original proposal, Granville saw no reason to reveal it by publicising this correspondence either. But he did decide that the general himself should be consulted. Again, Granville appears to have decided not to tell Gladstone of this meeting – or at least neither man committed any reference to paper.

Gordon was at that time a man adrift and careless. He needed rest and, as Verney had correctly said, was anticipating a long break in the Holy Land. His advice to Granville revealed him to be dramatically out of touch with developments in Sudan. He pronounced the reported scale of the Mahdī's uprising 'immensely exaggerated' and recommended that, with Wilson himself transferred from Cairo to Khartoum as Governor-General, an Egyptian force of just 8,000 soldiers and gendarmes, headed by serving British officers, would be sufficient.[89] That preference for Wilson was endorsed by Northbrook at the Admiralty, who was in regular correspondence with his friend Ripon and who no doubt had heard of Gordon's whimsical approach to his Indian posting. Northbrook expressed doubt that Gordon would wish to return to the scene of his former labours in Sudan or that it would even be 'wise to try him'.[90] According to Blunt, Gordon's views of the Sudan uprising revealed him to be dangerously out of tune with the cabinet.

> My recollection of Gordon's talk is that he expressed himself at the time in entire sympathy with the Mahdi as the popular leader of a revolt against an iniquitous Government, but . . . insisted on the retention of Khartoum as a necessity for Egypt in connection with the Nile water-supply, and as an outpost to be held politically. On this point alone we disagreed.[91]

The combination of Gordon's opinions and Northbrook's negative judgement seems to have tipped the balance and Granville buried the Gordon file. No word of the discussion leaked out into cabinet minutes, parliamentary papers or even personal journals. The clique's internal debate was concluded and Gordon was allowed to proceed to the Middle East, aimless, jobless, a man on the shelf, for a year of what his friend Demetrius Boulger called 'inglorious inaction', pottering about the Holy Land and indulging his enthusiasm for amateur archaeology and Biblical pseudo-scholarship.[92]

Still, the interest of the Foreign Office had been piqued, at least to the extent that they authorised the despatch of an experienced intelligence officer, Lieutenant-Colonel Donald Hamill-Stewart, to compile a report on the situation in Sudan, in collaboration with an Italian soldier and draftsman named Giacomo Messedaglia.[93] The cabinet acquiesced but was careful to maintain the arm's-length relationship. As Granville wrote to Gladstone on 17 November 1882, the day before his meeting with Gordon: 'We decline to have any responsibility for military operations in the Soudan, but the Mission of these officers to obtain information was asked for by [officials in Cairo] in order that they might have information, and not by the Egyptian Gov. Our War Office approved.'[94]

Stewart's own orders were couched in almost verbatim terms: 'under no circumstances,' Malet ordered him, 'should he undertake any responsibility with regard to military operations there'.[95] Stewart began his investigation with customary vigour in December 1882 and immediately began transmitting brief updates on the activities of the Mahdī and General 'Abd-al-Qādir to Malet and Dufferin in Cairo, who in turn passed them on to London.[96] Despite having to send these prolific updates, Stewart was able to complete his authoritative final report by 9 February 1883. But few in government were much interested: the first phase of Gladstone's Sudan policy was now set: tentative exploration, minimum engagement, zero responsibility.

CHAPTER 2

From Egypt into Sudan?

It is the abandonment of that splendid sympathy which the great power has always shown for the manacled slave throughout the world that is to be considered in estimating the cost of England giving up Egypt's authority over the Soudan . . . Has England considered that Khartoum . . . will be turned into a pandemonium of slave-traders busily plying their infamous trade in human beings?

General William Loring, *A Confederate Soldier in Egypt*[1]

The first phase of Sudan policy survived largely unchallenged into the autumn of 1883, when Hicks led a very large but very poorly equipped and ill-trained Egyptian force on a disastrous retaliatory strike against the Mahdī.[2] While he still lived, most diplomats in Cairo were experienced enough to stay 'on message' in respect of the strict arm's-length relationship with Hicks, as stipulated by existing policy. Dufferin described Hicks's employment, alongside 'a few retired European officers', in one of his lengthy updates on the Egyptian situation – still including Sudan – in appropriately careful terms: 'Both Colonel Hicks and his companions have entered the Egyptian service on their own responsibility, nor have either Sir Edward Malet or myself been concerned in the arrangement'.[3]

At least one senior civil servant, however, was reprimanded by Granville for copying Hicks's campaign reports to Malet, a courtesy that implied British complicity in the general's mission: 'It is unnecessary for me to repeat that Her Majesty's Government are in no way responsible for the operations in the Soudan, which have been undertaken under the authority of the Egyptian Government, or for the appointment or actions of General Hicks'.[4] Malet, stung by the rebuke, relayed these sentiments verbatim in an open letter to the Egyptian Prime Minister. Muḥammad Sharīf replied with heavy-handed sarcasm that he 'could not have entertained any doubt on the issue . . . so frankly expressed'.[5]

But the Gladstone government's political inconsistency on intervention – if Egypt, why not Sudan? – was compounded by moral ambiguity. Approval for Egypt's final military push against the Mahdī was implied by the overt role of the British high command in Cairo in Hicks's selection but was set against explicit disavowal of the expedition's aims. In other words, as Robert Wilson has written, 'the British Government sanctioned, but gave no aid to the expedition [so making] themselves morally responsible for its fate without taking steps to make its success a certainty.'[6] Charles Moberly Bell, Cairo correspondent of *The Times*, was scathing about the cabinet's repudiation of responsibility: 'it is hardly possible to suppose that such reasoning will influence the sentiment of the Egyptian fellaheen, who are not habitual students of Hansard or the Army List. To them the Soudan is a province depending on the Government of Egypt, which is itself dependent on the English.'[7]

Disasters in the East and West

On 4 November 1883, after weeks of being harried through the parched thorn-forests of central Kordofan, the 10,000-strong Hicks force was finally overwhelmed by the Mahdī's fighters, dubbed by him *al-anṣār* ('followers') in imitation of the Prophet Muḥammad's earliest adherents, at Sheikān, tantalisingly close to the revolution's new headquarters at al-'Ubeiḍ. News of the disaster filtered back to London only slowly, during which time four cabinet meetings were held, on 10, 13, 17 and 20 November 1883, just one of which discussed Sudan in even general terms.

But even as ministers reconvened at 2pm on 22 November, Gladstone was handed a telegram from Baring in Cairo, received just fifteen minutes earlier. It contained confirmation of Hicks's defeat and with it the death of Egypt's military pretensions in Sudan. Citing eye-witness reports, Lieutenant-Colonel Henry de Coëtlogon, a British officer serving as Egypt's acting Governor-General in Khartoum, had reported to Baring the previous night that 'Egyptian troops were totally destroyed, except 200 wounded.[8] All arms, ammunition, &c., were taken by rebels [who] numbered about 300,000'.[9] Four days later, de Coëtlogon sent a pessimistic despatch with the warning that, with a shortage of serviceable steamers and with soldiers that were 'the refuse of the army, mostly old and blind', 'the only way of saving what remains is to attempt a general retreat on Berber'.[10]

Within cabinet, Northbrook was compelled to concede, in a private letter to his friend Ripon, that 'the Soudan business is a serious one and the defeat of Hicks must bring some discredit upon us. We have, no doubt, carefully avoided all responsibility for the Soudan proceedings of the Egyptian Govt but we shall be told "why did you shrink from it? if you had interfered the disaster would have been avoided".'[11] Nor did the government's critics hold their fire. In Paris, *Liberté* was clear that 'the moral responsibility of this disaster recoils on Great Britain. The English generals laboured under a two-fold illusion. They underestimated the army of the Mahdi, and exaggerated the effects of the new organization given by them to the Khedive's troops. A painful experience shows that a single error of calculation suffices to derange the best conceived military plans'.[12] But the Hicks disaster at least forced the British government to address the Sudan issue with due seriousness at last, resulting in the first modification of policy.

Anxiety in Cairo over the massacre of Hicks's force was compounded by a second Egyptian defeat on the Red Sea Coast on the very same day, 4 November. This military setback was felt more keenly in London because Commander Moncrieff, the British Consul stationed at Sawākīn, was among the fatalities. Augustus Wylde, a well-connected and influential trader based at the Red Sea port, described Moncrieff as 'a hard-working and conscientious officer and an ornament to the service . . . [who] died deeply lamented and beloved by everyone'.[13] Attempting to lift the siege of Sawākīn, a crucial point of departure for the Sudanese interior, by Mahdist forces under the banner of 'Uthmān Diqna, one of the greatest heroes of the Mahdist uprising, Moncrieff's Egyptian force had been destroyed, leaving the eastern coastline highly vulnerable.[14]

These two disastrous engagements proved to be a critical turning point in Britain's relationship not just with Sudan but with Egypt itself. As Wylde wrote, the defeat of Hicks especially proved that 'Mahdism had to be recognised as a serious power aiming at the very security and life of the Egyptian nation'.[15] The Gladstone government was prompted, via its proxies in Cairo, to reconsider the withdrawal timetable of its own troops occupying Egypt. Secondly, a plausible strategic option with regard to Sudan itself – one that still involved British personnel at an absolute minimum – had to be worked out.

There were serious political and moral arguments involved in the debate over available strategic options. None of the possible variations of the status quo – continued colonial occupation of Sudan by Egypt, with tacit British oversight; by the Ottoman Sultan (in whose name the Egyptians purported to rule anyway); or by or another European power – received any significant support, inside or outside government. But the most powerful arguments were marshalled behind the most starkly contrasting alternatives: a full British military occupation of the northern portion of the Sudan territories – more importantly Sawākīn on the Red Sea coast and the Nile route to Khartoum via Dongola, Abū-Ḥamad and Berber – or the complete abandonment of Sudan to the Mahdī, with no military action to be taken against him.

There is no evidence that the Ottoman initiative was pursued with much purpose, unsurprising perhaps given Gladstone's previous virulent animosity toward the Ottoman Empire. In 1876, he had produced a powerful tract denouncing the Turks, who had perpetrated 'atrocities' in Bulgaria, as 'the one great anti-human species of humanity'.[16] Still, Gladstone did subsequently at least toy with the idea of dealing directly with Sultan Abdülhamit II over the 'Soudan question'. Hamilton noted on 9 June 1884: 'It occurs to Mr. G. that it may be just possible that Gordon's proposals should take practical shape in connection with Turkey, wholly severed from us. Mr. G. has always felt our position in the Soudan as regards the Sultan to be a dubious one, and questions our right to prevent Sultan from making war on Mahdi'.[17]

For those in favour of abandonment, primarily Liberals and their Radical allies, the most pragmatic strategy was to pull the northern garrisons of Khartoum, Berber and Dongola back to Wādī-Ḥalfāʾ and there establish an impregnable frontier. Military outposts further south, at Sinnār, Fashoda, Deim Suleimān and elsewhere in distant Equatoria, if still alive, would have to be left individually to negotiate terms of surrender. Both east and west had been comprehensively overrun by the Mahdī's forces; indeed, the fall of al-ʿUbeiḍ, followed by the Hicks disaster, had cut off the last escape route for the Darfur garrisons, forcing the surrender of the Austrian provincial governor, Rudolf Slatin, on 23 December 1883.[18] Even setting aside Gladstone's 'Midlothian principles', there were many practical arguments for such a withdrawal, articulated with typical briskness and clarity by Northbrook in early 1884.

> Our main lines of policy seem to me to be clear and right, that we are satisfied that Egypt should no longer be hampered by the attempt to govern a piece of the world as large as Europe when she cannot find a Corporal's guard fit to fight from her own people, or provide a hundred thousand pounds to pay troops without plunging deeper into bankruptcy. On the other hand that we are not going to spend the lives of Englishmen or of natives of India in either supporting Egyptian rule in the Soudan or of taking half Africa for ourselves and trying to govern it.[19]

By this argument, the Gladstone Bloc hoped to contain the threat from the Mahdī below the twenty-fourth parallel, enabling a return to the priority issue: withdrawal from Egypt. The sixty-four-year-old colonial connection between Egypt and Sudan would be cut, as would Egyptian losses, both financial and human. And this hard-headed policy, it could further be argued, was but a logical extension of an unofficial retreat from Khartoum that was already underway. Dismayed at the Mahdī's triumph over Hicks, many Europeans, Egyptian camp-followers and miscellaneous Ottoman expatriates were making their way downstream to Berber, still held by its government garrison. 'The exodus here is going on,' Frank Power, reporter-cum-consul, wrote to his mother on 1 December 1883; 'Greeks, Copts, Turks, Maltese, Bengalese, Madrasees, Algerians, Italians . . . all trooping down before the river to Berber is closed.'[20]

The counter-argument, territorial occupation by Britain, was supported by an impressive and rowdy coalition of Conservatives and Liberal imperialists, backed by a formidable number of newspapers and periodicals, including *The Times*, the *Pall Mall Gazette*, *Blackwood's Edinburgh Magazine*, *The Quarterly Review*, *The Nineteenth Century* and the *Anti-Slavery Reporter*. The most articulate and authoritative advocate of this 'forward' policy was Wolseley, hero of al-Ṭall al Kabīr, who now demanded the consolidation of Egyptian rule around just three garrison towns. In an important memorandum to Hartington at the War Office, he urged that 'a good garrison should be established at Assouan [i.e., in Egypt proper], that reinforcements should be sent to Suakin, Berber, and Khartoum, and that the two last places should be strongly held under British officers'.[21]

For his part, Hartington, a confirmed 'Liberal imperialist', observed that 'Egypt will never voluntarily give up the provinces east of the White Nile, which she has held for over sixty years, and I don't think she should be asked to do so . . . I think, however, that the district included in the great bend made by the Nile from Khartoum to Debbeh should be retained as part of Egyptian territory, although it is to the west of the Nile.'[22] After all, as Henry Patterson pointed out at the time, while the Mahdī's fortunes thus far had been 'rather chequered . . . the fact that this impostor can point to all this success – this dreadful slaughter – shows clearly that almost anything is possible in the Soudan, and that the evil requires nipping in the bud, or it may become very difficult to deal with at a later date'.[23]

The Times agreed, arguing that 'unless Khartoum is defended, and authority is maintained in Senaar, the Soudan will either be filled with European adventurers or will lapse into native anarchy, constituting a standing menace to Egypt'.[24] This was merely the latest formal objection by The Times, a paper whose position on Egypt was compromised by its financial dependence on the Rothschild family, one of the major investors in the Egyptian state. As well as joining other British bondholders in the attempt to force the annexation of Egypt or its declaration as a British protectorate, the Rothschilds used The Times, an 'obedient organ', to argue that 'the Sudan east and north of Khartoum was essential for the security of Egypt proper'.[25]

As the months passed, the debate grew more acrimonious, yet also more nuanced, as parliamentarians, soldiers, journalists, businessmen and lobbyists argued over British prestige, territorial loss to imperial rivals, a potential resurgence of the Equatorial slave trade, the pros and cons of agricultural and commercial development in the central Sudanese provinces and, above all, the security of Egypt proper. It was on the issue of slavery that the Gladstone cabinet found it hardest to maintain a satisfactory position. Forcing the Egyptians to abandon Sudan risked not only the general charge that 'civilisation' was retreating in the face of 'barbarism', but also a more specific denunciation: the inevitability of a resurgent slave trade.

But slaves were not the only commercially viable exports from the Sudan territories and many of the arguments over a policy of abandonment focused on trade, in which the monopoly was assumed to be an expatriate prerogative, as it had been since Muḥammad ʿAlī's invasion in 1820.[26] By this argument, direct British territorial control would produce a vigorous import/export market. Indeed, Ibrāhīm ʿAbbās goes so far as to say that 'nearly every individual Briton who had travelled, traded or joined the administration in the Sudan before the outbreak of the Mahdist revolution, was against the policy of the British Government to abandon the whole of the Sudan, with the exception of the port of Suakin, to the Mahdi'.[27]

Dufferin in Cairo was among those who believed that commerce was an important reason for the Egyptians to stay in Sudan. 'Under our superintendence,' he wrote, the month after the Hicks debacle, 'Egypt will undoubtedly become more or less a civilizing Power and if a good administration were established in the Soudan proper, with a railway from Suakin to Berber, a good deal of light could be let in the "dark continent".'[28] This was the first explicit British reference to a Sawākīn-Berber railway, an issue that would become of paramount importance during the summer of 1884. Over the previous quarter-century, interest in a rail link south of the Egyptian frontier centred on the Nile route between Wādī-Ḥalfāʾ and Kerma.[29] At any event, a railway to boost exports was now endorsed by the missionary Robert Felkin, who was convinced that Sudan 'had great capabilities which only required an outlet to the sea to enable its vast resources to be utilized by the civilized world'.[30]

The third strand of the debate centred on the security of Egypt itself: the strength of its southern frontier; its susceptibility to the spiritual call of the Mahdī; and its dependency on the waters of the Nile. As early as 9 January 1883, *The Times* had stated that a pull-out would not just mean 'the triumph of the slave holding class':

> It is not at all probable that a successful semi-military, semi-religious confederacy in the Soudan would be content to maintain a passive attitude towards its neighbours; and the tranquillity of Lower Egypt would be continually disturbed by the aggressive acts or threats of those who even now have a full belief to vanquish any number of [Egypt's] soldiers.[31]

The *Pall Mall Gazette*, meanwhile, fretted about the threat to Egypt and beyond of the 'conquering Mohammadan Power' emerging in Sudan.[32] And champions of intervention posited a more immediately urgent argument for retaining Khartoum at least: come the rainy season, the Nilometer at the junction of the Blue and White Niles gave Egypt between ten and twenty days' warning of the advance of the flood waters; its loss would represent a 'direct threat to the people living off the soil in Egypt'.[33] Prince Ibrāhīm Hilmy in Cairo wrote to *The Times* to remind readers of a second Nilometer at Berber, 'where the tributary Atbara enters the main stream', warning that 'the abandonment of Khartoum and Berber would involve the surrender of sources of knowledge which I believe are of vital importance to the well-being of the whole country'.[34]

Sir Samuel Baker, meanwhile, explicitly advocated the extinguishing of any independent identity for Sudan, calling instead for Khartoum to be formally instated as the capital of Upper Egypt. In a powerful contribution to *The Nineteenth Century* magazine, Baker lamented the loss of British prestige in retreating before 'ignorant barbarians, who extinguish all progress by a chronic inter-tribal strife'. Foreshadowing the Fashoda Crisis of 1898, he speculated about rival French ambitions in Central Africa, expressing the fear that 'in less time than many would believe, we should discover a rival colony firmly rooted at Khartoum'.[35] Baker also raised the spectre of a security nightmare even worse than the loss of the Nilometers:

> Not only will this inestimable result of modern science . . . be lost by the abandonment of Khartoum, but should a civilised, or even a semi-civilised, enemy be in possession of that point, the water of the Rahad, Dinder, Blue Nile, and the Atbara rivers could be diverted from their course, and dispersed throughout the deserts, to the utter ruin and complete destruction of Egypt Proper.[36]

There was some attempt to counter such alarmist language. John Cross, Liberal MP for Bolton and Lord Kimberley's deputy at the India Office, happened to be in Cairo shortly after the loss of the Hicks force. He concluded not only that there was zero risk of a direct attack by the Mahdī on British troops in Egypt proper – an incorrect assumption, as it turned out, though such an offensive would not be launched until several years later – but also that schemes to divert the course of the Nile 'to the ruin of Egypt' were simply 'chimerical'.[37]

Compelling Egypt to disengage

In the short term, there was little visible urgency in London's response to the losses of Hicks and Moncrieff, although three stop-gap measures were implemented. To address the problems on the Red Sea coast, General Valentine Baker, Commandant of Police in Cairo, was ordered to raise a force of 3,600 Egyptians and transport them south to relieve the garrisons around Sawākīn. Baker was a highly controversial figure, whose chequered history included an alleged sexual assault on a train: influential connections had enabled him to salvage something from his military career by securing him an Egypt posting. Still, following a protest from Northbrook over Baker's new prominence in Cairo, Gladstone had written in a memo of 20 November 1882: 'As to Baker, I think he would be best in the Soudan [i.e. instead of Hicks], next to this in the gendarmerie [which is where he ended up]'.[38] Once deployed on the Red Sea coast, Baker's force would fare no better than Moncrieff's three months earlier. Fully two-thirds of his men were subsequently slaughtered by 'Uthmān Diqna's fighters on 4 February 1884 a few miles inland from the small port of Trinkitat, a defeat that was vividly described in the *Evening Standard* two days later.[39]

On the diplomatic front, Baring was invited to provide an analysis as to the knock-on risk of the Mahdī's victory over Hicks at Sheikān to 'Egypt proper' and to 'tender advice about retirement from Soudan'.[40] Thirdly, the troop withdrawal from Cairo to Alexandria was frozen. On 11 December 1883, Granville wrote to Constantine Musurus, the Ottoman Ambassador in London, to say that, in view of the 'great disaster' in Sudan and 'in virtue of the responsibility thrown upon them under circumstances which will not have escaped your Excellency's recollection', the cabinet had decided to 'retain the troops provisionally in Cairo'.[41]

Annoyed at such distractions from an enjoyable break amid unseasonably warm weather at Windsor Castle and in Oxford, Gladstone wrote to the Chief Whip, Lord Grosvenor, to comment laconically that 'late incidents & especially the Soudan disaster have very much ruffled the aspect of foreign affairs & Egypt again looks as if it might work out into a serious difficulty'.[42]

Despite this prescient appraisal, it was not until 3 January 1884 that the cabinet reconvened to discuss what to do about Egypt's Sudanese holdings. As before, ministers benefited from analysis presented by Baring in a succession of telegrams over the preceding weeks. What those messages made clear was the absolute determination on the part of the Egyptian government to reclaim the initiative in its southern colony, despite Britain's abdication of responsibility. Indeed, the Egyptian ministers argued, maintaining a presence was no more than their constitutional obligation: Sudan, like its Egyptian rulers, fell under Ottoman rule. Indeed, the official document signed by Sultan Abdülhamit in Constantinople appointing Ṭawfīq as Khedive on 17 August 1879 had stated that he must never 'under any pretext or motive, abandon to others, in whole or in part, the privileges accorded to Egypt, and which are emanations of the rights and natural prerogatives of my imperial government, nor shall he abandon any part of the territory'.[43]

On 12 December 1883, Baring had been visited by Muḥammad Sharīf, Prime Minister in the post-invasion government, who had negotiated with first Dufferin and then Baring the now aborted withdrawal of British forces from Cairo to Alexandria. Well-educated, multi-lingual and originally from Kavala, in what is now north-eastern Greece, Sharīf's rise to prominence in Cairo was an example of the Ottomans' anti-native prejudice that had prompted Colonel Aḥmad 'Arābi to mount his uprising under the banner 'Egypt for the Egyptians' (miṣr li'l-miṣriyīn). Baring later described Sharīf as 'the least Egyptian of any of the Moslem Prime Ministers in recent times. . . . Whatever was not Turkish in his character, was French.'[44] Egypt, Sharīf Pasha now insisted, was not asking for British troops for Sudan; indeed the presence of Christian soldiers might stir up support for the Mahdī still further. Instead, the Prime Minister conveyed his cabinet's conviction that 'the best expedient in the present emergency is to resort to the Sultan; and they would be grateful if Her Majesty's Government would negotiate with His Imperial Majesty the conditions under which the assistance of Turkish troops can be obtained'.[45]

Three days after this visit, Baring received his instructions from the Foreign Office: 'Her Majesty's Government have no objection to offer to the employment of Turkish troops, provided they are paid by the Turkish Government, and that such employment be restricted exclusively to the Soudan, with their base at Souakin. . . . Her Majesty's Government recommend to the Minister of the Khedive to come to an early decision to abandon all territory south of Assouan, or at least of Wady Halfa.'[46] This response was partly informed by the receipt of a further briefing paper, delivered 'with the greatest diffidence and reserve', by Northbrook, who commended 'the deliberate abandonment of the attempt to govern the Soudan from Egypt, the withdrawal of Egyptian troops to such point as may be decided upon with our consent, coupled with the assurance that we will protect Egypt [from the Mahdī's expected advance], for a specified time'.[47]

The government had in this matter the reluctant support of the Queen, who 'acquiesced, though with regret, in the abandonment of the Soudan by Egypt'.[48] This new policy was, of course, more easily dictated than achieved: hence Henry Traill's acid observation that 'when they instructed the Khedive to abandon the Soudan ... they were presumably aware that the withdrawal from a territory by a former ruler is not quite so simple a matter as the *déménagement* of a householder, or even the surrender of possession of a private landowner's estate. There were such things to be considered as populations and garrisons, neither of which could quite properly be left to extermination by the incoming tenants.'[49]

This domestic analogy was more than matched by one offered to Baring by Granville (and thus of a distinctly more aristocratic flavour) as he mused on 28 December 1883 over Egypt's reluctant surrender of its Sudan territories: 'It takes away somewhat of the position of a man to sell his racers and hunters, but if he cannot afford to keep them, the sooner they go to Tattersall's [bloodstock auctioneers] the better'.[50] Muḥammad Sharīf's reply to the order from London, taking the argument to the next stage, had come just the day before the cabinet meeting:

> Under these circumstance, and taking into consideration that we cannot get any help from Her Majesty's Government as regards the Soudan, the Government of His Highness finds itself compelled to apply to the Porte,[51] without delay, for a contingent of 10,000 men to be sent to Suakin. If His Majesty the Sultan does not see fit to comply with our request, the Government of His Highness has determined to notify to the Porte their retrocession to the Empire of the administration of the shores of the Red Sea and of the Eastern Soudan. ... Egypt would be able to concentrate on the Nile her forces which are scattered from Harar [a major commercial centre in the hills of what is now eastern Ethiopia] to Suakin. This concentration would allow us, including the troops we have at Senaar, Khartoum, and Berber, to raise a force of about 15,000 men, which, in our opinion, is sufficient to command the Nile from Khartoum, and thus assure the safety of Egypt.[52]

The 'Granville Doctrine'

To the British, this offer by the Cairo government of a compromise, ceding responsibility for the Red Sea coastline but refusing to disengage from the upper Nile Valley, appeared little short of intransigence. On a domestic political level, it too closely resembled the arguments of the 'retention lobby', as articulated by

Wolseley, Samuel Baker and their allies in the Conservative press. More practically, the aspiration to 'command the Nile from Khartoum' seemed to be ill-founded optimism, as unrealistic as Muḥammad Sharīf's breezy confidence before the Hicks debacle that 'we shall give this gentleman [the Mahdī] a good thrashing'.[53]

'I can only say,' Baring now wrote, 'that I entirely disbelieve that any Egyptian force which can be got together will be capable of defending the whole length of the valley of the Nile from Khartoum downwards.'[54] This view echoed the consensus reached by the three British officers responsible for all military affairs in Egypt at a meeting in Cairo on 26 November 1883 – at least as reported by Baring. Generals Stephenson, Wood and Baker had been 'unanimously of opinion that the Egyptian Government will find it impossible . . . to hold the Soudan . . . They think that Khartoum should, if possible, be held sufficiently long to allow the more advanced posts and detached garrisons in the Soudan to rejoin'.[55]

This reflected accurately the views of Wood and Stephenson. Wood wrote to Queen Victoria the day after the meeting to state his clear belief that 'the happiest result would be that Egypt should lose all the interior country south of Assouan'.[56] Stephenson wrote to his sisters on 21 December to state that 'the Soudan must be abandoned – Egypt cannot hold it; there is not an atom of fighting power in the natives, and the administration of that distant country has been corrupt and oppressive. The Soudanese are better without a Government at all than with such a one as Egypt has furnished them with'.[57] But Baring was dishonest in attaching Valentine Baker to an otherwise triumvirate consensus. Baker, probably influenced by his brother Samuel, was still arguing as late as 17 January 1884 for the retention of what he called Eastern Sudan (i.e. east of the White Nile), a region that was, he insisted, 'a paying province' whose continued occupation would serve as a deterrent to a move by the Mahdī on Egypt proper and would maintain 'the only line of retreat open' to the other Sudan garrisons.[58]

Unaware of this partial but deliberate misrepresentation, the cabinet meeting on 3 January 1884 concluded by adopting two strategies, one overt, the other secret. The first was to be conveyed openly to Baring. Britain had no objection to any surrender of Egyptian sovereignty to the Sultan; indeed, the Turks would be welcome to take over Sudan's Red Sea ports, although with no 'pecuniary obligation to the Porte' by either London or Cairo.[59] Secondly, the withdrawal from Khartoum must be authorised by Sharīf Pasha's government in conformity with British 'advice'. And thirdly, the proposal that Egypt be formally declared a protectorate was rejected, despite the fact that such status might have enabled the Egyptian government to swallow London's orders with some measure of dignity and given them some legal cover with respect to the Sultan. 'It is of the greatest importance,' wrote Granville, 'that the Egyptian Government should, without delay, make up their minds as to the policy they are ready to adopt . . . that all military operations, except those for the rescue of outlying garrisons, should cease in the Soudan.'[60]

The second, secret, message removed any question of negotiation. 'Ministers and Governors [in Egypt],' the note read, 'must carry out this advice or forfeit their offices. The appointment of English ministers would be most objectionable, but it will no doubt be possible to find Egyptians who will execute the Khedive's orders under English advice. The Cabinet will give you [Baring] full support.'[61]

Afaf al-Sayyid has gone so far as to label this dramatic change in relationship, under which Egyptian ministers could be fired if they did not carry out British policy, the 'Granville Doctrine'.[62] This convenient label, however, is an oxymoron. Granville was incapable of articulating such an uncompromising approach. All the push came from Gladstone and attracted predictably sardonic commentary from domestic critics. 'The venerable Statesman,' wrote Traill, 'actually imagined that a Government which we had taken under our tutelage at Cairo might, outside a certain radius from the capital, have its authority shattered and its armies annihilated without our being thereby compelled to take any action on our own account in the matter. Comedy jostles tragedy.'[63] Officers and civilians in the field were equally dismayed. At Sawākīn, Augustus Wylde, an adherent of the retention lobby whose arguments were based on years of commercial experience, professed himself 'dazed' at the decision and added, with some hyperbole:

> No revolution, no change of dynasty or government was ever so sudden
> . . . It meant ruin to those who were left up country in the Soudan; it meant
> ruin to all those who had interests in the Soudan; it meant anarchy,
> murder, and the cessation of all law and order, and the plunging of the
> country back again into confusion and chaos, and the instant destruction
> of years of work that had partly civilized the inhabitants.[64]

The edict from London caused consternation in Cairo. Khedive Ṭawfīq was torn between his instinctive hostility to the British order and his gratitude to Gladstone for restoring his authority after the defeat of Aḥmad ʿArābi: 'I may not see the wisdom and advantage of evacuating the Soudan, but I concur in the present necessity and the course adopted, though Khartoum might perhaps have been saved . . . Let them say that I am weak and sold to England . . . my conscience tells me that I have done right.'[65] But it was too much for Muḥammad Sharīf and his cabinet colleagues, who resigned en masse, complaining that, 'since Sudan is a possession of the Ottoman Porte, entrusted to our charge . . . we resign our posts because we are prevented from governing in accordance with the constitution'.[66] 'Time and posterity,' Sharīf added, 'will judge between me and Mr Gladstone.'[67] Speaking more candidly to his German friend, Baron Karl de Malortie, Sharīf explained that, while he accepted his general subservience to the British, the Sudan policy was a step too far.

> No true Egyptian will subscribe to the abandonment of Khartoum and the
> Eastern Soudan, or renounce our autonomy. I have in many ways
> sacrificed my popularity in order to satisfy British demands, but I should

be unworthy of my post were I to consent to an act I consider suicidal. . . .
Generally a Cabinet falls because it is not in accord either with the
Sovereign or the country; in our case we fell *though*, and perhaps *because*,
we are all agreed on the question of the Soudan.[68]

Although such formal legal terminology would never have been admitted in
London – and, indeed, had been explicitly rejected in the cabinet meeting of 3
January 1884 – General Stephenson was surely right to 'consider the present
state of things as virtually the commencement of our Protectorate'.[69] The new
Prime Minister of Egypt was the more compliant Nūbār 'Boghos' Nubārian[70], an
Armenian Christian who had worked as a secretary and private trade ambassador for every Egyptian ruler since 1848. His loyalty to the royal family,
currently represented by the Khedive Ṭawfīq, coupled with decades of bureaucratic and political experience, made him a perfect candidate for the
premiership. The detail of how Nubārian worked with Baring was entirely abdi-
cated by ministers in London. 'Baring exercising his best judgement on the
present necessities and means of Egypt,' noted Gladstone after a cabinet meeting
on 22 January 1884, 'and we approve of Baring's proceeding and shall be glad if
he finds that he can come to terms with the Egyptian Govt.'[71]

Two different rationales may be found for Baring's willingness and ability to
do so with relatively little trouble. On the one hand, as Roger Owen has written,
Baring now 'took the lead in exposing what he had begun to believe as the illogic
of the British cabinet's original assumption that an immediate military evacuation was possible on the grounds that (a) the only way to ensure post-occupation
stability would be a return to the type of Khedivial absolutism that Britain was
attempting to replace, and (b) if Britain were to leave before this stability was
assured it might well be forced to reoccupy the country in defence of its imperial
interests in more difficult diplomatic and military circumstances a few years
hence'.[72] Less creditably, Baring's was a truly paternalistic approach to colonial
administration, in which, as he later wrote, 'each special issue should be decided
mainly with reference to what, by the light of Western knowledge and experience tempered by local consideration, we conscientiously think is best for the
subject race'.[73]

Baring's readiness to implement tough orders from London prompted some
in Cairo to view him as an abnormally ruthless diplomat. The English Controller-
General of Egyptian Customs, Baron de Kusel, noted that the Egyptians 'were not
used to the hand of steel without a covering of some soft textile fabric. . . . It may
well be that his particular characteristics were more suitable and needful in
Egypt at that time than the more polished diplomacy; but it has always seemed
to me that a little tact is not really harmful in dealing with most people, nor need
it detract from the powers of a strong man'.[74] General Wood, by contrast, divided
the personal from the professional. On the one hand, he found the administrator
'singularly undemonstrative'.[75] But at work Baring was 'one of the biggest men
now serving the Queen's Government – clever – patient and determined'.[76]

Baring's mind-set had been shaped by British India, an experience that left him diametrically opposed to the views of men such as Sir John Seeley, convinced that self-rule was both unlikely and unsuitable, as 'it will never be possible to make a Western silk purse out of an Eastern sow's ear'.[77] Ibrāhīm 'Abbās has ascribed to Baring even less charitable motives, chiefly 'his desire to be virtually responsible for the government of Egypt proper. He had anticipated that the policy of abandonment might serve this supreme object of his . . . to assume absolute power in Egypt because this would enable him to fulfil the role he had envisaged for himself as the maker of "modern Egypt"'.[78]

The scale of the proposed withdrawal from Sudan was immense. The best evidence available put the total number of Egyptian troops, their families and camp followers, as well as civilian bureaucrats and administrative assistance whose loyalty to the Egyptian proxy regime at Khartoum might put their lives at risk, at more than twenty thousand.[79] In fact, officials in Cairo had already begun issuing military orders in line with the new policy. On 9 January 1884, Baring relayed to London an alarming message from de Coëtlogon in Khartoum, supported by Egyptian generals in the city, to the effect that 'one-third of garrison are unreliable, and that even if it were twice as strong as it is it would not hold Khartoum against the whole country . . . [so] preliminary instructions have been given to prepare for a retreat'.[80]

On 16 January, Cairo ordered its garrisons on the Blue Nile and much further south in distant Equatoria and on the Bahr al-Ghazāl to fall back on Khartoum immediately. There they should join the 2,000 men of the Fashoda garrison who had already abandoned their post on the White Nile, making their way down to Khartoum three weeks earlier. But for most, the orders were already too late. Sinnār and Deim Suleimān were both under siege, while smaller outposts were picked off one by one by the Mahdī's men and their soldiers killed or subsumed into the ranks of the anṣār. The command to withdraw was not made public in Khartoum itself. As late as 21 January, Power was reporting that 'the order for evacuation has not yet been definitively given, nor it is publicly known that such an order is contemplated'.[81]

Only one element of the new Sudan policy now needed to be resolved: identifying both a mechanism for achieving the complete withdrawal of the distant garrisons and the man to lead the exodus. As General Stephenson put it, 'it will be an operation of difficulty and serious danger unless the wild tribes can be conciliated'.[82] The decision taken by the government at this crucial stage – the second-chance selection of General Charles Gordon – would prove to be the most fateful twist, one that would lead not just to radical policy revision but, by the end of the nineteenth century, full-scale military invasion, the abandonment of overseas retrenchment as an ethical norm and active participation in the 'scramble for Africa'.

The decision to send Gordon was the result of increasingly frantic, last minute and behind-the-scenes negotiation, conducted entirely within the small foreign policy cabal. While press debate was increasing, the decision certainly had nothing to do with parliamentary consultation. By the time MPs and Lords gathered at Westminster on 5 February 1884 for the state opening of parliament, they had not sat since the previous August: fully 163 days. But members were well aware, from their newspapers and periodicals, of the growing storm over the 'Soudan Question', so when it came to the Queen's Speech, formally setting out the legislative agenda for the session ahead, 'the customary placid language was,' as John Bowen put it, 'strangely at variance with the feelings of those who listened to it'.[83]

As defended in the Lords by the Lord Chancellor, the Marquess of Tweeddale, the relevant section of the address made it clear just how seriously Egypt and its southern colony would dominate the government's legislative agenda for the foreseeable future.

> Having had every reason to be satisfied with the tranquillity of Egypt, and with the progress made in the establishment of orderly institutions, I gave, during the autumn, instructions for the evacuation of Cairo, for the further reduction of my military forces, and for their concentration mainly in Alexandria.
>
> But in the month of November the Egyptian Army, appointed to maintain the rule of the Khedive in the Soudan, was defeated and broken up with heavy loss.
>
> Upon the occurrence of this defeat, I deemed it wise to recall the order I had given, as a precaution against the possible effects of the military reverse in Egypt itself, and to preclude all doubt as to the certain maintenance of its tranquillity. . . .
>
> I have offered to the Egyptian Government such counsels, as appeared to be required by a prudent regard to the amount of its resources, and by the social condition of the country. I have also dispatched Major-General Gordon to report on the best means of giving effect to the resolution of the Khedive to withdraw from the Interior of the Soudan, and have permitted him to act in the execution of the measure.[84]

Barring the transparent falsehood in the final paragraph, that a comprehensive Egyptian withdrawal from the Sudan colony was anything other than a British order, the greater part of the Egypt section of the Queen's Speech was a straightforward admission of policy shift, grudgingly conceded by Gladstone. More problematic, however, indeed an ambiguity that was to haunt his government, was the question of Gordon's authority in Sudan, and the scope of his permission 'to act in the execution of the measure'.

It was just one more element of uncertainty in a policy that was being patched up on a contingency basis. 'Up to this moment,' wrote Henry Traill in the aftermath of the ensuing debacle, 'it was still possible for them to avoid the abyss of discredit towards which events and their own half-hearted counsels were hurrying them.'[85] But the appointment of Gordon was one ad hoc measure too far; or, as Winston Churchill later put it, 'the Ministers looked about them, wondering how they could assist the Egyptian Government without risk or expense to themselves, and in an evil hour for their fame and fortunes someone whispered the word "Gordon"'.[86]

CHAPTER 3

'Gordon for the Soudan!'

I can well understand all the perplexities of the Gordon appointment . . .
Baring's doubt . . . comes from the impossibility of inducing him to carry out
any policy of which he does not approve. This arises from a very noble frame
of mind, but it is obviously a drawback. . . . When I start by saying I regard
Gordon as the grandest character in 1884, you will not I hope misunderstand
my stating I think his heart is better than his head. Either because he takes
his inspirations from the Bible, and applies them literally to daily life; or
because there is some want of fixity of purpose in his mind; he is occasionally ludicrously inconsistent.

General Sir Evelyn Wood, 1 February 1884[1]

By early January 1884, when the Gladstone cabinet began searching in
earnest for an officer to lead the forced Egyptian evacuation from Sudan,
it was more than a year since Granville and his coterie had discussed the
possible casting of Major-General Charles Gordon in some as-yet-undefined
primary role in Khartoum. Gordon himself had thrown no shadow over
proceedings during the intervening months: skulking in the Holy Land, he had,
after decades of intermittent national attention, effectively disappeared from
view.

The poet Wilfrid Blunt – aesthete, former diplomat, property-owner in Cairo
and champion of Aḥmad ʿArābi's 'Egypt for the Egyptians' campaign – had been
a regular correspondent with Gordon for years.[2] In a journal entry for early
January 1884, Blunt noted that 'except for a few reviews of Hake's book
"Chinese Gordon", which had been published at Christmas time, I can find
nothing about him in any of the London newspapers'.[3] Indeed, as one such
reviewer noted, Gordon's current whereabouts were 'unknown to all except his
friends and such of his admirers as make a point of following with the keenest
attention the course of his strange and adventurous life'.[4] Confusion over
Gordon's nickname, earned for his exploits during the China wars of the 1860s,

suggests that his was no longer a name to be conjured with in all quarters. 'So little was General Gordon known at this time by his countrymen,' notes Seton Churchill, 'that a country gentleman . . . remarked, on seeing the fact mentioned in the paper that "Chinese Gordon" was going out [to Sudan], "I see the Government have just sent a Chinaman to the Soudan. What can they mean by sending a native of that country to such a place?"'[5]

Had Gordon taken employment on the Congo under King Leopold of the Belgians, as planned, this oblivion may have been lasting. Such an appointment had been at the centre of a protracted flirtation between Gordon and the king dating back more than four years. As early as October 1879, hearing rumours that Gordon was to resign as Governor-General of Sudan, Leopold authorised Sir William Mackinnon, a well-connected shipping magnate, to sound out Gordon as to his interest in sharing the management of the king's Congo territories with Henry Moreton Stanley.[6] Stanley himself wrote that, by 1882, his own responsibilities were 'so serious that they threaten to become unmanageable' and 'feeling an intense interest in the growth of the territory which was rapidly growing into a State, I suggested to His Majesty . . . that I required as an associate a person of merit, rank, and devotion to work, such as General Gordon, who would undertake either the management of the Lower or Upper Congo, while I would work in the other section'.[7]

Despite the frustrations of his recent stuttering career, however, Gordon regarded a Congo expedition with little enthusiasm; indeed, in his more self-flagellatory moments, he seemed to view it as more of an opportunity for personal suffering than advancement. But he had no qualms about serving Leopold, and certainly no premonition that the monarch, in his lavish palace at Laeken, currently lauded across Europe for his professions of humanitarian concern, would be revealed in time as one of the worst perpetrators of abuse in European colonial history. Nor was Gordon alone in his misplaced confidence in Leopold: Charles Allen, Secretary of the British and Foreign Anti-Slavery Society, believed that the world owed a debt of gratitude to a monarch 'whose generosity enables such men as Stanley and Gordon to bear the torch of civilization and the banner of freedom into the heart of the "Dark Continent"'.[8]

A coalition of interests

Gordon's improbable return from obscurity was engineered by a small but vocal cabal of influential personalities, Wolseley primary among them but including Sir Samuel Baker, veteran of Sudan service and tireless advocate of a retention policy, Hugh Childers, the Chancellor of the Exchequer, William Stead, editor of the *Pall Mall Gazette*, Demetrius Boulger, a prolific writer and editor of the *Asiatic Quarterly*, as well as the Anti-Slavery Society and several other individuals who admired Gordon for his religious convictions. Personal motivations varied but the common denominator was anger: at the abandonment of Hicks, at the weakness of Egypt's southern frontier, at the potential resurgence of slave-raiding in Sudan and at the betrayal of a fundamental philosophical principle, never surrendering to the 'savage'.

Some, like Lord Northbrook, admired Gordon's 'enormous power over uncivilised people'.[9] Among Gordon's many friends and admirers within the army was Colonel Gerald Graham, who spent several days with his hero in Egypt as Gordon passed through the last diplomatic ordeals of mission definition (see Chapter 4) and who left a vivid contemporary description of a man to whom he accorded an almost embarrassing degree of reverence.

> Not over 5 feet 9 inches in height, but of compact build, his figure and gait characteristically expresses resolution and strength. His face, though in itself unpretending, was one that, in common phrase, "grew upon you". Time had now streaked with grey the crisp, curly brown hair of his youth, and traced lines of care on his ample forehead and strong, clear face, bronzed with exposure to the tropical sun. His usual aspect was serene and quiet, and though at times a ruffling wave of constitutional impatience or indignation might pass over him, it did not disturb him long . . . [and] outer disturbance was to him like the wind that ruffles the surface of the sea, but does not affect its depths. The force and beauty of Gordon's whole expression came from within, and, as it were, irradiated the man, the steadfast truthful gaze of the blue-grey eyes seeming a direct appeal from the upright spirit within.[10]

Even before Gordon's mission became defined, this broad coalition of interests embraced various material ambitions. Baker himself was among the 'business lobby' arguing for retention on the grounds that Sudan had great potential as a source of cotton and wheat for Britain. 'There is no possibility of internal improvement [in Sudan],' he argued, 'without the employment of foreign capital; and there will be no investment of such capital until confidence in the stability of the administration shall be established. . . . If that should be accomplished, we should quickly see reforms in the Soudan that would within two or three years exhibit an extraordinary change both in the people and in the resources of the country.'[11]

Charles Burnett, an Aberdeen-based trader, wanted Gordon to be the agent of active British intervention. Otherwise, he warned in an 1884 pamphlet, 'Germany, Italy and France would turn their ships and armies to establishing a central African dominion, with its outlets on the Red Sea . . . [and] they would take out of British hands the management of, and all future interference with, the destinies of Egypt itself and its highway to India.'[12] Burnett's solution was the installation of Gordon as nothing less than Khedive of Sudan, with 'resources in men, arms and money to enable him to undertake the necessary preliminary task of pricking the pseudo-theological wind-bag, by killing or capturing the would-be prophet [i.e. the Mahdī]'.[13] Other voices joined the debate, usually on the side of greater, rather than reduced, British intervention.

Baker was Honorary Secretary of a group called the Patriotic Association, made up of 'able and illustrious' establishment figures, most of them graduates of Christ Church, Oxford, and all affiliated in some way to the Conservative Party.[14] The association's membership is nowhere listed in full, but certainly included the Earl of Cadogan as President, as well as the Earl of Dunraven and several serving Conservative Party MPs.[15] The association's manifesto, condensing political and moral objections to current policy, was discussed at the Guildhall on 20 January 1884 under the headline 'Requisition against the abandonment of the Soudan':

> We feel that . . . the abandonment of Khartoum and of the extensive provinces of which it is the emporium to a fanatical barbarism would be discreditable to England, would greatly enhance the reputation and power of the Mahdi, and would be a cause of serious danger to Egypt and to the neighbouring countries; that such a course would leave the garrisons and civilian population of Khartoum and many other places to great suffering and massacre; that the commerce with the Soudan and with Central Africa is considerable and increasing; and that the slave trade, which formerly inflicted such misery upon those regions, and which England has made such efforts to repress, would be revived with desolating effect.[16]

The military was well represented in the informal cabal intriguing for Gordon's despatch. Affection for Gordon was matched by contempt for government. Wolseley despised politicians in general but reserved especially vitriolic disdain for Gladstone, whose policy of imperial retrenchment was the antithesis of everything he had spent his professional life as a true 'soldier of empire' trying to achieve. The Prime Minister, he was to write later, was simply 'contemptible', a 'rampant self seeking politician': 'Never have I hated a man as I did Mr. Gladstone then, but it was not the hatred I felt for the honest devils whom I would kill, it was the loathing & the contempt that all men feel for the ignoble, the unworthy & the base'.[17] 'I have never been enamoured of Quacks in any calling', Wolseley wrote, 'but it is a sad spectacle to see the Land Forces of our Empire handed over to the charge of some chance firework politician in search of a reputation for administrative ability.'[18]

The force of these combined interventions, in which the cream of the aristocracy joined forces with decorated officers, the most articulate spokesman on the Opposition benches and the most widely-read newspapers and periodicals in the land, was easily enough to sway the Foreign Office, led by the chronically indecisive Granville. Yet the two-fold premise of the Gordon candidacy, that he had scored tremendous successes during his earlier tenure as Governor-General in Khartoum and was therefore an authority figure loved and respected by the Sudanese, was easily refutable even at the time.[19]

Lobbying for Gordon had resumed in February 1883, just a few months after the first abortive (and unpublicised) initiatives to recruit the general to the Sudan cause. Boulger wrote twice to *The Times*, arguing that 'in the interests of Egypt, of civilisation, and of the mass of the Soudanese . . . General Gordon should be sent back with plenary powers to the old scene of his labours'.[20] 'On this occasion', Boulger later reflected ruefully, 'I was snubbed, being told by one of the ablest editors I have known . . . that "Gordon was generally considered to be mad".'[21]

Following this reverse, pressure intensified markedly toward the end of the year. On 24 November 1883, Childers received a letter from Sir Andrew Clarke, acting Major-General in the Royal Engineers, Gordon's own regiment, and Inspector-General of Fortifications, urging that 'if the Mahdi is a prophet, Gordon in the Soudan is a greater' and enclosing a second letter from a fellow officer in the Engineers, who declared that, were it to be announced 'that Charlie Gordon has been appointed to assist the Khedive with supreme power, and authorised to ask for a division from India . . . then the Government will reinstate themselves in favour with the country'.[22] The officer's letter urged specifically that 'Gordon should be sent to the Soudan with a force from India of two European and four or five native battalions, and that he should advance from Suakin to Berber, 270 miles'.[23] The chancellor responded positively, relaying the recommendation to Granville, who on 27 November sketched in turn a short note to Gladstone:

> Do you see any objection to using Gordon in some way. He has an immense name in Egypt – he is popular at home – He is a strong but very sensible opponent of slavery – He has a small bee in his bonnet. If you do not object I could consult Baring by telegraph.[24]

Two days later, Gladstone noted in his diary that he would discuss Sudan with Granville the following day: 'I should not wonder if it became necessary to call the Cabinet'.[25] But another thirty-five days would pass before such a meeting was convened and, with no explicit objection from the Prime Minister forthcoming, Gordon's name was first placed in the official record of correspondence between government personnel. On 1 December 1883, Granville telegraphed Baring in Cairo: 'If General Charles Gordon were willing to go to Egypt would he be of any use to you or to the Egyptian Government, and if so, in what capacity?'[26]

Baring wasted little time in swatting the suggestion away. What he failed to reveal to his superiors, however, was a long-standing mutual antipathy between himself and Gordon, suggesting that Boulger was right to claim later that 'Gordon's appointment and departure were retarded by personal animus and an old difference'.[27] This 'old difference' had its roots in their first meeting five years earlier, in March 1878, when Colonel Gordon first encountered Major Baring, newly appointed as British Commissioner, in Cairo. Gordon promptly confided in a friend that Baring had 'a pretentious, grand, patronising way about him . . . when oil mixes with water we will mix together'.[28] For his part, Baring observed that, in the context of Gordon's possibly joining the Commission charged with resolving Egypt's national financial crisis, he was 'about as much fit for the work in hand as I am to be Pope'.[29] Keeping his own reasons for rejecting Gordon to himself, Baring received the Foreign Secretary's query shortly before six on a Saturday evening and was able to reply before noon the following day, apparently having made consultation with the then Prime Minister, Muḥammad Sharīf, his immediate priority. Baring relayed what he described as Sharīf's 'strong objections', gently reminding his master in London of the existing 'hands off' policy.

> The Egyptian Government is very much averse to employing General Gordon, mainly on the ground that, the movement in the Soudan being religious, the appointment of a Christian in high command would probably alienate the tribes who remain faithful. I think it wise to leave the whole responsibility of Soudan affairs to them, and not to press them on the subject.[30]

And so it was left for another month, until the press entered the fray. As the new year began, Sir Samuel Baker made an explicit case to a wider public through the letters column of *The Times*: 'Why should not General Gordon Pasha be invited to assist the Government? There is no man living who would be more capable or so well fitted to represent the justice which Great Britain should establish in the Soudan.'[31] Such a statement was clear enough; still less equivocal was the contribution of William Stead and his *Pall Mall Gazette*. Its edition of 9 January 1884 dropped a bomb into London's salons, clubs and ministerial offices. Under the headline 'Chinese Gordon for the Soudan', Stead argued that the general should be given *carte blanche*, sent 'with full powers to Khartoum, to assume absolute control of the territory, to treat with the Mahdi, to relieve the garrisons, and to do what he can to save what can be saved from the wreck in the Soudan. . . . No one can deny the urgent need in the midst of that hideous welter of confusion for the presence of such a man.'[32]

Stead himself had taken the trouble of interviewing Gordon in Southampton, where the general was spending what he expected to be his last days of leave before departing to the Congo River on behalf of King Leopold. The interview is a fascinating digest of Gordon's insights on affairs Sudanese and Egyptian. On many points his judgment is acute, pragmatic and even prescient. He describes the strategic value of the Red Sea coast; the risk to Egypt and beyond of a charismatic Islamic leader on the warpath; the immense challenge of withdrawing remote garrisons; the rapacity of earlier Egyptian administration in Khartoum; the widespread resentment against the occupiers that fuelled the uprising; and – a most surprising concession – the difficulty of ending slavery. 'It should be proclaimed in the hearing of all Soudanese,' he told Stead, 'and engraved on tablets of brass, that a permanent Constitution was granted to the Soudanese by which no Turk or Circassian would ever be allowed to enter the province to plunder its inhabitants . . . and that no immediate emancipation of slaves would be attempted'.[33]

That reference to Sudan as a 'province' indicates that Gordon concurred with the view of Sudan as part of a Greater Egypt. More importantly, he makes some ultimately fatal misjudgements, insisting that 'there is no hurry . . . the garrisons can hold their own . . . until disunion and tribal jealousies have worked their natural results in the camp of the Mahdi'. Worse, Gordon states his conviction 'that it is an entire mistake to regard the Mahdi as in any sense a religious leader . . . I strongly suspect that he is a mere puppet put forward by Ilyas [Ilyās Aḥmad Umm Bireir] . . . the largest slave-owner in Obeid, and that he [the Mahdī] has assumed a religious title to give colour to his defence of the popular rights.'[34] And on the central point, Egypt's abandonment of Sudan, Gordon stated his disagreement with government policy as it had thus far evolved: an ominous indicator of dissent ahead.

> There is one subject on which I cannot imagine any one can differ about. That is the impolicy of announcing our intention to evacuate Khartoum. Even if we were bound to do so we should have said nothing about it. The moment it is known that we have given up the game every man will go over to the Mahdi. All men worship the rising sun. The difficulties of evacuation will be enormously increased, if, indeed, the withdrawal of our garrison is not considered impossible.[35]

Stead's exclusive sparked mass copy-cat reporting. The interview with 'Chinese Gordon on the Soudan' was picked up and reproduced almost verbatim the following day by *The Times*, the *Leeds Mercury* and the *Bristol Mercury and Daily Post*, on 11 January by the *Newcastle Courant* and *Freeman's Journal* in Dublin and on 12 January by *John Bull*. Despite the fact that the loudest voices were emerging from the opposition press, and despite Gordon's evident lack of identification with government policy, political reaction from within the vacillating cabinet was predictably swift.[36]

The following day, Granville again wired Baring: 'Would General Gordon or Sir C. Wilson be of assistance under altered circumstances in Egypt?'[37] Again, Baring rebuffed the suggestion, this time having consulted Nūbār Nubārian, who proposed instead sending the former Governor-General of Sudan, 'Abd-al-Qādir Hilmi, back to Khartoum to supervise the troop withdrawal and evacuation of civilians and families. The Queen was kept informed that Baring had 'agreed first with Sherif, and now Nubar, in negativing the [Gordon] proposal'.[38] Doubts, however, were beginning to emerge as to Baring's objectivity, with Granville reporting to Gladstone on 12 January that there was gossip about 'an old quarrel between Baring and Gordon'.[39]

Wolseley's pincer movement

Wolseley now entered the fray, with decisive effect. Indeed, Sir Henry Gordon, the general's brother, was right to state that 'it was Lord Wolseley who caused them [the government] to send him out'.[40] The conqueror of Egypt had been an admirer of Charles Gordon since the Crimean War, when they met in 1855 in the trenches before Sebastopol. 'He was full of courage and determination,' remembered Wolseley later, 'honest in everything he did or ever thought of, and totally indifferent to wealth.'[41] Their relationship was rarely renewed in either personal meeting or correspondence, yet even in advanced age Wolseley looked back on his meetings with Gordon with affection, modesty and a sense almost of amazement. 'I cling tenaciously to every remembrance of our intimacy,' he wrote, 'because he was one of the very few friends I ever had who ever came up to my estimate of the Christian hero. . . . His absolute single-mindedness of purpose startled me at times, for it made me feel how inferior I was to him in all the higher qualities of character, and how inferior were all my aims in life to his.'[42]

Unlike other Gordon enthusiasts, with their manifestos and editorials, Wolseley now mounted a campaign in the shadows, exploiting his influence in the Ministry of War to thwart Gordon's Congo mission and divert him instead to Sudan. As early as 16 October 1883, Wolseley had written to Hartington at the War Office, emphasising for the time being Gordon's short-comings in an attempt to forestall any Congo mission: 'Looking at the fanatic character of the man, and the chance of collision with French adventurers, I think it very doubtful whether the permission should be given'.[43] Now, he took up his campaign in earnest, first writing Gordon a warm and personal letter, stating explicitly that, were he to have his way, Gordon would be 'the first person I should ask to take employment' and expressing opinions on strategy that meshed with Gordon's own.

> I wish I could have a long talk with you on Egyptian affairs, & learn your views on this Soudan question . . . You have had enough of liver-grilling climates, and the world does not seem bounded with the clear horizon that would warrant . . . our very best man burying himself amongst niggers on the equator. . . . The fact is the Egyptian Gov^t is totally incapable of ruling that or indeed I might say any other province whether in Upper or Lower Egypt or on the Equator. To reorganise the Soudan would require an army of 20,000 Indian or Turkish Troops. . . . Is the English taxpayer to pay for the reconquest of this province? Cui bono ['For whose benefit?']?[44]

Technically, in fact, Gordon should have been turned out of the army months earlier. According to Granville, the general had forfeited his career when his formal request for a further sabbatical to take up the Congo job had been denied on the grounds that 'an officer on full pay should not be placed at the head of this association, which is not self-supporting . . . and which may lead to international difficulties'.[45] But the terse response from London – 'The S.S. [Secretary of State] declines to sanction arrangement' – had been scrambled en route, with 'declines' becoming 'decides'. Still, according to strict army regulations, even by travelling to Brussels Gordon forfeited both rank and pay.

In a gesture of mercy, however, the authorities relented – although the aftermath of this clerical error was, as Granville observed in a typically mild note to Gladstone, 'rather a mess'.[46] Among Gordon's supporters were Sir Andrew Clarke, who wrote persistently to the Military Secretary, Lieutenant-General Sir Edmund Whitmore, to urge a compromise solution, even though Gordon had written to Clarke from Brussels on 4 January to express the hope that, upon his own departure for the Congo, Clarke would get his 'step', i.e. his substantive major-generalship.[47]

'Although the original objections remain,' Granville concluded, 'we thought it better to avoid subjecting the Queen's service to such a loss, and inflicting such a heavy penalty on so distinguished a man. He is a genius, and of a splendid character. It is a great pity that there should be some eccentricity.'[48] Gordon himself, presumably unaware of that final sentiment, appreciated the government's gesture in allowing him to keep his rank. On 17 January, he asked Northbrook to convey to Hartington and Granville his thanks 'for their consideration in not obliging me to quit H.M.'s Army. I have been a deal of trouble to the Govt but it is my failing, and I hope now it is ended for I shall not come back [from the Congo].'[49]

This was the point at which Wolseley matched his powers of personal persuasion with direct action within his own military competency. The second part of his pincer movement was a formal order that thwarted the Congo mission by denying Gordon permission to resign his commission. The official ruling of 5 January, the day after the letter of entreaty quoted above, was scribbled in haste over an illegible signature on the notepaper of the Royal Engineers at Horse Guards. Addressed to Gordon at the Hotel Bellevue in Brussels, it was a flat refusal to countenance either his mercenary appointment or his retirement.

> With reference to your telegram of the 3rd instant, I am directed by His Royal Highness the Field Marshal Commanding-in-Chief to inform you that the Secretary of State for War declined to sanction your employment on the Congo, and further, that as you have not as yet been three years unemployed as a General Officer, you are precluded, under the provisions of Art. 91 of the Royal Warrant of 11th March 1882, from retiring at the present time with a pension.[50]

Even this uncompromising notice failed to dent Gordon's determination to leave for the Congo. Still, even as he travelled to Belgium to finalise details of his mission, he kept an eye on Sudan, where his sympathies appeared to be entirely with the oppressed and mutinous population. 'I arrived here on the 1.1.84 & saw the King on 2.1.,' he wrote to Miss Felkin, a fellow activist in the anti-slavery movement, 'and am going to leave the Army & go to Congo on 5 Feby. . . . I feel for the rebels & am proud of their prowess, and our Lord will work good for them out of it.'[51]

By 11 January, he was still committed to the Congo venture, no doubt partly motivated by the king's generous offer to remunerate him for lost pension rights. After intense negotiations involving Sir Henry Gordon, a 'generous and cordial' £7,288 was to be paid into a trust fund, 'furnishing,' as Boulger put it, 'a marked contrast with the grudging and parsimonious spirit of the British Government'.[52] On 6 January, Gordon wrote to Stanley, confirming his willing-ness to serve 'with and under' him: 'We will, God helping,' he added, 'kill the slave-traders in their haunts, for if we act together in the countries where they hunt, and make treaties with the chiefs, we can prevent their raids and truly stop the slave trade. . . . No such efficacious means of cutting at the root of [the] slave trade was presented as that which God has, I trust, opened out to us through the kind disinterestedness of His Majesty.'[53]

As for the Sudan crisis, Gordon had now somehow been given to understand that it would be left in the capable hands of Samuel Baker.[54] So, expanding on his comments to the *Pall Mall Gazette*, Gordon wrote to Baker with some specific political advice, based on the assumption that the Sultan in Constantinople would never allow the Mahdī to succeed, for fear of abdicating his authority in the Ottoman provinces of Hedjaz, Syria and Palestine.

> I take it for granted, then, that you will go; and I would recommend (1) permission to be got from the Sultan to engage 4,000 of his reserve troops, both officers and men, which will be under your brother's [General Valentine Baker's] command and be volunteers, with a promise of remuneration at end of their service; (2) that some 2,000 Beloochees under the native officers should be enlisted in India, who have been soldiers of Her Majesty, old sturdy warriors; for cavalry, you can horse them in the Hedjaz, Palestine, and Syria; (3), that Her Majesty's Government will allow you to purchase from Her Majesty animals, paying a percentage on all purchases; (4), that Her Majesty's Government should allow military store officers to aid you, but not to go into field.[55]

Wolseley had one stratagem left to try: a direct appeal to Gordon's sense of duty, his patriotism and his endless desire, whatever his protestations to the contrary, to be indispensable. Crucially, this initiative had the personal endorsement of Granville and Gladstone, though in a note to the Prime Minister on the eve of the Wolseley/Gordon meeting, the Foreign Secretary was fretful: 'If he says that he cannot go to Egypt, or that he cannot go without a consider-able force . . . we shall be on velvet [i.e. in a slippery position]. If he says he believes he could by his personal influence, excite the tribes to escort the Khartoum Garrison, & inhabitants to Suakim, a little pressure on Baring might be advisable.'[56] Gladstone responded the following day to say that he agreed with Granville's analysis 'throughout'.[57]

Face-to-face with Gordon, Wolseley pledged that issues of leave, pay and commission could all be resolved amicably and the Congo mission only deferred – providing that he agree immediately to address the Sudan crisis. 'What would you do in my position?' he asked Gordon, receiving the modest reply: 'I would send myself'. Wolseley concurred, but he was still not in a position to convey openly the endorsement of the government, let alone the offer of a formal position. All he could tell Gordon, as he recalled in notes for his unfinished memoir, was that the Cabinet 'fully appreciated his public spirit in volunteering to go there should such a step be deemed advisable'.[58]

But this was not enough for Gordon. 'I thought he was disappointed at the decision,' Wolseley recalled, 'but he only said, "Very well, I shall go to Brussels to-night and will start at once for the Congo."'[59] Granville could not conceal his disappointment that the meeting had been 'not very satisfactory', although he was pleased that Wolseley 'did not mention us' [i.e. the government] during the conversation.[60] Wolseley appeared to have fallen at the last hurdle.

But the situation in Cairo was still evolving rapidly. Perhaps unsurprisingly, given what appeared to be a poisoned chalice, ʿAbd-al-Qādir Hilmi reneged on his agreement to travel to Khartoum. Baring now had little room for manoeuvre and, on 16 January, he was obliged to relay the message that the Egyptian government 'would feel greatly obliged if Her Majesty's Government would select a well-qualified British officer to go to Khartoum instead . . . He would be given full powers, both civil and military, to conduct the retreat.'[61] Baring even conceded later the same day that 'General Gordon would be best man'.[62] Not that he had changed his mind: as early as 4 March 1884, he wrote to Northbrook to lament that, 'of all the things I have done here, what I most blame myself for is having ever approved of Gordon's mission':

> I hesitated very much about it, partly on account of my knowledge of Gordon's character, but more still because I feared his being caught in a trap, and of thus involving us in the affairs of the Soudan. . . . In England, public opinion appeared to be unanimous on the subject, and the Government seemed to wish it. At last I yielded, rather against my judgement, and I have never ceased to regret it since.[63]

Baring's endorsement now enabled Granville, briefing the Queen by coded telegram on 18 January, disingenuously to shift the onus of responsibility for the mission to Cairo: 'Sir E. Baring having now expressed a wish to have Chinese Gordon, Lord Granville has assumed that your Majesty will approve of his proceeding to Egypt. He starts to-night.'[64]

It had been an eleventh-hour decision. On 17 January, Gordon, unimpressed by the parameters set out by Wolseley for a return to Sawākīn – not even Khartoum – merely as a government observer, was still expecting to go to the Congo. 'I am bound to King Leopold,' he wrote to Northbrook from Brussels; 'all I might have done [in Sudan] is to write a report, but I am not at all enthusiastic to do so.'[65] The precipitate nature of Gordon's decision-making gives the lie to Boulger's assertion that, for the previous three days at least, Gordon had been secretly complicit in a conspiracy with Wolseley to hoodwink Leopold. Boulger seeks to mitigate Gordon's guilt in reneging on his promise to the king by arguing that Gordon's arrangement was always 'coupled with this proviso, "provided the Government of my own country does not require my services". The generosity of that sovereign in the matter of the compensation for his Commission did not render that condition void, and however irritating the King may have found the circumstances, Gordon broke neither the spirit nor the letter of his engagement with His Majesty by obeying the orders of his own Government.'[66]

Wolseley's trump card, played at the last possible moment, was a gathering of the cabinet, or at least the four members not currently at their country seats. Joining Wolseley's ally Hartington at the War Office were Granville, Northbrook and Sir Charles Dilke: a minority taking upon themselves a huge moral responsibility. Fitzmaurice, Granville's Under-Secretary at the Foreign Office, had prepared 'an elaborate memorandum' to brief the ministers.[67] Granville for one subsequently regretted his involvement in the Wolseley/Hartington scheme, noting later that Lord Derby, despite his presence in London, had not been among their number, as 'his cautious mind would probably have led him to object to the whole plan as premature'.[68] And Kimberley, who did not come up to London until 21 January, was quoted as saying that 'if he had known in time . . . he would have shown Gordon to be unfit for the work, for he knew him well'.[69]

Still, Gordon could only be flattered by the attention. Faced with the combined authorities of the Foreign Office, the War Office and the Admiralty, he was at last persuaded by what appeared to amount to a government order. As Dilke himself put it, 'Gordon, although he had no wish to go to Egypt, would go if he were ordered'.[70] So, setting aside his own reservations, the general agreed to the parameters set out by the assembled ministers. Gordon's own notes of the meeting included four central observations on what was to be a very circumscribed mission:

> To proceed to Suakin and report on military situation of Soudan and return. Under Baring for orders, and to send through him letters, &c . . . Nubar and Baring to be notified, so as to give all assistance. . . . Letters to Brussels saying leave is given to me to go to Congo after my mission to Suakin. I understand H.M.G. only wish me to report and are in no way bound to me.[71]

Northbrook's account of the meeting stressed Gordon's concluding phrases: 'I was very glad to find that he readily & even cordially accepted our policy that the Egyptians shall give up the administration only holding on to the sea coast. He is not at all alarmed at the situation, & does not believe in the immense power some think the Mahdi has, either spiritual or physical.'[72] Northbrook's memoir, however, recalls a phrase that, if remembered accurately, should have raised alarm at the time. Gordon, he writes, accepted that his mission was 'to report on the best way of withdrawing the garrisons, *settling the country* [my italics] and to perform such other duties as may be intrusted to him by the Khedive's Government' through Baring.[73] Dilke, too, recalled what turned out to be Gordon's unduly optimistic appraisal of the Mahdī's military threat: 'Gordon said that he believed that the danger at Khartoum had been "grossly exaggerated", and that the two Englishmen there [Power and de Coëtlogon] had "lost their heads"; he would be able to bring away the garrisons without difficulty.'[74]

Gladstone himself telegraphed his 'concurrence in the proceedings' the following day from his home at Hawarden Castle on the Welsh borders.[75] Seeking later to distance his master from an uncharacteristically meek abdication of policy oversight, Edward Hamilton wrote that the decision to send Gordon was taken 'in a desperate hurry' and that the Prime Minister 'had to acquiesce by telegram knowing next to nothing of the Commissioner [Gordon] or what he is to do'.[76] Gordon himself described his final hectic hours in London in a scribbled note to his sister Augusta.

> I arrived in town very tired, at 6 A.M. yesterday, went with Brocklehurst to Barracks, washed, and went to Wolseley. He said Ministers would see me at 3 P.M. I went back to Barracks and reposed. At 12.30 P.M. Wolseley came for me. I went with him and saw Granville, Hartington, Dilke, and Northbrook. They said, 'Had I seen Wolseley, and did I understand their ideas?' I said, 'Yes', and repeated what Wolseley had said to me as to their ideas, which was *they would evacuate Soudan*. They were pleased, and said, 'That was their idea; would I go?' I said, 'Yes'. They said, 'When?' I said, 'To-night,' and it was over. Lord Granville said Ministers were very much obliged to me. I said I was much honoured by going. I telegraphed King of the Belgians at once, and told him "Wait a few months". I started at 8 P.M. H.R.H. The Duke of Cambridge and Lord Wolseley came to see me off. . . . I have taken Stewart with me, a nice fellow.[77]

As a travelling companion, Gordon could not have asked for a sturdier or better-informed aide-de-camp than Lieutenant-Colonel Hamill-Stewart, a man whose wilderness adventures had far exceeded even Gordon's and whose steady intelligence would prove an invaluable counter-balance to Gordon's increasing mania. Aged thirty-eight and still acclaimed for his 1883 report on the Mahdī's burgeoning uprising, Stewart had been diverted from a 'confidential civil mission' on behalf of the colonial administration in Canada and

brought back to London to contribute his expertise to an early draft plan of a
Khartoum evacuation.[78]

Stewart's conclusions were bracing, prescient and should have given the
cabinet pause. A concerted push into eastern Sudan was required, he wrote,
preferably involving a detachment from India to secure an exit route from
Khartoum via Kassala to the Red Sea port at Massawa. Without such a 'forward
movement' he added, 'a retreat from Khartúm will practically mean the dissolution of the retiring force'.[79] Nor did he scruple to berate the government for
their hesitation: 'Ministers appear to stand shivering on the brink, afraid to
take the responsibility of ordering the retreat of the garrison for fear they
should be massacred on the homeward march, and on the other hand afraid to
take measures to hold the Eastern Súdán.'[80]

As Gordon and Stewart made a hurried departure from London for the
Channel crossing and the train to Brindisi, a sense of satisfaction was felt by
those who had pushed so hard for the mission to be undertaken. It would be an
understatement to say that Gordon departed with the goodwill of Britain's
newspaper editors. In his exhaustive scrutiny of the London dailies and periodicals, Todd Willy reveals the true extent of the collective hero-worship: 'The
following is a list of terms used to describe General Gordon in January of 1884;
it is not complete, but it is representative: "hero"; "Christian hero"; "true
soldier of Christ"; "humane soldier"; "reverent"; "benevolent"; "transparently
upright"; "truly good and great"; "gallant"; "thoroughly dauntless"; "born
warrior of infinite resource"; "trusty leader"; "great and valorous soldier";
"gallant countryman"; "genius"; "distinguished officer"; "gallant officer";
"famous general"; "grand old soldier"; "ever-victorious"; "deeply religious";
"highminded and highspirited"; "illustrious".'[81]

Precisely because so many different factions had campaigned for the Gordon
mission for so many different reasons, there were few overt critics of the
mission. Wolseley could justifiably feel smug that his hard work had paid off,
even though he was saddled with the chore of finding a replacement to satisfy
the irate King Leopold.[82] Favourable coverage was guaranteed in *The Times*,
which opined that the government had selected 'the most competent agent for
the development of its policy in the Sudan'.[83] But there was approval too in the
Standard ('a wise and important step'), the *Daily News* ('an earnest of the determination of the Government to take every possible means for the rescue of the
garrisons'), the *Morning Advertiser* ('Let us hope it is not too late') and the *Daily
Telegraph* ('At the eleventh hour, a faint chance has arisen'), as well as all the
main provincial papers. The *Pall Mall Gazette* noted contentedly that Gordon and
Stewart were seen off at the station by three of the most powerful figures in
British foreign policy: 'Lord Wolseley carried the General's portmanteau, Lord
Granville took his ticket for him, and the Duke of Cambridge held open the
carriage door'.[84]

Lord Salisbury, however, was reported to have reacted with 'bewildered
indignation' to the selection of 'the last possible man to be entrusted with any

form of diplomatic mission', saying: 'They must have gone quite mad!'[85] Queen Victoria's approval of the 'employment of General (China) Gordon' was leavened with a customary tetchiness about the dilatory nature of politics: 'Why this was not done long ago and why the right thing is never done til it is absolutely extorted from those who are in authority, is inexplicable to the Queen. Over and over again she has urged by letter and by cipher that energetic measures were necessary; but not till the whole country became alarmed – and, she flatters herself also, in deference to her very strong pressure – was anything done.'[86]

The remuneration for Gordon's new job was hardly generous: the government declared itself to be 'not indebted beyond passage money and £3 *per diem* travelling expenses'.[87] Fewer than a dozen people were even aware of his volte face over King Leopold's mission. Even his admirers in the Anti-Slavery Society failed to realise that he was going to the Nile, not the Congo, instead celebrating what they expected would be a dramatic and sudden 'incursion' by Gordon and Stanley from the Congo territory into the Bahr al-Ghazāl, 'one of the richest hunting-grounds of the man-stealer'.[88]

And even as Gordon sped south, by train and boat to Port Said, his mind considered and reconsidered the most desirable options for a free, independent Sudan. Despite his swift acknowledgement of the mission parameters as laid out by the rump cabinet, he appears to have paid scant regard to the actual content. From Gladstone's perspective, Gordon's instructions were clear: it was simply 'a mission to report'.[89] Close collaboration between Baring, Hartington and Granville, however, produced a set of considerably more elaborate instructions. These are worth setting out in full, not least because they would be subject to such swift and comprehensive alteration.

> Her Majesty's Government are desirous that you should proceed at once to Egypt, to report to them on the military situation in the Soudan, and on the measures which it may be advisable to take for the security of the Egyptian garrisons still holding positions in that country, and for the safety of the European population in Khartoum. You are also desired to consider and report upon the best mode of effecting the evacuation of the interior of the Soudan, and upon the manner in which the safety and good administration by the Egyptian Government of the ports on the seacoast can best be secured.
>
> In connection with this subject, you should pay especial consideration to the question of the steps that may usefully be taken to counteract the stimulus which it is feared may possibly be given to the Slave Trade by the present insurrectionary movement, and by the withdrawal of the Egyptian Government from the interior.

You will be under the instruction of Her Majesty's Agent and Consul-General at Cairo, through whom your Reports to Her Majesty's Government should be sent, under flying seal.

You will consider yourself authorised and instructed to perform such other duties as the Egyptian Government may desire to intrust to you, and as may be communicated to you by Sir E. Baring. You will be accompanied by Colonel Stewart, who will assist you in the duties thus confided to you.

On your arrival in Egypt you will at once communicate with Sir E. Baring, who will arrange to meet you, and will settle with you whether you should proceed direct to Suakin, or should go yourself or dispatch Colonel Stewart to Khartoum via the Nile.[90]

CHAPTER 4

Gladstone struggles to retain control

I could do no more than delegate to Gordon my own powers . . . Whatever he does will be well done; whatever propositions he will make are accepted in advance; whatever combinations he may decide upon will be binding for us; and in thus placing unlimited trust in the Pasha's judgement, I have only made one condition – 'That he should provide for the safety of the Europeans and the Egyptian civilian element'.

Khedive Ṭawfīq, January 1884[1]

Taken at face value, Gordon's mission parameters were, for the most part, unimpeachably careful, although the loophole instructing him 'to perform such other duties as the Egyptian Government may desire to intrust to [him]' was soon exploited by the Khedive in pursuit of his own agenda. Gordon himself seemed initially clear, if sardonic, about his orders. A personal postcard written during the Mediterranean crossing aboard the *Tanjore* summarised the project thus: 'As *H.M.G. will not guarantee future good government* it seems *evacuation* is the only thing that could be done'.[2] More formally but equally sarcastically, he drafted a long memorandum, setting out on his views on the mission ahead:

I understand that Her Majesty's Government have come to the irrevocable decision not to incur the very onerous duty of securing to the peoples of the Soudan a just future Government [so] have determined to restore to these peoples their independence, and will no longer suffer the Egyptian Government to interfere with their affairs. For this purpose, Her Majesty's Government have decided to send me to the Soudan to arrange for the

58

evacuation of these countries, and the safe removal of the Egyptian employés and troops.[3]

So far, so clear – although 'report on' had already become 'arrange for'. And before a month had passed, Gordon had subjected his parameters to extreme stretching, with several more initiatives, no sooner invented than publicised – but rarely carried through. Within hours of his departure from London, Gordon drafted no fewer than eight telegrams for Baring to forward to Granville, including a proclamation from himself to the tribes of eastern Sudan and a memorandum on a new Sultan of Darfur, all suggesting that Gordon intended to play a central role in shaping a new, independent Sudan.[4]

This incontinent stream of inventive schemes, evidence of Gordon's hyperactive mental condition, continued to pour forth. Among these initiatives were renewed military action against the Mahdī; a solo journey south into Equatoria; the unilateral award to the Mahdī of the hitherto non-existent post of Sultan of Kordofan; the identification of tribal or religious rivals to counter the Mahdī; and the public announcement of the planned abandonment of Sudan, gainsaying his own stated creed that such a declaration would amount to mission suicide. The most worrying of these ad hoc proposals, no sooner thought up than committed to the telegraph, came on 6 February 1884, when Gordon proposed that, in the light of what then appeared to him to be a better than feared security situation, evacuation should be at least postponed:

> To disturb, if not annihilate, this system at a moment's notice would appear to me to hand over the country to complete anarchy. . . . Hence I would suggest that the Government of Egypt should continue to maintain its position as a Suzerain Power, nominate the Governor-General and Mudirs [provincial governors], and act as a Supreme Court of Appeal. . . . I would therefore earnestly beg that evacuation, but not abandonment, be the programme to be followed.[5]

The most important moment in this 'mission creep' was Gordon's promotion, in Cairo, from observer to Governor-General. Gordon's brother, Sir Henry, may have believed that 'without having power from Egypt as Governor-General he would have not have had any power and could have done nothing', yet Khedive Ṭawfīq's motives must certainly have been suspect.[6] After all, had not John Cross of the India Office warned in January that, on the popularity or otherwise of a withdrawal, it was chiefly 'among the influential and political classes [in Egypt] that the loss of the Soudan was unpopular', while the lower classes who ran the risk of actually being sent there, as soldiers or administrators, were 'much less disposed to object'.[7]

Gordon's role thus changed in three crucial ways. Instead of a British uniform, he donned the brocade tunic and fez of khedivial service. The advisor, based at Sawākīn, charged with recommending how best to achieve a withdrawal, became the executive officer, based at Khartoum, responsible for the withdrawal. And, under Gordon's new orders, the withdrawal of Egypt's forces became but a preamble to the establishment of a secure indigenous Sudanese administration.

To complicate matters further, there were two proclamations of investiture, both dated 26 January 1884. In the public pronouncement, Gordon's numerous qualities were praised: 'We do hereby appoint you Governor-General of the Soudan, by reason of your perfect knowledge of that country, and we trust that you will carry out our good intentions for the establishment of justice and order, and that you will assure the peace and prosperity of the peoples of the Soudan'.[8] The second, secret pronouncement was much more explicit. As well as being ordered to 'carry into execution the evacuation of those territories, and to withdraw our troops, civil officials, and such of those inhabitants, together with their belongings, as may wish to leave for Egypt', Gordon was instructed to 'take the necessary steps for establishing an organised Government in the different provinces of the Soudan, for the maintenance of order, and the cessation of all disasters and incitement to revolt'.[9]

Confusion was compounded by additional mission parameters dictated by Baring. After endorsing the Egyptian government's agreement with Gordon's plan to form a 'confederation' of 'petty Sultans', he went on to state: 'You are therefore given full discretionary power to retain the troops for such reasonable period as you may think necessary, in order that the abandonment of the country may be accomplished with the least possible risk to life and property. A credit of £100,000 has been opened for you at the Finance Department.'[10] So, in addition to 'carrying into execution the evacuation', Gordon now had 'full discretionary power' over the Egyptian army in Sudan.

Executive status, executive decisions

Such rapid escalations would not have happened had Gordon not been diverted to Cairo. His reluctance to do so was based on personal antipathy towards not just Baring but also the Khedive Tawfīq, whom Gordon mistrusted profoundly. As recently as 17 January, just a day before his abrupt departure from London, Gordon had written to Northbrook: 'The man I fear most is Tewfik he is a little snake and Nubar [the Egyptian Prime Minister] must be the ferret to get rid of him or to keep him in order'.[11]

For his part, Baring too may well have preferred to avoid a face-to-face meeting. But when Gordon reached Port Said on 24 January 1884, he found an almost pleading letter from Cairo. Made aware by Granville of Gordon's unrelenting hostility, and knowing that a diversion to Cairo would be 'personally distasteful', Baring argued that there were 'strong public grounds' for such a diversion, 'to arrange a common plan of action and prevent any risk of working at cross-purposes'.[12] Baring further insisted that Gordon's only safe route to Khartoum was via Cairo and the Nile, a view endorsed during a meeting at

Ismailia with ʿAlī Tuhami, an elderly retainer from the Khartoum secretariat during Gordon's previous tenure as Governor-General, who provided a bracing update on affairs in eastern Sudan.

The tribal leader of the Hadendawa in the Red Sea Hills, Sheikh Maḥmūd Mūsa, had died, leaving his followers divided.[13] As Stewart recorded the conversation, 'the minor part of the tribe sided with the son of Mahmoud Moussa . . . while the larger portion followed Osman Digna & is now in rebellion'.[14] Sir Charles Wilson certainly believed that this news 'weighed heavily' in convincing Gordon and Stewart to abandon their plan to sail to Sawākīn and the Red Sea itinerary was abandoned.[15]

The diversion created the opportunity for two eventful days in Cairo and, on 25 January 1884, Gordon progressed from his audience with the Khedive to a conclave with Baring, Wood and Nūbār Nubārian to fix a twenty-two-point set of mission parameters agreeable to the British and the Egyptians. Small surprise, then, that by evening Gordon professed himself 'precious tired of long wearisome talks'.[16] The salient points, as transcribed by Stewart, are worth highlighting:

1) That the Govᵗ should place a credit of £E100,000 at Gordon's disposal.

2) That the evacuation of the Soudan should be gradual.

3) That 2 firmans [proclamations] should be given Gen Gordon appointing him Gov. Gen of the Soudan in one of which the evacuation should be mentioned.

4) that [General Valentine] Baker Pasha should be named Gov. Gen of East Soudan which includes the coast line from Ras-el-Haya to Massawa & inland so as to include Toka, Sinkat & Bogos [in Abyssinia]. . . .

7) That Gordon's suggested proclamations were accepted & that the British Govᵗ be mentioned therein. . . .

9) That the Egyptian Govᵗ within reasonable limits will take into its service any of the Mahdi's black troops who will come & offer them the same terms as in the Soudan. . . .

11) Zebeyr [al-Zubeir Raḥma Manṣūr[17]] & Gordon to have an interview tomorrow before Sir E Baring & Nubar Pasha

12) Gordon to have the power to grant within reasonable limits & chargeable on the Egyptian Govᵗ small sums to divers persons in the Soudan.

13) The Egyptian Govᵗ to pay Gen Gordon's staff.

14) Gen Gordon's & Lt Col Stewart's salaries to be paid by the English Govᵗ.

15) Wady Halfa to form the new Egyptian frontier.

16) Gen Gordon to use his own judgement as to the disposal of stores & steamers now in the Soudan.

17) The Dongola Mahdi [Stewart's error: it should be *mudīr*, *'governor'*] to lend if possible 300 Camels to assist in removing Slatin Bey[18] from Darfur.

18) No orders to be sent Gordon Pasha except through Sir E Baring or Nubar Pasha.

19) Khedive no longer to telegraph on his own authority.

20) Gordon to communicate only with Sir E Baring & Nubar Pasha.

21) Baker's troops to be withdrawn from Suakin after the relief or fall of the beleaguered places.

22) An Egyptian Cypher to be given Gordon & Nubar.[19]

It is striking that this agenda makes no mention of replacing Egyptian rule with an indigenous leadership. Gordon, however, did not drop the idea. By 1 February 1884, Stewart dutifully noted that 'Gen. Gordon's present idea is to clear out the whole of the present Egyptian officials from the Soudan & to replace them by a purely native administration. He is convinced that however badly the native Administration may work that it will in any case be better than the present miserable Egyptian one.'[20]

Stewart himself believed that it was essential to get the job done before the abandonment plan was revealed: 'It seems to me that at present the most suitable plan is not to publish abroad throughout the Soudan that we mean to leave. Before doing so, we ought at any rate to place the kinglets in their several districts. Whether it will be possible to induce Gordon to remain silent in the matter is, however, more than doubtful.'[21] Indeed, the general only managed to contain himself as far as Berber, where on 12 February he woke Stewart at 5 am to tell him that he had 'come to the decision of opening the Pandora Box & openly proclaiming the divorce of the Soudan from Egypt'.[22]

The campaign to install 'al-Zubeir Pasha'

At this point in the evolution of Gladstone's Sudan policy, Gordon's initiative in advancing the cause of al-Zubeir Raḥma Manṣūr, a question that continued to preoccupy the general until late autumn 1884, was highly significant. It was not, however, the first time that the name had come up in the context of military operation in Sudan. The previous December, a report from Cairo said that 'Zebehr Pasha . . . will probably accompany Baker Pasha in command of the Bedouins [fighting in eastern Sudan]. It is hoped that he may prove loyal; but the appointment is not generally approved'.[23]

Later the same week, it was reported that 'with respect to the appointment of Zebehr Pasha to a command under Baker Pasha, the suggestion has been mooted that he should be rewarded with the government of Kordofan and Darfour as the price of his loyalty', though in Khartoum itself 'the news of the appointment of the archrebel Zebehr Pasha has been received with astonishment and consternation. It nullifies the work of General Gordon and Sir Samuel Baker.'[24] The Khedive's ambassador to London, Ibrāhīm Hilmi, commented that such a deployment was 'simply incomprehensible, and I fear it bodes no good as far as a solution of the Soudan difficulty is concerned'.[25] The inevitable conclusion of this first effort to involve al-Zubeir was reported just eight days before Gordon's departure from London: 'The projected despatch of a force of black troops to the Soudan, under the command of Zebehr Pasha, has been abandoned.'[26]

Gordon's typically contrarian argument was simple enough: a powerful figure with a record of military success and a career in commercial slaving would counter the Mahdī's argument that rule by outsiders would deprive the Sudanese people of their traditional lifestyle and rights. For Gordon, that outweighed the morally reprehensible conclusion that domestic slavery would have to be allowed to continue in Sudan, a position he made public on arrival in Khartoum on 18 February 1884.[27] Frank Power, facing dual obligations as reporter and consul, was obliged to transmit a translation of the relevant section both to *The Times* and to his master, Baring, in Cairo.[28]

> Proclamation. To all the inhabitants. Your tranquillity is the object of our hope. And as I know that you are sorrowful on account of the slavery which existed among you, and the stringent orders on the part of the Government for the abolition of it, and the punishment of those who deal in them . . . henceforward nobody will interfere with you in the matter, but everyone for himself may take a man into his service henceforth.[29]

Gordon's unilateral abrogation of the 1877 Slave Trade Convention was done for strictly local and practical reasons, all based on the impossibility of policing. 'The question asked me was this,' he telegraphed to Baring on 21 February; 'did I insist on the liberation of slaves in 1889 as per Treaty 1877? I answered that the Treaty would not be enforced in 1889 by me, which, considering the determination of Her Majesty's Government respecting Soudan [i.e. abandonment], was a self-evident fact. The question is one of slave-holding, not of slave-hunting, and, in my opinion, that Treaty of 1877 will never be carried out in Cairo as to slave-holding.'[30] Baring himself supported Gordon's decision, arguing that 'knowing that he is powerless to stop slavery in the future, General Gordon evidently intends using it as a concession to the people which will strengthen his position in other matters'.[31]

Gordon's unilateral move prompted consternation and anger back in London. Amid strident protests from the Anti-Slavery Society, questions were asked in parliament. On 21 February in the House of Commons, Edward Gibson asked Gladstone, following extensive quotations from the convention, whether 'the recent Proclamation of General Gordon relieves the Egyptian Government from the obligations of the said Convention?' An embarrassed Gladstone was forced to prevaricate, claiming that clarification of Gordon's text was still awaited from Baring, though the Prime Minister did concede that Power's version in that morning's edition of *The Times* 'approaches to accuracy'.[32] In the Lords, meanwhile, Salisbury asked Granville sarcastically whether he was 'at all aware of the species of conveyance Sir Evelyn Baring is using . . . The newspapers have received it by telegraph. Is Sir Evelyn Baring waiting for a Nile boat?'[33] Late on 25 February, the full transcript of Gordon's announcement was before MPs, though Gladstone still felt able to say that the government did 'not regard it in the main as a political Proclamation' and that 'our confidence in General Gordon on this subject is absolute and unabated'.[34] By 29 February, the opposition had organised a rather tepid debate on the issue in the House of Lords.[35]

On the question of al-Zubeir, Gordon's argument was simple: he might be a ruthless thug but at least he's *our* ruthless thug. By mid-1884, as Henry Jackson has written, al-Zubeir had spent 'nine years in semi-captivity, a prisoner at large. In Egypt he had few friends, but in the Sudan he could command an enormous body of supporters.'[36] Such friends as he had in Cairo, however, were loyal indeed. Baron de Kusel described al-Zubeir as 'extremely generous with all who came in contact with him; many slaves chose his service in preference to others, and were enrolled by him in his army. . . . He was energetic, resolute, extremely courageous, and of great ability.'[37]

But the furore over slavery made support for Gordon's purely political nomination of al-Zubeir as a possible indigenous alternative to the Mahdī much less likely. Shock at the perceived volte face over slavery reached even America, where General Charles P. Stone, a veteran of Egyptian service, wrote to the *New York Sun* on 22 February 1884, quoting in full Ismā'īl's orders to Gordon on the occasion of his first appointment as Governor-General of Sudan in 1874.[38] Stone concluded wryly: 'It may be doubted . . . if his faithful execution of orders which make him declare that tens of thousands of human beings, because they are of a different color, are merchandise, by order of Queen Victoria, will bring him . . . much applause from the civilized world.'[39]

Gordon was certainly right to anticipate opposition. But he was so caught up in his increasingly manic oscillation between instant solutions to the Sudan problem that he failed to anticipate simple bewilderment, not least because his personal antipathy towards al-Zubeir had been a matter of public record for at least five years. As Governor-General in 1879, he had authored a pamphlet denouncing al-Zubeir's 'inhumane and violent' activities.[40] Only a fortnight before his own departure from London, Gordon had predicted a radically different outcome for any mission by al-Zubeir to Sudan. In a long memorandum on affairs in Egypt and Sudan sent to Boulger, Gordon declared that, were al-Zubeir to be allowed to return to Sudan, 'he will, most probably, be taken prisoner by the Mahdi, and will then take the command of the Mahdi's forces'.[41]

In fact, barely twenty-four hours earlier, freshly arrived in Egypt and travelling by steam launch from Port Said to Ismailia, Gordon had shown Wood a memorandum advocating al-Zubeir's immediate detention in Cyprus. So Wood was, in his own words, 'reduced to astonishment when in council on Friday [25 January] he expressed a wish that Zebehr might accompany him to the Sudan'.[42]

That astonishment was shared by other officials in Cairo. The follow-up meeting, referred to as Point 11 in Stewart's minutes (above), degenerated swiftly into an acrimonious slanging match over Gordon's execution of al-Zubeir's son, Suleimān, seven years earlier. In his own handwritten account, al-Zubeir dismissed Gordon's claim to have seen seditious correspondence between al-Zubeir and Suleimān, instead accusing Gordon of betraying his responsibility to Suleimān, who was by the time of his death a senior government employee in Bahr al-Ghazāl.

> You embarked on a series of acts of aggression against my interests all over the country . . . you looted all my property, including furniture and personal effects, as well as the belongings of my supporters in rural areas. You also destroyed my farms and their water-wheels. You seized my Arabian horses, my river-boats and much besides from my farms and warehouses – all against the *Shar'īa* [Islamic law] and against the laws of humanity.[43]

It is now conventional wisdom that Gordon's suggestion that al-Zubeir accompany him to Khartoum was universally ridiculed. Certainly, when Lieutenant-Colonel Watson's opinion was canvassed at the end of the meeting, he answered tersely that both he and 'natives thoroughly conversant with both men were of opinion that such a policy would entail the death of either one or other of them'.[44] There was immense political pressure on the government in London to reject al-Zubeir out of hand. A typical intervention came from Edward Sturge, Chairman of the British and Foreign Anti-Slavery Society, who wrote to Granville to response to a swell of rumour that had 'of late increased in force and consistency':

> In the records of the devastations and murders inflicted by the Slave Trade on North-eastern Africa this man has stood the foremost and the principal actor, and his career is specially marked by perfidy and crime. . . . Countenance in any shape of such an individual by the British Government would be a degradation for England and a scandal to Europe. The Committee express no opinion on the policy of a permanent maintenance of British authority at Khartoum, but they earnestly hope that in the event of HMG making an arrangement for its independent rule, the conditions will be such as will secure the country alike from a reign of anarchy and barbarism, and from that of the slave-dealer.[45]

Despite such interventions, however, the cabinet very nearly endorsed al-Zubeir's extraordinary phantom candidacy, not least because of Baring's advice. Baring was concerned about more than al-Zubeir's history: he was also worried that al-Zubeir might in future pose as great a threat to Egypt proper as the Mahdī himself. Still, with the approval of the Egyptian Prime Minister, Nūbār Pasha,

Baring concluded unequivocally that 'Zebehr Pasha should be permitted to succeed General Gordon'.[46] Gladstone's own notes following cabinet on 29 February 1884 chime readily with his declared policy that an indigenous alternative to the Mahdī, however unsavoury, was preferable to any British or revived Egyptian involvement: 'Viewing Gordon's & your recommendation Cabinet ready to approve choice of Zebir as Governor but not to make appointment. This should be by Egyptian Governor & should not invade Sultan's sovereignty.'[47]

It is not clear, however, that this message was sent: after the same cabinet meeting, Granville's formal reply to Baring stated baldly that his arguments were 'under the consideration of Her Majesty's Government'.[48] Even when the cabinet rejected the proposal on 5 March, the actual note from Granville left open the possibility that the government could yet be persuaded.[49] Indeed, revisiting the question ten days later, the cabinet was evenly divided, 6-6: Hartington, Derby, Childers, Chamberlain, Dodson and Carlingford vs. Granville, Northbrook, Kimberley, Dilke, Selborne and Harcourt.[50] Gladstone, who had missed a series of four meetings on Sudan within six days because of illness, was confident that his casting vote would approve the despatch of al-Zubeir to Khartoum.[51]

At the last minute, however, Childers and Chamberlain changed their votes: strategic policy did not weigh as heavily as public anxiety over a resurgence of slavery. The al-Zubeir mission was scotched, to the chagrin of Gladstone, who concluded that his cabinet colleagues had 'gone wrong . . . in this most strange of all cases'.[52] The fullest explanation for the refusal to send al-Zubeir was transmitted by Granville to Baring on 28 March:

> If reliance could safely have been placed upon Zebehr to serve loyally with General Gordon, to act in a friendly manner towards Egypt, and to abstain from encouraging the Slave Trade, the course proposed was undoubtedly the best which could have been taken under the circumstances; but upon this most vital point General Gordon's assurances failed to convince Her Majesty's Government. . . . They could not satisfy themselves of the probability that the establishment of Zebehr's authority would be a security to Egypt . . . There seemed to Her Majesty's Government to be considerable risk that Zebehr might join with the Mahdi, or if he fought and destroyed him, that he would then turn against Egypt.[53]

By rejecting al-Zubeir, of course, the government contradicted its declared policy of non-interference in Sudan. As Winston Churchill put it, 'the refusal to permit his employment was tantamount to an admission that affairs in the Soudan involved the honour of England as well as the honour of Egypt. When the British people – for this was not merely the act of the Government – adopted a high moral attitude with regard to Zubehr, they bound themselves to rescue the garrisons, peaceably if possible, forcibly if necessary.'[54] Baron de Malortie in Cairo agreed, arguing that it had been wrong 'not to sanction the *only* demand made by Gordon, though he had been assured, on leaving for Khartoum, that he had … *carte blanche* to do what he thought right'.[55] Gladstone may have respected the cabinet majority but he explicitly shared the blame.

Gordon was in no way deterred by the rejection of his scheme. On 17 April 1884, after two months in Khartoum, he telegraphed al-Zubeir in person to notify him that he had been formally appointed Deputy Governor-General. There are two subtly different accounts of al-Zubeir's response to this summons. De Kusel, who believed that the cabinet refusal was based on 'crass obstinacy', described al-Zubeir as 'pleased and very much affected' by Gordon's unilateral move but quoted him as saying: 'What can I do? I am virtually a prisoner, and after this telegram, if I went as far as the railway station I should be stopped, you may be sure that copies of the telegram are now in the hands of the Khedive and Baring. No, I cannot go! the English do not want me in the Soudan. I am sorry for Gordon, because I would have sent him safely back to Cairo.'[56] De Malortie, who visited al-Zubeir the following day and saw the same telegram, quoted his host only as saying that, while he had forgiven Gordon for past grievances, he dared not travel to Sudan because 'if anything happened to Gordon they would lay it at my door, and say that it was my doing to revenge my son'.[57]

Baring's response was typically resolute: he deported al-Zubeir to Gibraltar. Gordon, stymied, pursued the scheme, doggedly and fruitlessly, for many months. As late as 3 December 1884, seven weeks before his death, Gordon was still speculating pleasurably on the political turmoil that would follow a successful resolution of his plans for an al-Zubeir-led, Ottoman-funded administration in Khartoum.

> The opposition will be perfectly wild at seeing the Ministry get out of the mess, with what one may say [is] really credit, while Anti S. S. [Anti-Slavery Society] and Europe at large will empty their vials of wrath on me.[58] Towfik & his Pachas will wring their hands *openly* over such an act. . . . For my part, I shall get out of any of those wretched honors, for the Ministry will be only too glad to say "we could not, you know, confer any honors on him, after such very disreputable conduct", knowing well enough I would not take them, if offered, and as I am not going to England again, & shall not see the Papers, I shall not much mind the abuse. I think it is a splendid programme.[59]

Evacuation of the garrisons

The al-Zubeir distraction was not the only example of Gordon's manic scheming. Late in the spring, he fired off a note that added to the confusion in Cairo by implying a wholly imaginary desire on the part of the Mahdī for the services of al-Zubeir Raḥma. 'It is possible,' he wrote, 'that I may go to the Mahdi, and not be heard of for two months, for he might keep me as a hostage for Zebehr.'[60] Not surprisingly, as soon as Baring came to hear of the idea, he stamped on it firmly:

'I hope you will give me a positive assurance that you will on no account put yourself voluntarily in the power of the Mahdi. . . . There would, in my opinion, be the strongest political objections to your risking a visit.'[61]

Still, despite this continued lack of focus, once in Khartoum Gordon's military competence came to the fore and the mission began with remarkable effectiveness. The core purpose was evacuation and the 'exodus' referred to by Power the previous December was continued. Priority was given to civilians and Egyptian military personnel unfit for service. Stewart's campaign journal entry for 26 February records: 'After some trouble we managed to get off 237 sick Egyptian soldiers. This is the first instalment of those bound for Egypt.'[62]

In fact, official records show that, by the time the official evacuation procedure was terminated by the capture of Berber on 18 May 1884, several hundred civilians and serving personnel had travelled safely to Egypt. On 4 May, Reuter's news agency reported from Aswan that 'nearly 2,000 refugees have reached this place from Korosko, and more are daily arriving'.[63] Gordon's own figures were somewhat higher: by 30 July, he claimed that 'we have sent down over 600 soldiers and 2,000 people [i.e. civilians]'.[64]

Final statistics were compiled by Colonel Francis Duncan, an artilleryman seconded to the Egyptian Army and stationed at Korosko, the point at which the arduous journey across the Nubian Desert from Abū-Ḥamad finally reached the green bank of the Nile.[65] Duncan found that, of the 2,138 refugees processed by his unit, 1,178 were 'men and boys', 960 'women and girls'. Differentiating between military personnel and civilians, he recorded that 185 were 'officers and men of Egyptian Soudan army . . . nearly all invalids, and a more wretched, broken-down set of men it would be hard to conceive'. A further 155 were described as 'Bashi-Bazouks', members of a predominantly Shaiqīa militia, denounced by Stewart in his 1883 *Report on the Soudan* as 'mostly swaggering bullies, robbing, plundering, and ill-treating the people with impunity . . . a constant menace to public tranquillity'.[66]

The vast majority, 1,798 individuals, were 'civilians and families of officers and of soldiers'; of these, sixty-five were 'Government civilian officials, telegraph clerks, &c.' Duncan ended his reckoning with two important caveats. Not included in his tally were 'a good many merchants, some Copts, and teachers, a few European priests and converts, and some prisoners'. More tellingly, 'the number of soldiers would have been greater if his Excellency Gordon Pasha had not recalled from Berber all the men who had started for Egypt and who were fit for service'.[67]

Duncan's own account of the exodus, delivered during a fevered election campaign in 1885, left no room for doubt as to who deserved credit for the success of the evacuation as far as it went: 'Gordon, who was not a mere sentimental philanthropist, but a man of business as well as a man of courage':

> With marvellous monotony, I might say, batch after batch of the sick and
> the injured, of women and children, used to be sent by Gordon to me. They

used to arrive in an almost perfect state of comfort, with all the necessary papers enabling me to disperse them among their different villages in Egypt. One of the first messages the General sent to me was this, 'Do try and find a motherly European woman to receive these poor women and children, for they have never been in Egypt yet before'. With the regularity of clockwork over 2000 refugees arrived, all the arrangements for their transport from Khartoum to Berber having been made by Gordon. . . . Two thousand five hundred men, women, and children were saved by the direct action and the direct humanity of Gordon himself, long before the [relief] expedition set out for Khartoum.[68]

CHAPTER 5

'No end to our responsibilities'

The British flag flies free amidst the slain,
Our slain, alas! too many. At what cost
The vantage here was won! not to be lost,
If England's voice have power, by faltering will
Or Fiction-muddled fancy. GRAHAM's skill . . .
Matched with such worthy foes, must not in vain
Mark the right watchword, "Rescue and Remain!"

Punch, 22 March 1884[1]

Gladstone gives ground

With Gordon and Stewart hard at work in Khartoum, the Gladstone government now attempted to regain the more solid ground from which it had been shaken by the defeat of General Hicks the previous November and resume planning for the future of Egypt where it had left off. In the short term, there were apparent grounds for confidence. As Edward Hamilton noted in his journal on 23 January, 'the despatch of "Chinese Gordon" . . . has been very well received and has for the moment satisfied public opinion'.[2] But there were two well-attended protest meetings in London over the weekend of 15–16 February, at the Guildhall and the Prince's Hall, Piccadilly.[3] At the second rally, Lord Randolph Churchill denounced the government as being 'solely responsible for the anarchy which prevails in Egypt, and the bloodshed which has occurred and which is imminent in the Sudan,' adding that 'the vacillating pusillanimous policy of the Ministers deserves the severest censures of the country'.[4]

Even before these rallies, a powerful leading article in *The Times* on 21 January should have caused Gladstone a frisson of alarm. The leader is believed to have been largely the work of Gordon's former protégé turned Wolseley agent,

Captain John Brocklehurst of the Household Cavalry.[5] The pro-retention paper echoed 'the feelings of relief and satisfaction inspired by the knowledge that General Gordon has undertaken the *pacification* of the Sudan' (my italics) and hinted strongly that the establishment of a proxy indigenous government would be the outcome of the mission. The editorial further emphasised the difficulties facing any evacuation, deliberately exaggerating the numbers of troops in the scattered garrisons by claiming that 'a mass of Egyptian soldiers and officials, variously estimated at from 25,000 to 40,000 men, has been let loose upon the country in the name of occupation'.[6] In fact, according to a tally calculated by Baring just the previous month, the maximum military strength of all the Sudan garrisons was 24,025 – and more than half of these men were already either dead or subsumed into the ranks of the Mahdī's forces.[7]

Two important but premature assumptions underpinned Gladstone's optimism that the 'Sudan Question' could be sloughed off for good: that the withdrawal of the Egyptian garrisons was now irreversibly underway and that some kind of indigenous leadership would be found to assume power in Khartoum in the aftermath of Gordon's mission. Still, the Prime Minister was only too aware that the position in Egypt and Sudan was 'getting too like a dance on the tight rope'.[8]

Gordon's mission aside, the diplomatic and financial headaches that had followed the 1882 invasion of Egypt were becoming increasingly time-consuming and would eventually prompt a unilateral British effort to secure an agreement whereby European rivals would pledge not to occupy Egypt in the aftermath of the British evacuation.[9] After protracted diplomatic manoeuvring, a trilateral Conference was arranged, involving Britain, France and Germany, but, following seven occasionally acrimonious sessions, it broke up on 2 August 1884 without agreement, leaving Britain definitively but reluctantly in possession of Egypt.[10]

More immediately, a clear restatement of core intentions in respect of Sudan was required. It came in a cabinet memorandum, dated 4 March 1884, illustrating Gladstone's determination to pursue the active abandonment of Sudan, to cede responsibility for any retention of territory on the Red Sea coast to the Ottoman Sultan and to return once more, step by careful step, to the original schedule for military withdrawal from Egypt, whose government, as before, would have no say at all in unfolding events.

Soudan
Sultan to recognise Gordon's mission. The two Powers [Britain and Turkey] to concert as to a successor when the time comes. Successor to be subsidised for a time on Baring's plan.[11] Turks to take over custody of Suakim & any other ports of Red Sea it may be deemed necessary to hold. The two Powers agree to prohibit slave trading therein & use force agst it by land or sea.

Egypt
Should it be found that the military system hitherto contemplated – viz. Egyptian force under British Officers – cannot be relied on, then might we perhaps entertain the idea of a convention with the Sultan for the maintenance of order & the Khedive's throne in Egypt? Wood's army would then be disbanded in due course. Sultan to be limited in numbers: 4000 or 5000? . . . English to hold Alexandria for the same time, or less, if they think they can remove without prejudice to public order . . . *The case arising*, should Baring be brought home to consult: all depending on the decision as to an Egyptian force.[12] Present basis cannot *long* be held.[13]

This reiteration that retrenchment was back on the agenda ruled out any further reinforcement of British forces in Egypt, let alone Sudan. Rejecting a proposal from Childers at the Treasury for the deployment of battalions composed 'entirely of English soldiers under the Egyptian Flag', Gladstone wrote that 'my eyes will not readily be turned to any measure for strengthening the military & governmental hold of England upon Egypt, in which I see no advantage whatever, & the seed of every possible future difficulty'.[14] Put more pithily by General Stephenson in Cairo, the government's 'one object is to shake themselves clear of Egypt as quickly as they can and almost at any price . . . [despite the fact that] this country is now in a very unsettled and unsatisfactory state'.[15]

Military intervention in the east

In terms of policy drift, however, any such restatement was already much too late. The deployment of British troops to Trinkitat and Sawākīn created a bridgehead that proved hard to abandon, especially as the Ottoman Sultan showed no enthusiasm for relieving the British of their Red Sea coast holdings. Indeed, for all the Gladstone cabinet's efforts to formulate an exit strategy, with British troops taking on the levies raised by 'Uthmān Abū-Bakr Diqna on behalf of the Mahdī in a series of high-casualty encounters, it was already embroiled de facto in the First Sudan War.

On 11 February 1884, the cabinet in London began seriously to examine the possibility of increasing military activity in eastern Sudan, both as a demonstration of British military power on the Red Sea Coast and as a way of drawing off the Mahdī's military resources from Khartoum. The following telegram was accordingly sent to Gordon, who was still on his long journey south: 'It has been suggested by a military authority that, to assist the policy of withdrawal, a British force should be sent to Suakin sufficient to operate, if necessary, in its vicinity'.[16] Gladstone himself, anxious to secure a prompt reply on the Red Sea question, apparently hoped to forestall Gordon's arrival in Khartoum, expressing 'no objection to keeping him (or trying to keep him for he moves sharply) at Berber, until . . . he will give us his views'.[17]

The following day, 12 February, the cabinet developed its plan 'to collect a force at Suakim with the object if possible of relieving Tokar garrison if it can hold out: if not, of taking any means necessary for defence of ports'.[18] To that end, Northbrook wrote to Admiral Sir William Hewett, newly appointed as Governor of Sawākīn.[19] But it was Kimberley who highlighted Gladstone's continuing resistance to British military involvement in the face of more bellicose cabinet colleagues: 'After an hour's stubborn resistance the chief consented to measures being taken. Pity they were not taken immediately after Baker's defeat [on 4 February]. Hartington proposed an expedition two or three days ago.'[20]

At Sawākīn itself, therefore, Augustus Wylde was wrong to believe that 'England and the English nation had at last awoke to a sense of the serious state of Soudan affairs'.[21] On 7 March 1884, the cabinet discussed the state of negotiations with the Ottoman court, which had been carried between Granville and Constantine Musurus, the 'Turkish Minister to England'. Items on the agenda of Granville's 'conference' included: '1. Recognition of Gen G; 2. Confer as to successor; 3. Turk in Red Sea ports on terms; Union as to Slave Trade'.[22] Musurus Pasha had his own orders from the Sultan, who had been angered by Egypt's decision, albeit forced by its British occupiers, 'to evacuate the Soudan without consulting the Porte'.[23] Subsequent negotiations also involved the Egyptian ambassador, Ḥassan Fahmī, but, having failed to interest the Turks in taking over the security of the Red Sea coastline, a cabinet meeting on 18 March concluded that it was at least necessary to seek the approval of the Ottoman Sultan for the British deployment: 'Explain expe[ditio]n to S[uakin] conformable to our obligations & not derogatory to Sultan's rights. It will give us much satisfaction if he expresses his concurrence.'[24]

Using only British troops, General Graham achieved his first resounding victory over the Mahdī's army in the Red Sea Hills on 29 February 1884 at the 'Place where Camels are Hobbled', an oasis that retains its place in British military lore as 'El Teb'.[25] For the Sudanese, it was the 'Third Battle of the Coast', the first and second having been the attack on Sawākīn on 4-5 November 1883, in which Commander Lynedoch Moncrieff was killed, and ʿUthmān Diqna's destruction of Valentine Baker's force on 4 February 1884.[26]

The fatalities on each side reflected the grotesque mismatch in fire-power. While Graham lost just thirty-four men, there were more than 2,100 anṣār bodies counted on the battlefield.[27] The Sudanese suffered even larger casualties in Graham's second big victory on 13 March at al-Tamainaib (abbreviated by the British as 'Tamai'), where ʿUthmān Diqna's cousin, Mahsūd Mūsa, led his forces to destruction at the hands of Graham's ranked Highlanders. 'The slaughter of the Arabs was terrible,' noted Thomas Archer, 'over four thousand having fallen before the fire of our men.'[28]

British respect for the Sudanese, who had repeatedly and fearlessly charged into overwhelming rifle and artillery fire, did not preclude the systematic execution of the Mahdist wounded, carried out by both soldiers and ancillary civilian staff, many of whom were 'of a particularly bloodthirsty nature where savages were concerned'.[29] Frederic Villiers, war artist for the daily *Graphic*, painted as vivid a close-up in words as he ever managed in pictures:

> Unless when a bullet smashed a skull or pierced a heart, they came on furiously; and even when the paralysis of death stole over them, in their last convulsions they would try to cut, stab, or even bite. . . . When once in the square, an absolute melee ensued. In rallying groups our men tried to stand their ground, but slowly, yet surely, a retrograde movement was compulsory. We were getting the worst of it. Enveloped in smoke we could hardly distinguish friend from foe. For a moment or two firing ceased, and an appalling silence seemed temporarily to reign, but the struggle had now devolved into a deadly hand-to-hand conflict in which both sides were too busy to give tongue. . . . Regulation revolvers are not much use against the Fuzzy Wuzzy. He seems to swallow the bullets and come up smiling.[30]

With 'Uthmān Diqna's forces temporarily in disarray, some perceived that the route to Berber and Khartoum was now clear. Graham himself opined that 'at the price of much bloodshed . . . the opportunity for rescuing Gordon, and for saving Berber and Kartoum, was actually within England's grasp'.[31] Nor did those in London calling for a more robust attitude to Gordon's vulnerability at Khartoum lose any time in pressing for the use of Sawākīn as the launching-point for a strike into the interior.

As with the deployment of Gordon in January, the most active and vocal agitator for pre-emptive military action in eastern Sudan was Wolseley. On 8 February 1884, with Gordon still only at Abū-Ḥamad, en route to Khartoum, Wolseley had submitted a lengthy and prescient memorandum to Hartington, proposing the despatch of four battalions of infantry, with cavalry and field artillery support, to Sawākīn. Perfectly aware that such a deployment would amount to a policy reversal, he argued that a forceful intervention was required to dislodge the Mahdī's military and psychological grip and distract him from the target that Gordon would present once he arrived at Khartoum.

> I would advise, therefore, that Gordon, in announcing to the inhabitants of the country his appointment as Governor-General, should announce his intention to retain possession of the country to the east of the White Nile; that, in future, it will not be ruled by Egyptian Pashas; that it will be ruled by Soudanese officials under British officers until a stable native government can be established . . . Unless this is done, I do not see what he can effect there. He will be besieged, and . . . the result I foresee is an irresistible demand on the part of our people to have him relieved, and to relieve Khartoum under such circumstances would mean a costly war of considerable proportions.[32]

Wolseley's memorandum travelled rapidly through Whitehall. It provoked dismay among Gladstone's cabinet allies, who saw in his proposal nothing but the potential for further entanglement. There were good reasons to retain the Red Sea coastline: denying exit points to slave-traders; denying access points to European rivals; and maintaining a secure shipping route from the Suez Canal to Aden and on to India. But as for the Sudanese hinterland, Edward Hamilton insisted, 'we have no interest; and when once we exceed that line, there would be no end to our responsibilities'.[33]

But the growing pressure on the government was only increased on 9 February when the Queen, resident at Osborne House on the Isle of Wight, sent her government a characteristically forceful expression of confidence in the Wolseley memorandum: 'The Queen *trusts* Lord Wolseley's plan WILL be considered, and our *whole position remembered*. . . . We must make a demonstration of strength and show determination, and we must not let this fine and fruitful country, with its peaceable inhabitants, be left a prey to murder and rapine and utter confusion. It would be a *disgrace* to the British name, and the country will *not* stand it.'[34]

Parliamentary skirmishing

Remarkably, the government continued to evade serious political damage at Westminster, despite several acrimonious debates on the Sudan crisis between the Queen's Speech on 5 February 1884 and the break-up of parliament for the summer recess on 18 July. It was, as Granville's biographer put it, 'a war to the knife' in which 'it rained attacks and votes of censure'.[35]

The evening of 12 February marked the beginning of a five-day Commons debate on the government's Sudan policy.[36] The formal motion stated that 'this House . . . is of opinion that the recent lamentable events in the Soudan are due, in a great measure, to the vacillating and inconsistent policy pursued by Her Majesty's Government'.[37] Gladstone's own speech on the 'history & controversy' lasted one hour and fifty minutes.[38] For all the bark, however, the opposition had little bite. It was Northbrook who spotted the Conservatives' error in 'accusing us of vacillation instead of taking the only good ground for attack which was that the abandonment of the Soudan was right, but from our mismanagement it had been too long delayed and that thus we were responsible for the disasters . . . The result has been that the attack of the opposition has signally failed.'[39]

After a marathon fifth night of argument, ending at 2am, the motion was defeated in the Commons 262-311 – although the opposition carried the motion in the Lords by a majority of 100. Commenting in his journal three days later, Kimberley reflected on the government's good fortune that news of the loss of Tokar to the Mahdī 'did not fall before the division on Tuesday (the 19th). Our majority (49) was as good as we could wish & rather better perhaps than we deserved.'[40]

Having survived this first vote, another ordeal was faced a month later, when Ellis Ashmead-Bartlett rose on 15 March to propose a motion calling attention to 'the enforced abandonment of Khartoum, and of the Eastern Sudan' and moving that 'it will be highly discreditable to this Country if Her Majesty's Ministers, who are responsible for Egypt, abandon these territories to slavery and barbarism, and that the only satisfactory settlement of the disorders in the Soudan will be the appointment of a British Governor General to restore order and to develop civilization in those Countries, in friendly co-operation with the Sovereign Power'.[41]

On coruscating form, Ashmead-Bartlett lampooned what he called Gladstone's chronic indecision, citing no fewer than six different policies over the previous sixteen months. The phases he identified were, first, 'the policy of drift and shirking which was pursued after the battle of Tel-el-Kebir [in September 1882] up to the 4th of January, 1884 . . . when . . . they drove Cherif Pasha from Office in the most offensive way'; second, the 'reckless, helter-skelter withdrawal or scuttling out of Soudan anyhow . . . regardless of the consequences, caring nothing for the garrisons, for the Egyptian soldiers, for the civil population, or anything else'; third, the decision 'to send out General Gordon to conduct the withdrawal of the garrisons'; fourth, the decision to venture 'a sort of reconstruction of the Administration of the affairs of the Soudan'; fifth, 'a period of hesitation and dispute in the Cabinet as to the extent of military operations to be undertaken'; and sixth, 'the indefinite prolongation of the period of General Gordon's Governorship of the Soudan'.[42]

As Dilke, answering for the government, struggled to get a word in, Henry Labouchère waded in with an amendment adding that 'this House is of opinion that the necessity for the great loss of British and Arab life, occasioned by our Military operations in the Eastern Soudan, has not been made apparent'.[43] This time it was Fitzmaurice's turn to flounder in the face of firebrand oratory from Lord Randolph Churchill. Technically, it was not a vote of confidence, but defeat would still have been damaging and, on an evening when the Commons was less than full, it took a vigorous effort by Liberal party enforcers to gather MPs in sufficient numbers to see off both motion and amendment by a margin of 111-94. It was, as Kimberley noted, 'a very narrow escape' and did not bode well for the government's prospects: 'We shall have to come to a Dissolution before very long, & all the signs point to our defeat.'[44]

Gladstone was again forced to defend his position in the House on 3 April, when Northcote demanded clarification of existing policy on 'the government of the Eastern Soudan; the relations which are to be maintained with the Western Soudan; the Government of Khartoum; the relations between the Soudan generally and the Egyptian Government; . . . General Gordon's present position and views; and, whether it is the intention of Her Majesty's Government to afford him any material support?'[45] As there was no formal motion, there was no vote, but the Prime Minister himself mounted a vigorous defence, backed by a feisty Hartington.[46]

Again on 22 April, Gladstone was quizzed in the Commons, this time by Ashmead-Bartlett, who came to the chamber armed with 'the statements of a Catholic Missionary, who has just reached Cairo from the Upper Nile, that it is impossible for General Gordon to maintain himself with the present garrison'.[47] Focusing on the deep trench dug outside Khartoum's southern perimeter earthworks, a defensive barrier that, in high season at least, filled with Nile water, Ashmead-Bartlett quoted his source: 'For defending the Canal alone, he [Gordon] requires 6,000 men. Both Niles are now beginning to sink, and with blocks of wood the Arabs will cross from bank to bank. An attempt to escape by way of Berber would be absolutely vain.'[48]

Again, Gladstone held his ground. Nettled by Ashmead-Bartlett's direct question as to 'whether, after the statements which have been made as to the imminent peril of General Gordon at Khartoum, the House is to understand that Her Majesty's Government are taking no steps whatever for the relief of Gordon?', the Prime Minister replied tartly:

> I must say he puts a Question in the preamble of which he asserts and implies that which I have repeatedly and positively denied – namely, that we know that General Gordon is in imminent peril. . . . In our view that is an entirely erroneous opinion, and it is entirely and absolutely contradicted by the language of General Gordon himself.[49]

Even Gladstone's cabinet colleagues were amazed at the way he got away with brazen hair-splitting and prevarication in the Commons. Dilke described an amusing scene in cabinet, where he and Chamberlain exchange furtive notes like naughty schoolboys, lamenting Gladstone's 'inconvenient habit of giving information at question time'. Dilke quotes a short poem extemporised by Chamberlain: 'Here lies Mr. G., who has left us repining, / While he is, no doubt, still engaged in refining; / And explaining distinctions to Peter and Paul, / Who faintly protest that distinctions so small / Were never submitted to saints to perplex them, / Until the Prime Minister came up to vex them'.[50]

Exemplary stalling tactics aside, this minor skirmishing prefaced a second formal vote of censure, tabled on 12 May by Sir Michael Hicks-Beach, the Conservative MP for East Gloucestershire: 'That this House regrets to find that the course pursued by Her Majesty's Government has not tended to promote the success of General Gordon's Mission, and that even such steps as may be necessary to secure his personal safety are still delayed'.[51] The debate was shorter than in February, two long nights instead of five, but Dilke for one did not expect to see it 'excelled for interest and fire'.[52] Of his own contribution 'on the Gordon question', Gladstone noted almost defensively in his journal that he had spoken 'with an active & absolute desire to speak according to truth & justice'.[53]

The result was another close call, with the government securing a narrow majority of 28: 303-275.[54] 'On the failure of the conspiracy,' commented a relieved

Prime Minister, 'the Liberal cheering was perhaps the most prolonged I have ever known.'[55] More importantly, Tory impotence had again been exposed. Still, notwithstanding Gladstone's own protestations that evidence of Gordon's 'imminent peril' was still lacking, his cabinet colleagues were acutely aware that the impetus for some kind of rescue expedition was well nigh irresistible. Where they differed was in interpretation.

Some, like Dilke, saw in the failure of the parliamentary opposition the opportunity for the administration to wash its hands of Gordon and put the 'Soudan Question' behind it for good. 'Here ended our responsibility,' he wrote later; 'from this moment we had only to please ourselves as to whether we should disavow him and say that he was acting in defiance of instructions, and must be left to his fate, or whether we should send an expedition to get him out.'[56] Others, like Kimberley, feared the worst. Writing in the immediate aftermath of the second vote of censure, he lamented the 'clamour for an expedition to Khartoum' from opponents in the press and in parliament, 'the former from ignorance, the latter because it is the best mode of embarrassing us':

> The interest of the nation is to get quit of the Soudan and the Egyptian occupation as soon as possible. But Gordon is a tremendous obstacle. If he cannot be got out in any other way, an expedition, (a frightful undertaking) is inevitable. Of course it is not an impossible undertaking, but it is melancholy to think of the waste of lives and treasure which it must involve, and except the rescue of Gordon & Stewart, no good end is to be attained. We shall have to fight the Soudanese with whom we have no quarrel and to support the rascally Egyptians whose cowardice and cruel Govt. have been the cause of the whole calamity.[57]

Opportunity in the East declined

If the cabinet in London was willing to regard Gordon as expendable, Baring in Cairo was woefully off-message, even if he was sympathetic with the strategic imperative of evacuation. Baring, of course, read all the military intelligence that he transmitted to London, but his conclusions were strikingly different from those reached by his political masters. As early as 24 March, when Gordon had been in Khartoum for barely five weeks, and following extensive consultations with his own military colleagues in Cairo, Baring pressed for an acknowledgement that the evacuation of Egyptian personnel was doomed to failure. Given that Gordon and Stewart were likely to take a highly moral stance, refusing to leave without the soldiers and civilians they had been sent to save, it was time for a pre-emptive strike from the east.

> Only two solutions appear to be possible. The first is to trust General Gordon's being able to maintain himself at Khartoum till the autumn, when, by reason of the greater quantity of water, it would be less difficult to

conduct operations on the Suakin-Berber road than it is at present. . . . The only other plan is to send a portion of General Graham's army [at Sawākīn] to Berber with instructions to open up communications with Khartoum. . . . General Gordon is evidently expecting help from Suakin, and he has ordered messengers to be sent along the road from Berber to ascertain whether any English force is advancing. . . . General Stephenson and Sir Evelyn Wood, while admitting the very great risk to the health of the troops, besides the extraordinary military risks, are of opinion that the undertaking is possible. . . . We all consider that, however difficult the operations from Suakin may be, they are more practicable than any operations from Korosko [i.e. across the Nubian Desert to Berber] and [thence] along the Nile.[58]

This intervention was bold and, given the government's declared opposition to military action of any kind, personally risky. It was also the first salvo in what would become, over the summer, 'the battle of the routes'. The government's terse but emphatic negative was telegraphed the following day. No such initiative was possible, given 'the climate of the Soudan at this time of the year, as well as the extraordinary risk from a military point of view'; as for Gordon, he had 'full discretion . . . to remain at Khartoum, if he thinks it necessary, or to retire by the southern or any other route which may be found available'.[59]

This careless answer ignored Baring's observation that Gordon and Stewart would simply decline to abandon those they had been sent to save. Dilke, who found Baring's telegram 'very unpleasant [and] . . . pointing, we thought, to a possible resignation', applauded the government's 'absolute refusal'.[60] But Queen Victoria endorsed Baring's 'alarming' message, writing to Hartington at the War Ministry on 25 March: 'Gordon is in danger: you are bound to try and save him. Surely Indian troops might go from Aden: they could bear the climate. You have incurred fearful responsibility.'[61]

Responsibility, of course, was exactly what Gladstone did not want, either for his erratic agent in Khartoum or for the wider territory, and the Queen's accusation triggered a sustained broadside from cabinet. Granville convened a meeting at the Commons the same evening with Hartington and Northbrook. Agreeing a common position, they subjected the Queen to a barrage of explanatory letters. Granville observed that Baring's call for an advance on Berber ran 'contrary to his former opinion', while Hartington enlisted the backing of the Duke of Cambridge, Commander-in-Chief of the British Army and a relative of the Queen's, for the argument that an expedition to Berber across the eastern desert from Sawākīn would be 'too hazardous'.[62]

Gladstone himself weighed in two days later with a long-winded exposition of the current state of affairs. Joining the personal attack on Baring, who may have 'shown conspicuous ability and excellent sense in the office that he holds: but the difficulties are such that it is no wonder if occasionally he treads awry', the Prime Minister noted that 'on this occasion he makes a recommending (in what can hardly be considered as an official document) that amounts to a reversal of policy'. Citing inadequate military intelligence, he complained of 'the very imperfect knowledge with which the Government are required at the shortest notice to form conclusions in respect to a peculiar, remote, and more than half-barbarous region, with which they have but a very slight and indirect connection in the ordinary sense'. The repeated assertion that more information was required was a device used by this master of legalistic evasion with remarkable frequency and effect for much of the summer. 'When adequate intelligence shall have been received from General Gordon,' he concluded, 'there will be every disposition to support him to the full extent which national interests will permit, and without too nice a computation of risks merely Ministerial.'[63]

Hard upon this broadside, the cabinet stamped firmly on the Baring plan, issuing immediate orders for General Graham and his troops to withdraw from the Red Sea coast to their Egyptian barracks.[64] They had travelled no more than twelve miles from Sawākīn. Graham later regretted that he had not taken a unilateral decision to march on Berber. 'Though not allowed the honour of being Gordon's deliverer,' he reflected, 'it is yet some small consolation to me to know that Gordon, in the midst of his bitter reflections when alone at Kartoum, acquitted me, and the gallant little force I had the honour to command, of all unreadiness, or disinclination to advance to his rescue'.[65] Thus was the first of two real opportunities to reach Gordon in time squandered.

Nor did the cabinet wish Gordon to continue to delude himself as to prospects of military relief. A comprehensive reminder of standing policy was telegraphed by the Foreign Office to Khartoum on 28 March 1884. Given Gordon's refusal to leave without the garrison he had come to evacuate, this despatch was, in Henry Traill's words, not just a series of 'laboriously ex-cogitated excuses but in effect Gordon's death-warrant. Whatever was to be done to save him from beleaguerment in Khartum should have been done during the next fortnight at latest.'[66]

Granville used the telegram to rehearse the mission parameters, stressing that 'the Mission of General Gordon, as originally designed and decided upon, was of a pacific nature, and in no way involved any movement of forces'. Observing that the 'full discretionary power' given Gordon in Cairo en route to Khartoum 'virtually altered General Gordon's mission from one of advice to that of executing, or at least directing, the evacuation not only of Khartoum but the whole Soudan', Granville voiced approval of Gordon having 'the largest discretion . . . hampered as little as possible by criticisms and objections'. After some disingenuous comments on the Red Sea campaign, where Graham's successful campaign might 'enable the road from Suakin to Berber to be opened, by the friendly action of the tribes, without the necessity of further military measures', Granville fell back on the stalling tactic of requesting further information on 'General Gordon's actual position, his resources, and his requirements'. Finally, offering Gordon the doubtful palliative that 'his mission, even though it be not successful, will have added to his very high reputation', Granville came to the real point of the long message.

The presence of British forces in Egypt, and the part which Her Majesty's Government are taking in the administration of the country, are for a special and temporary purpose, which has been clearly defined in declarations to Parliament, and in diplomatic communications to other Powers. It is their desire to keep within the limits so laid down, and not to extend the scope of British intervention more than is necessary . . . With regard to the Soudan, Her Majesty's Government adhere to the policy which formed the basis of the advice which they pressed upon the Khedive . . . It appeared to them to be an obvious fact . . . that to reconquer the interior of the Soudan was a task beyond the powers of Egypt alone, and they were firmly resolved . . . not to lend any military assistance for the purpose of regaining for Egypt vast territories, which, far from being of use, had created a constant drain of blood and treasure since their conquest sixty years ago. Her Majesty's Government laid down in the most distinct terms their determination not to use British troops for this purpose.[67]

Evacuation ended by siege of Khartoum

Even as the political arguments continued in London, the evacuation from Khartoum was curtailed by several irrecoverable reverses, the most severe of which was the Mahdī's final encirclement of the city on 13 March 1884. This was the completion of a pincer movement by Sheikh Muḥammad Badr al-ʿUbeiḍ, advancing down the east bank of the Blue Nile at the head of at least 30,000 men, and an alliance of Muḥammad wad al-Baṣīr and Sheikh Muṣṭafa al-Amīn, moving up the west bank of the White Nile toward Omdurman with another 15,000 fighters between them.[68] This development prompted some alarm in London, with Gladstone prompted to re-examine Gordon's request for al-Zubeir Raḥma. After a crisis cabinet meeting on 15 March, the Prime Minister noted:

1. Increase in danger and difficulty through cutting of the [telegraph] wires, and rising of tribes between Khartoum & Berber.

2. Impossible under these circs. to send peremptory order for retreat from Khartoum. . . . If Baring, with or without further support from Gordon, thinks it best to send Zobeir, and can make what he may think a proper arrangement with him, we will support him. (I much regret that we have been much frightened about Zobeir though the proposal was certainly not one to be hastily adopted or without testing the opinion entertained in Egypt).[69]

Gordon's capacity to break out in substantial numbers was then badly damaged by a serious defeat six days later. On 16 March, an expedition to recapture the village of Ḥalfāya, to the north of the Nile confluence, was thwarted by the treachery of two senior Egyptian officers, generals Ḥassan Ibrāhīm Shallāli and Saʿīd Ḥussein al-Jimiʿābi, and from then on Gordon was restricted to occasional and minor sorties from the city.[70] Only a day earlier, Gordon had written to Watson to lament that he was 'not strong enough to do more than annoy them, for I do not like to risk Kartoum . . . We are all right & in good spirits. It is queer to hear their drums so close to us.'[71]

The fall of Berber on 13 May killed off any remaining hope of retreat to the north, certainly for a party numbering in the thousands that still remained in Khartoum. The loss of Berber, however, had long been expected. As early as 7 April, Baring was warning London that the siege by fighters under the banner of the Mahdī's regional chieftain, Muḥammad ʿAbdallah Khojali, was tightening dangerously.[72] In fact, Ḥussein Khalīfa, a senior figure in the ʿAbābda tribe currently serving a second term as Governor of Berber, had warned a full month earlier that 'if we are not relieved by a sufficient force, there is danger of the routes of communication between the Soudanese districts and the north being cut off'.[73] And on 15 April, a group of expatriates in Berber signed a joint letter imploring both Cairo and London not to forget them:

> We Europeans, Turks, Egyptians, Hijazis and Algerians, came to the Soudan relying on the support and protection of the [Egyptian] Government. Now if it abandons us today, through indifference or weakness, its honour will be everlastingly tarnished by the handing over of its servants and subjects to death and dishonour. If Egypt has given the Soudan up to England, we implore that great, chivalrous, and humane power to come to our help . . . for if the same state of things continues for ten days or a fortnight more, our country will be ravaged and we shall be lost.[74]

Unmoved, the cabinet waited a full fortnight before even authorising an 'inquiry as to means of helping Berber'.[75] The inquiry came in the form of a Foreign Office telegram to Egerton in Cairo, conceding that the danger to Berber appeared to be 'imminent' and instructing him to 'report, after consultation with Nubar, Wood, and Stephenson, whether there is any step, by negotiation or otherwise, which can be taken at once to relieve it'.[76] After immediate telegraphic consultations with Ḥussein Khalīfa at Berber, who begged for two battalions of reinforcements in addition to more ammunition, Egerton relayed back to London the Egyptian Prime Minister's agreement to the despatch of additional troops.[77] Generals Wood and Stephenson, he added, had argued for an Anglo-Egyptian force to be sent to Berber. The least that could be done in the short term would be to give Berber an assurance that 'English material aid shall be rendered as soon as is practicable'.[78] Egerton then proceeded to undermine this expert testimony by offering the personal opinion that 'it would be almost madness to run the risk of sending an English or Egyptian force now by the routes suggested'.[79]

That last observation, albeit unsolicited and unqualified, enabled the cabinet to reject all conflicting advice in unequivocal terms and the reply effectively doomed Berber. 'We cannot sanction attempt to send English force at this season to Berber,' came the reply, 'or to send Egyptian troops alone. Tell Hassan [sic] Khalifa that no immediate assistance can be given to him.'[80] Cabinet notes reveal that Hartington alone was 'dissentient', a hint of trouble to come.[81] As for evacuation, now clearly impossible, it was left to Granville to transmit the blandly disingenuous advisory that 'the original plan for the evacuation of the Soudan has been dropped'.[82] From now until the late autumn, Gordon was sent message after message, usually in 'Cypher O' code, repeated with only minor variations.[83]

> Gordon ... should keep us informed, to the best of his ability, not only as to immediate, but as to any prospective danger at Khartoum; that to be prepared for any such danger he advise us as to the force necessary in order to secure his removal, its amount, character, route for access to Khartoum, and time of operation; that we do not propose to supply him with Turkish or other force for the purpose of undertaking military expeditions, such being beyond the scope of the commission he holds, and at variance with the pacific policy which was the purpose of his mission to the Soudan; that if with this knowledge he continues at Khartoum, he should state to us the cause and intention with which he so continues.[84]

It is hard to believe that the precise wording of this 'decisive' missive had been discussed at several meetings between Gladstone, Granville and Hartington before being agreed by the wider cabinet on 23 April.[85] As late as 21 June, the cabinet was still wavering over the relief expedition and, in Dilke's words, 'it was decided to wait ten days before settling anything, and to see whether we heard from him [Gordon] in reply to the silly questions which had been asked'.[86] Gordon's response to the message was scornful: on 19 September, he wrote sarcastically that the 'cause and intention' of his remaining in Khartoum had been 'those horridly plucky Arabs'.[87]

Eye-witnesses to the siege of Khartoum

We have three main sources for events in Khartoum, military and civil, during the summer of 1884: Gordon's official despatches, surviving elements of Stewart's campaign log and Power's reports for *The Times*. Many messages, however, failed to reach London, especially once the Mahdī's siege was completed and the severing of the telegraph lines from the city forced a reliance on covert, hand-carried communications. Power's longhand despatch dated 14 April 1884, sent by courier to his colleague in Cairo, Moberly Bell, was not published until 1890. Fearing capture and punishment as a spy, the messenger hid the despatch between bricks in a wall and was unable to return to the site until several years later. 'Since we heard that we had been abandoned by the

British Government,' Power's report began, 'General Gordon has been indefatigable in carrying on this unequal war against the Arabs. He is putting down mines in all directions and the steamers are almost daily engaged with the Arabs.'

Three further despatches, dated 28 April, 30 July and 31 July, took many weeks to be smuggled by messengers via Kassala and the Abyssinian port of Massawa to the British at Sawākīn. These vivid and atmospheric accounts of the siege were published to popular acclaim several months later.[88] One contemporary writer described the 'bright and eventful day' when Power's accounts were published, 'astounding us with the recitals of extraordinary feats, amazing us with some idea of the surpassing power and genius of the noble-hearted defender of the city in the desert'.[89] For Gordon's many admirers back home – and for the Stewart and Power families – the resulting silences made for long periods of anxious waiting. During these silences, gossip and rumour replaced hard news.

Power's despatches conveyed not only military detail and dramatic eyewitness evidence of life within the besieged city, but also opinionated commentary, which greatly influenced the mood in London and provided emotional ammunition for those who were dissatisfied with government policy. Power's views clearly bear the stamp of Gordon's own opinions, reflecting not just hero-worship but the almost claustrophobic physical proximity of the shared executive suites in the Governor-General's residence. On 2 April 1884, Power wrote:

> The rebels, being gradually emboldened, are approaching the town on all sides. Khartoum for the present is safe, and pretty well provided. The people are naturally asking, "Are we to continue for ever like this, or to be released by the English, the Turks, or the Egyptians!" . . . The total ignorance which exists among us as to the intentions of Her Majesty's Government is far worse than the certainty, however bad. . . . Would it not be more honest of the Government, if it cannot carry out its self-imposed duty towards us by means of British troops, to hire Turkish regiments?[90]

Five days later, another despatch presented the same mixture of reportage and commentary: 'The rebels' tents are within sight, and their bullets often strike or go over the palace, in which a man was thus killed last week. We have killed several of the rebels, but our store of Krupp [artillery] ammunition is rather short. The situation is now very critical . . . I have had only two sources of hope in this crisis – first, the expectation of an English relieving column; secondly, the plan of a retreat across the Equator . . . To retreat on Berber is impossible.'[91]

With such a loyal amanuensis, Gordon scarcely needed to transmit reports himself. Needless to say, he did not hesitate to do so, although the blizzard of often contradictory messages that had characterised the early weeks of the mission diminished and became at times calmer, even carefully reasoned. His

Portrait of William Ewart Gladstone by John Everett Millais. Gladstone's stern demeanour was mirrored by his inflexible approach to Sudan policy, especially his refusal to become embroiled in a conflict in which he thought Britain had no part and no strategic interest. This is not a portrait of a man prone to 'drift and shirking'. But even Gladstone could not prevent his career and his reputation being fatally undermined by the publication of Gordon's posthumous Khartoum Journal.

Major-General Charles Gordon, the man many hoped would bring the 'Soudan Crisis' to a speedy end. Instead, his unilateral actions subverted the policy he was sent to enforce – and his posthumously published journals were cannily exploited to end the career of William Gladstone.

The last surviving fragment of Stewart's campaign journal, a meticulous account of a city under siege. The final entry reads: '7th July. Monday. Two steamers went up the White Nile. Were not fired on by the Arab fort. At 3 PM they reached Jebel Auli [south of Khartoum]. The banks were raided . . .' The author is planning to publish a full annotated edition of the entire journal in 2013.

Ordeh. (Dongola) Nov: 7. 1884.

My dear Gordon. I sent you a long message 2298 5216 3944 3513 6522 2298 5216 5321 1611 I had no answer to 3042 1179 7849 shall have a considerable force concentrated in neighbourhood of DEBBEH or AMBUKOL 5426 3378 6386 2267 6756 6574 2996 7502 5395 6554 2267 8153 especially made for the purpose in England. Besides force 2996 5359 7310 7810 1468 4217 on Camels 1906 3223 7043 5523 6220 3723 4991 3513 4782 5562 English Cavalry Regiment.

I should like if possible 2267 2767 8049 2267 6672 1330 4687 5848 7842 6645 ABU HAMED, BERBER and S'HENDY 6361 6744 6259 7985 1851 5204 6164 2267 SHENDY 7456 2156 1030 2267 2753 6361 7414 5426 3811 1468 7969 1058 Camels.

Inclosed is a copy of 4293 6727. Do you know any one — 3157 7775 1906 6495 3236 6802 8273 — 6495 5242 6170 8093 6104 2267 6009 1114 2921 KHARTOUM 3519 3362 1115 3126 6958 2298 2290 4427 3240 EGYPT 2267 7091 5249 2895 7030 5678 3513 5724 7030 7527 7810 3214 5123 4170 7643 4770 2915 3603 4967 2319 2267 7091 4967 4434 6518 6097 5305 SOUDAN 3513 7065 4967 3224 4926 3684 2580 1906 3513 8184 4967 7951 8206 1179 3280 2267 1816 3171 1394 5783 2531 5123 1020 1635 2944 1144 6220 DONGOLA, BERBER and KHARTOUM 2267 1816 4857 3147 1751 7475 1906 6781 2267 1816 7988 7537 4660 1851 4618 Trade routes 3513 5069 4411 7625 6877 1565 1672 4134 1906 3513 2267 1401 2944 6924 4907 1179 4434 1035 1020 1904 to be reserved. 1565 3305 2267 3362 WADY HALFA KOROSKO, and ASSOUN. SOUAKIM 2267 1816 6584 7514 5497 6011 7514 1144 1635 2944 5409 3223 2426 I can think of as likely 2267 6593 3790 1175 7840 1111 2748 2839 4707 4489 1783 1906 6097 7414 3000 and the Mudir here. The former behaved well 7193 6267 2087 6128 3513 6260 1137 4967 2267 5309 1115 3126 4427 7414 Mohamet Achmet 5242 4873 4967 7490 3513 8171 4321 2626 8105 would suit. If you think 6909 6744 1906 4020 5242 6744 3271 6658 3513 2324 4967 2944 4427 I have described 7310 2208 Satin Bey 4770 8186 5237 7377 3261 1488 4770 8255 6356 2267 HUSSEIN PASHA KHALIFA.

One of a series of coded telegrams sent to Gordon, conveying policy instructions from London. The first numerical section of this message reads: 'Sir Evelyn Baring having gone [to] London I [am] charged by Her Majesty's Government [to] tell you to keep you informed not only as to immediate but as to any [?] danger at Khartoum . . .' After 9 September 1884, Gordon was unable to read such messages, having sent his codebook down-river on Stewart's last mission.

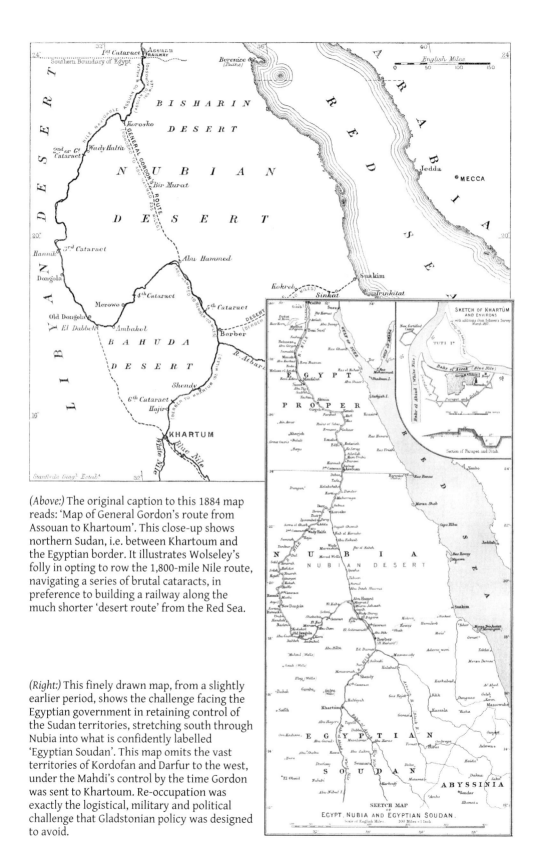

(*Above:*) The original caption to this 1884 map reads: 'Map of General Gordon's route from Assouan to Khartoum'. This close-up shows northern Sudan, i.e. between Khartoum and the Egyptian border. It illustrates Wolseley's folly in opting to row the 1,800-mile Nile route, navigating a series of brutal cataracts, in preference to building a railway along the much shorter 'desert route' from the Red Sea.

(*Right:*) This finely drawn map, from a slightly earlier period, shows the challenge facing the Egyptian government in retaining control of the Sudan territories, stretching south through Nubia into what is confidently labelled 'Egyptian Soudan'. This map omits the vast territories of Kordofan and Darfur to the west, under the Mahdi's control by the time Gordon was sent to Khartoum. Re-occupation was exactly the logistical, military and political challenge that Gladstonian policy was designed to avoid.

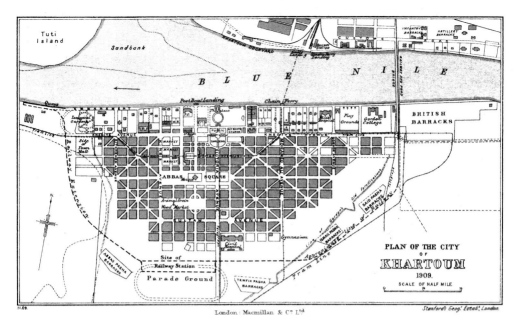

This map, drawn only a decade after British occupation, shows the rapid development of the capital, reinstated at Khartoum after 14 years of Mahdist rule from Omdurman. Elsewhere, the guidebook describes the reconstruction of a battered nation in partisan terms: 'Trade is slowly reviving, as confidence is established and the tribes realise that the Dervish power is at an end.'

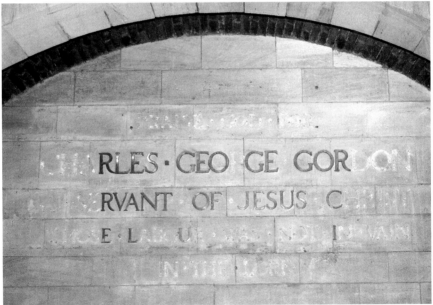

Remnants of a colonial-era British memorial to Gordon in the now deconsecrated Anglican cathedral in Khartoum. Most of the brass letters have been picked off the stone mount, probably by souvenir-hunters. The damaged script reads:

PRAISE · GOD · FOR
CHARLES · GEORGE · GORDON
SERVANT · OF · JESUS · CHRIST
WHOSE · LABOUR · WAS · NOT · IN · VAIN
IN · THE · LORD

The tomb of the Mahdi in Omdurman, after deliberate bombardment by Anglo-Egyptian forces, 1898. The tomb, known locally as a *qubba*, was built over the place where the Mahdi died of typhoid on 22 June 1885, five months after the death of Gordon. In the first phase of Kitchener's occupation, British soldiers had the Mahdi's body exhumed and his skeleton, minus the skull, thrown into the Nile – a deliberate echo of Gordon's decapitation by the Mahdi's fighters.

The tomb of the Mahdi in Omdurman today. The *qubba* is still one of the most important gathering points for followers of the al-Mahdi family, a powerful political force known collectively as the Ansar. In the modern era, splits within the family over the clan leadership and over finances have diminished the capacity of the al-Mahdis' political wing, the Umma Party, to resist military rule.

During the long siege of Khartoum, the government mint printed small bank-notes in denominations of 1, 5, 10, 20, 100, 500, 1,000, 2,000, 2,500 and 5,000 piastres (100 to the Egyptian pound). The central, hand-written inscription reads: 'This amount is approved and is to be paid from the Treasury of Khartoum or of Egypt six months from the date of issue'. This note bears the date 25 April 1884 and is endorsed with Gordon's signature and his personal stamp in Arabic ('Ghūrdūn').

LORD WOLSELEY INVESTING THE MUDIR OF DONGOLA WITH THE ORDER OF K.C.M.G.
From a Sketch by Our Special Artist, Mr. F. Villiers

Graphic 13/12/84

THE NILE EXPEDITION FOR THE RELIEF OF GENERAL GORDON

(*Above:*) The original captions read: 'Lord Wolseley investing the Mudir of Dongola with the order of K.C.M.G.' and 'The Nile Expedition for the relief of General Gordon'. Mustafa Yawar, the Governor of Dongola and the northern region of Sudan, was a Circassian officer with religious leanings. He proved to be a loyal ally, providing assistance to Wolseley during the slow build-up of British forces for the failed Gordon Relief Expedition.

(*Right:*) The original caption reads: 'Mirage.' '*What* is it that i seem to see across the sand waste? Is it the quick gleam of English steel, or but a desert-dream? Help—or, that last illusion of distress, the mocking *mirage* of the wilderness?' Critics of the Gladstone administration were quick to paint Gordon as having been abandoned by the government who sent him out. They did not take account of Gordon's refusal to leave, a clear and unilateral attempt to blackmail Gladstone into a policy reversal.

PUNCH, OR THE LONDON CHARIVARI.—APRIL 12, 1884.

"MIRAGE."

GENERAL GORDON. . . . . . "*WHAT* IS IT THAT I SEEM TO SEE ACROSS THE SAND WASTE? IS IT THE QUICK GLEAM OF ENGLISH STEEL, OR BUT A DESERT-DREAM? HELP—OR, THAT LAST ILLUSION OF DISTRESS, THE MOCKING *MIRAGE* OF THE WILDERNESS?"

Remains of the Melik gunboat, used by Kitchener's force in the invasion of Sudan, 1896-8. There has been a determined campaign in recent years by the Melik Society to prevent the *Melik* and another well-known Nile vessel, the *Bordein*, from falling into irreversible disrepair.

The original caption reads: 'A deed without a name.' *Macbeth*. 'ABANDONED.'

ABANDONED.

The original captions read: 'Stand not upon the order of your going, But go at once.' *Macbeth*. 'THE NILE PICNIC.' The pace of Wolseley's advance was carefully calibrated, clearly under-estimating the state of crisis in Khartoum. This cartoon pokes fun at the luxury extras enjoyed by senior staff on a mission that should have been leaner and much more expeditious. These cartoons by George Stronach and George Halkett are reproduced in *The Egyptian Red Book* (Edinburgh: William Blackwood & Sons, 1885) pp. 20, 26.

THE NILE PICNIC.

telegram of 17 March, for example, described the previous day's disastrous military encounter in punchy detail, leaving Baring to refer to Power's report of the same day 'as I have not time to write more'. Gordon's follow-up six days later described the court martial, death sentence and execution of the two officers whose treachery had led to the defeat of the Ḥalfāya sortie.[92]

By 30 July, with communications reduced to a minimum, Gordon's long message to both Baring and Nūbār Pasha in Cairo and hand-smuggled east to Sawākīn via Massawa proposed that Kassala, then still held by the pro-government Khatmīa leader, Muḥammad 'Uthmān Mīrghani, be 'the route for your despatches'.[93] By 23 August, however, Gordon was again in confused form, harping on themes that would be rehearsed endlessly in his subsequent journal, including the despatch of al-Zubeir, both British and Turkish troops and the recapture of Berber.[94]

Gordon's greatest mistake was his insistence that the threat from the Mahdī had been exaggerated and that all was well in Khartoum. One particular phrase, 'trumpery revolt', which illustrated his continuing lack of understanding of the spiritual and social underpinnings of the Mahdī's uprising, was first used by him in a private letter to Wood on 18 April 1884.[95] Such expressions played into Gladstone's hands and contributed to a grotesque misreading of the strategic situation by Gordon's most loyal supporters. In June 1884, Sir Henry Gordon professed himself convinced that his brother was in no personal danger, no doubt persuaded by his brother's 'impression of the truly trumpery nature of this revolt, which 500 determined men could put down'.[96]

'He under apprehension!' he exclaimed in an interview with *Contemporary Review*; 'Not the slightest. Talk of danger! Look at the story . . . when he marched into the camp of slave-dealers at Shakka [in Darfur during his first term as Governor-General].[97] That was danger.' Sir Henry was also deluded as to an imminent and satisfactory compromise outcome with the Mahdī himself: 'I should not be the least surprised to see the veil lifted between Khartoum and Berber by a telegram coming from Gordon: "We are all right. I have formed a Government, and have put the Mahdī in charge of Khartoum."'[98]

Nor was Sir Henry alone in the fog. As late as the end of July, Henry Stanley felt confident enough to pronounce that the man who was still due to succeed him on the Congo would have no difficulty in escaping from Khartoum, 'by means of the Congo, the Nile, and across the desert to Zanzibar'. Accordingly, noted his interviewer, 'Mr. Stanley derides the suggested expedition to Khartoum, and says the men would die like flies when the summer sun is waning'.[99]

The third and perhaps most immediately vivid account of the siege is contained in Stewart's campaign log, still diligently maintained but considerably thinner than in the early, optimistic days of the mission. Few fragments, unfortunately, survived following the last substantial mail-boat collection on 11 March. Gordon now needed his entire fleet of steamers for the defence of Khartoum and the risks involved in attempting to break through the Mahdī's blockade simply to run mail shipments were unjustifiable. The meagre fragments describing a period in late spring, however, show that Stewart lost none of his brisk and succinct reporting style. On 27 April 1884, for example, he noted: 'Rebels returned fire vigorously. Report that our Mails from Berber have been seized. Report rebels repelled from Shendy. News arrived that Saleh Pasha[100] with 1500 troops, supplies, ammunition & one Steamer had surrendered to the rebels under Wad-el-Bessir [Muḥammad al-Ṭayyib al-Baṣīr].[101] This surrender occurred 11 days ago.'[102]

Stewart maintained the official campaign journal throughout the long summer of siege, winning the approbation of his commanding officer, who pronounced it 'a gem'.[103] Like Gordon, we can only lament its subsequent disappearance amid the other official records of the siege, for after one last surviving extract from the beginning of July, a fragment that picks up mid-way through an entry, the voice of Stewart is silenced for good.

[2 July] . . . Shendy & that he had already defeated the Arabs with considerable loss. Also that Mah Osman [Muḥammad 'Uthmān Abū-Qarja] with another force was advancing on Shendy by the Atbara & that the rebels were very dispirited & falling away having lost heavily ? on 30th June. Another spy coming from a different direction corroborated above news. Ther [thermometer] in shade 97°. Hear that Cuzzi is going to Kordofan.[104]
. . .

4th July. Friday. One of the writers [secretaries] to the Police Officer deserted to the Arabs during the night or else was drowned as his clothes were found on the bank. Enemy's parades to day poorly attended.

5th July. Saturday. At 1.30 PM two steamers went up Blue Nile & shelled the forts. After some firing the forts were silenced. The Mansura steamer went up the White Nile & attacked the fort there.

6th July. Sunday. At 1 PM the Steamers went up the White Nile & attacked the fort. The firing lasted till dusk. The Ismailiyeh steamer unfortunately went aground. Two steamers also went up the Blue Nile & attacked trenches there. . . .

7th July. Monday. Two steamers went up the White Nile. Were not fired on by the Arab fort. At 3 PM they reached Jebel Auli [south of Khartoum on the White Nile]. The banks were raided . . . [105]

Fight or flight?

With the disappearance of so much important documentation from Khartoum, questions about any disagreement between Gordon and Stewart over how best to respond to the closure of the primary evacuation route must remain a matter of conjecture. Baring wrote later that relations between Gordon and Stewart were, in the early days at least, 'much strained'. Gordon had been irritated to have Stewart sent along as his 'wet-nurse', while Stewart found it hard to contain the general's 'impulsive flightiness'.[106] There were certainly rows, reported confidentially by Stewart to Baring, in which Gordon resorted to Power as his conduit for messages to Cairo when Stewart hesitated to send them in the form dictated.[107]

Sir Charles Wilson later wrote that, 'though in none of Stewart's letters is there a single disloyal word', there was a 'sharp discussion' over this question of exploiting the popular press to put pressure on the government. Stewart's opinion was that 'an officer who had accepted a special mission from Government should on all occasions state his views openly and fearlessly, and loyally accept their decision'.[108] Closer to disloyalty, to Gordon at least, was Stewart's sympathetic note of 4 March 1884 to Baring, in which he commiserated 'about the many & rather divergent telegrams you get. Gordon telegraphs directly an idea strikes him. There is no use in trying to stop it. Were I you I should always wait for a few days before acting unless the subject matter is so evident that there can be no doubt about it.'[109]

The question of whether the two beleaguered officers should make good their own escape, leaving the Egyptian garrison, its Sudanese employees and the civilian population of Khartoum to make the best terms possible with the Mahdī, must have provoked intense discussion. Sir Henry Brand, Speaker of the House of Commons, believed that Stewart had quarrelled with Gordon 'on the ground that . . . there was no further useful work to be done in Khartoum, that the longer he and Gordon stayed the greater would be the risk to the population, because . . . those unfortunate people if overpowered would meet with no mercy at the hands of the Mahdi'. There is no extant evidence to prove the point either way, but Edward Hamilton commented that 'if this be a correct representation of Stewart's views, they do him credit and they bring out in strong relief the sense of a sane man against the heroic foolishness of a scatter-brain'.[110]

One point on which Stewart agreed with Gordon was on the creation of an indigenous power-structure to rival that of the Mahdi. Even taking into account such dignitaries as Sheikh al-Amīn al-Darīr, head of the 'ulamā', the corps of state-sponsored religious and legal scholars, there was no one in Khartoum with the combination of religious credentials, administrative skills, tribal military following or sheer charisma to challenge the uprising. Most of the senior military personnel in the city were either Egyptian or unimpressive soldiers or both; the kind of men who put their name to a desperate appeal to the authorities in Cairo to the effect that 'if the Government persists in its inactivity, and abstain from quickly sending us aid to put down the revolt during the two months of high Nile, the whole Soudan will surely be lost, and the crisis culminate in our ruin!'[111]

Hence Gordon's obsession with al-Zubeir Raḥma. But without him to lead resistance in the short term and then head a new administration, Stewart

concurred that there was 'no means of terminating the state of affairs here . . .
Even if we could sneak away I am convinced Gordon is the last man in the world
who would do so.'[112] Once the cabinet had opted to imprison al-Zubeir for the
duration of the crisis, neither Gordon nor Stewart could decisively identify an
alternative candidate for the leadership.

Three options appear to have been considered. The Governor of Dongola,
Muṣṭafa Yāwar, was proving to be a reliable bulwark against the spread of
Mahdist sympathies in the north. Towards the end of the year, he would provide
invaluable assistance to Wolseley in his advance on Khartoum. But he was a
Circassian, and his appointment would have been little more than another
foreign imposition. The governor's own reasons for declining such an appointment were less to do with his military or administrative reservations than his
spiritual inclinations. In December 1884, the message he conveyed through an
interpreter to the visiting travel agent, John Cook, was simple: "Tell Mr. Cook I
have not lived with a desire to govern anywhere. I have lived with the great
desire of ending my days at Mecca and Medina."[113]

By contrast, his fellow governor in Berber, Ḥussein Khalīfa, was one of the
most senior indigenous Sudanese in the occupation government. He was rated
highly by Sir Samuel Baker, who in January 1884 had ascribed him a central role
in his proposals for the vigorous military suppression of the Mahdī's revolt. In
Baker's plan, Ḥussein Khalīfa would have been charged with transporting troops
across the desert, as well as raising 'those Arab tribes that are faithful to the
Government' and mounting an attack on the Mahdī from the west in collaboration with a simultaneous attack from Sawākīn.[114] Baker's stratagem, of course,
found no favour with the Gladstone government. Instead, with the fall of Berber,
Ḥussein Khalīfa was captured and promptly transferred to face the Mahdī in
person at al-Rahad, the main rebel camp outside al-ʿUbeiḍ.

Gordon's third alternative to replace him was a man closer at hand in
Khartoum. Muḥammad ʿAlī Ḥussein, a highly experienced officer, was one of
Gordon's most trusted colleagues and a perfect candidate. Born just outside
Khartoum, he had served the Egyptian administration since the 1860s.[115] His
primary responsibility during the early part of the siege was to command the
troops guarding the eastern ramparts at Burri Fort and Massallamīa Gate. On 27
July 1884, he achieved the highest military rank, promoted from colonel to liwāʿ,
full general, on the strength of a successful sortie in which four armoured
steamers and a force of around 800 men inflicted heavy casualties on the
followers of Muḥammad ʿUthmān Abū-Qarja.[116]

By 23 August, Gordon was confident enough to state that the general was 'the
only person in the Soudan on whom I can rely and who can replace me'.[117] But
this final option, too, was short-lived. On 5 September, Muḥammad ʿAlī Ḥussein
was killed in a disastrous sortie at al-ʿAilafūn on the Blue Nile, in which several
hundred members of the Khartoum garrison were killed or made prisoner by

fighters under the flag of Sheikh al-ʿUbeiḍ and, to add insult to injury, 75,000 rounds of Remington ammunition were seized.[118] According to one critical report by a Khartoum military officer, 'the troops were not formed in a square but were scattered in the wood and unprepared. The Dervishes jumped up from their ambush and rushed upon them like wolves.'[119]

CHAPTER 6

'A snob and a self-interested man'

I consider that every moment's delay in preparing an expedition diminishes Gordon's chances of escape. I think that the Government will ultimately, but too late, send a relieving force, not because Mr. Gladstone wishes it, but because public indignation will compel him, *nolens volens* [unwillingly or willingly], to do so; and, little as the Prime Minister may value Gordon, the Prime Minister cares a great deal for Mr. Gladstone. . . . The more pressure is brought to bear upon Mr. Gladstone to compel him at once to commence preparations for an expedition, the better chance for Gordon's life. Every day wasted is one more nail in the coffin of himself and [his] garrison.

Col. Frederick Burnaby, 16 May 1884[1]

Public pressure, private initiatives

Baring's prolonged visit to Britain in the late spring of 1884 was a significant factor in exploding the government's comfortable monopoly of information. Hitherto, Granville's selective release of material telegraphed from Cairo had enabled him to control the public debate. But Baring was forthright with all he met during his long stay in Britain, including the Queen herself. Victoria granted Baring an audience on 18 May 1884 and in her journal described him as 'very anxious about the state of affairs, which he considers very serious, and has spoken in strong terms about it to the Government, with, however, little effect. . . . Sir E. Baring has enormous difficulties to contend with, owing to the Government having no decided policy, and changing it continually.'[2]

That was the Queen's interpretation; Baring's own strategic view was less expressly judgemental. With the deployment of al-Zubeir vetoed, 'there were but two alternatives – either to give Gordon up altogether or to send an expedition'.[3] Despite the regrettable necessity of British or Indian troops, he went on, 'having sent Gordon to Khartoum, it appears to me that it is our bounden duty, both as a matter of humanity and policy, not to abandon him'.[4] Having made this strongly moral point, Baring may have been stung by a personal aside in one of Gordon's messages the following month:

> I do not see the fun of being caught here, to walk about the streets as a Dervisch with sandaled feet not that D.V. [*deo volente*, 'God willing'] I will ever be taken alive it would be the Climax of meanness after I had borrowed money from the people here, had called on them to sell their grain at a low price etcetera, to go and abandon them without using every effort to relieve them whether those efforts are diplomatically correct or not and I feel sure whatever you may feel diplomatically I have your support and of every man professing himself a gentleman in private nothing could be more meagre than your telegram.[5]

Gladstone's obstinate refusal to accept the seriousness of Gordon's plight failed to convince the electorate; instead, he came over as self-serving and mealy-mouthed. In a typically legalistic protest in the Commons on 21 April, he insisted that Khartoum was merely 'hemmed in, that is to say, there are bodies of hostile troops in the neighbourhood forming a more or less complete chain around it. I draw a distinction between that and the town being surrounded, which would bear technically a very different meaning.'[6] But by late spring, Gordon was widely accepted to be in dire straits. And when the Mahdī's siege and the severing of the telegraph caused 'a curtain of impenetrable mystery' to close over Khartoum, as Lytton Strachey put it later, 'the growing uneasiness manifested itself in letters to the newspapers, in leading articles, and in a flood of subscriptions towards a relief fund'.[7]

This extraordinary series of interventions and initiatives by private citizens and associations at all levels of society, representing a vague but growing sentiment that Gordon must have been betrayed, reached its climax in May. The first rallying call came from the Primrose League, a Conservative organisation whose motto was *Imperium et Libertas*, Empire and Freedom.[8] Its inaugural banquet in London on 3 May 1884 was addressed with panache by Colonel Frederick Burnaby, a celebrated cavalry officer, adventurer, imperialist and Conservative, then on home leave to recuperate from a wound inflicted at the battle of 'El Teb'.[9] After dinner, the League mandated its members to contribute to a national petition protesting against Gordon's 'abandonment' by the government.[10]

Then, as it had in January, the Patriotic Association came to the fore, organising a protest meeting on 8 May at St. James's Hall, London's premier classical concert venue.[11] Under the presidency of the Earl of Cadogan, a succession of speakers spoke out in support of the resolution 'That this meeting condemns the abandonment of General Gordon by Her Majesty's Government as dishonourable to them, and discreditable to the country'.[12] The Patriotic Association followed this well-attended gathering with a bigger rally in Hyde Park on 17 May.

In addition to the predicament of Gordon, this intensification of Conservative activity had a domestic political spur. The previous month, Socialist activists had convened in Manchester under the banner of the International Arbitration and Peace Association and passed the following resolution:

> That this Committee rejoices to notice the resolute position taken by the Government in refusing to send British troops to be decimated by drought and disease in the deserts in Africa, and trusts that they will continue to withstand the clamorous outcry of those who are ever ready to make pretexts for war.... Gordon went to the Soudan to show how much more might be done by justice and generosity than by bayonets and guns. Gordon is not abandoned, and he has not asked for any armed force to be sent for his rescue. Those who clamour for this to be done have other ends in view.[13]

Inflamed by this argument and by the collision (if not exactly coalition) of interests between Socialists and Liberals, several influential individuals now began to pester newspapers and periodicals with letters agitating for action. In early May, Lord Burdett-Coutts, who had close family ties to the Conservative Party and whose philanthropist wife could have effortlessly financed an entire invasion army from her own pocket, wrote to *The Times* to volunteer his assistance 'in the organising by public subscription of a volunteer movement to attempt the relief of General Gordon':

> A "Gordon Rescue Fund" would have existed ere this, had a rallying point been found upon which the country could have concentrated its efforts. ... We, the people, have never assented to an inscrutable policy of repudiation, and it may be some consolation to have recorded, by these emphatic proofs, the deep and wide-spread sympathy which has so stirred the national spirit.[14]

Even when the idea of a voluntary and amateur relief force was in its earliest stages, contributions appeared from some unlikely sources. One Englishman resident in Lyon wrote to *The Times* to pass on a 20-franc contribution from a French factory labourer, to be added to what he had heard was a 'subscription for the relief of General Gordon'.[15] Some had innovative schemes for the money donated by the public. On 24 April 1884, Hamilton referred to a 'somewhat chimerical idea' from Wilfrid Blunt 'that much might be done towards extricating not only Gordon but also the garrisons by liberal offers of bribery through Arab agents with whom he [Blunt] is acquainted.'[16]

The religious community, too, insisted that it had a part to play. Strachey recorded one intervention from a country vicar: 'Why should not public prayers be offered up for General Gordon in every church in the kingdom? ... "Is not this what the godly man, the true hero, himself would wish to be done?"'[17] When taken up by the Archbishop of Canterbury, however, this proposal was vetoed personally by Gladstone, who insisted that no public prayers had been offered 'for the army of Wolseley [in 1882] or Graham [in the Red Sea Hills], when they were running into considerable danger. But Gordon according to his own (I believe true) account is not (what is called) in danger.'[18]

Still, on 3 May, the editor of *Punch*, London's leading satirical weekly, moved to reply to a growing post-bag, mulled over possible captions for a cartoon depicting Gordon as a doomed gladiator. The source of this theme was probably a telegram from Power in Khartoum, dated 7 April 1884, containing the lament that 'the English Government have turned down their thumbs while General Gordon is struggling here'.[19]

> MR. PUNCH begs to thank numerous Correspondents for the suggestion of *"Pollice Verso"* [Latin: 'thumb turned down'] as a subject for one of his immortal Cartoons, representing GORDON down, the MAHDI about to strike, and only waiting the signal from — but here they almost all shirk the difficulty: the few who do not suggest "the spectators", others BRITANNIA, and some the Ministers, while TIBERIUS is represented by the PREMIER. At the moment (when these suggestions arrived) the MAHDI has *not* got General GORDON down, and we sincerely trust that, as far as he and Khartoum are concerned, that there are sure indications, not of a *pollice verso*, but of a "policy re-verso" in fact an entire change of policy.[20]

Such expressions of public discontent with government inaction were matched by increasingly open discussion of the specific military options for a relief expedition. The private offers of finance, meanwhile, found their counter-part in a range of freelance initiatives. Among the first, briskly shot down by the government, was a tentative reopening of the 'al-Zubeir file'. The retired Controller-General of Egyptian Customs, Baron de Kusel, reported that his friend al-Zubeir had 'volunteered to proceed to the Soudan, and said he would under-take to send Gordon back alive to Cairo [i.e. staying on himself]. . . . Confident that it was perfectly bonâ fide, and that he would, and could, do what he claimed to be able to do, I offered to accompany Zobehr to Khartoum . . . [But] Zobehr's offer was refused, and so was mine.'[21]

The first credible independent plan was proposed by the Conservative MP for Thirsk, Colonel Guy Dawnay, who advocated an advance on Khartoum from the port at Massawa via Kassala. On 28 April 1884, he asked whether, 'in the event of a sufficient sum being raised by public subscription . . . Her Majesty's Government will afford all necessary facilities for the expedition? He would mention that he has already an offer of £1,000 in one sum for the purpose.'[22] The offer was rebuffed by Gladstone in the Commons: 'I must only say to him that, in our opinion, the safety of General Gordon being a matter which would involve us in an obligation to consider the question in a practical view, we do not see how we could devolve that upon any volunteer effort. It appears to me that it is a matter which would devolve upon us.'[23] Dawnay's proposal was discussed in cabinet the same evening and again on 1 May, when the following conclusion was reached: 'Thank but are unwilling that his personal safety should be brought into question'.[24] Displaying scant regard for his personal safety, however, Dawnay left immediately for eastern Sudan, where he put his marksmanship and leadership qualities to good use in the military defence of Sawākīn.[25]

In the absence of any evidence that the matter had 'devolved' in any meaningful way upon the government, another initiative was put forward by James O'Kelly, an Irish nationalist MP who attempted in his capacity as correspondent for the London Daily News to visit the Mahdī himself at al-'Ubeiḍ and lobby in person for Gordon's safe passage. O'Kelly explicitly sympathised with the Mahdī's revolutionary aims, writing of Muḥammad Aḥmad that 'the new champion of Islam might strike hands with the French and German socialists as a man after their own hearts only somewhat more thorough'.[26] Travelling with his brother Aloysius, an artist working for Pictorial World, O'Kelly managed to reach Dongola, where he was brusquely informed by the governor, Muṣṭafa Yāwar, that he could go no further. An amusingly vague explanation for the termination of the mission was given by Fitzmaurice, who told parliament on 1 May that O'Kelly had been 'stopped on grounds of public policy, having reference to the relative positions of the Mahdi, Mr O'Kelly, and the Egyptian Government'.[27]

The majority option: Sawākīn to Berber

The government might be able to abort such missions, but it could not control growing speculation about a relief expedition. As spring passed into summer, two questions arose: over the route to be taken and the size of a possible force. From the beginning, the weight of expert opinion was emphatically behind the 280-mile Sawākīn-Berber route that had been opened by General Graham's victories in the Red Sea Hills and then, as abruptly, closed again by Graham's reluctant return to Cairo. This was almost universally preferred to the far longer Nile voyage to Berber via Assyūt, the Upper Egyptian Railway's southern terminus. There were only two significant advocates of the Nile route: Wolseley, who calculated the entire distance to be 1,728 miles, from 'Cairo to Assiut by rail, thence by River to Khartoum,' – and Sir Samuel Baker.[28] Sir Samuel Baker's plan envisaged a 'flotilla of 30 steamers, 10 steam launches, 4 Thorneycroft boats and 100 first class "kyassas" [twin-masted timber sailing boats] and "diahbeeahs" [similar] + 9,000 men'.[29]

Two further options won still fewer supporters. Sir Henry Gordon back Dawnay's approach from Massawa on the Red Sea, a 'splendid route' through 'a well-watered district'.[30] The desert short-cut from Korosko to Abū-Ḥamad, meanwhile, measuring approximately 230 miles, seems to have been ignored. The sole champion was James Grant, whose adventures with John Hanning Speke on the Upper Nile had made him a mid-Victorian celebrity. Grant capitalised on the contemporary fascination with Sudan by publishing a well-mapped account of his own 1863 desert crossing.[31] Still, as John Bowen wrote in hindsight, 'the desert journey is not altogether pleasant, as the line of skeletons of men and beasts who have perished on the way testifies; but there is a well at the midway station, and a flying column could have carried along enough water with it'.[32]

The most accurate assessment of the Sawākīn-Berber route had been made, ironically, by Gordon himself. An expert draftsman and accomplished engineer as well as tireless traveller, Gordon supplied his superiors throughout his career with precise and carefully annotated charts of his journeys. His 1874 map of the 'road' snaking through the arid hills calculated the route at 288 miles, though later assessments of the distance cut up to 40 miles off Gordon's figure.[33]

In principle, then, were a body of troops to achieve just ten miles a day, the trek could be accomplished within a month. The primary objections, of course, were two-fold: the lack of water and the certainty that 'Uthmān Diqna, even after the stinging defeats inflicted by Graham, would attempt to contest an advance. Military opinion was divided on the water problem. Stephenson in Cairo had reported in December 1883 that 'the wells along the line of route have been destroyed ... and that nothing but a brackish water is left'.[34] Lieutenant-Colonel Andrew Haggard, an officer serving at Sawākīn, thought the argument that water shortages made the route impossible was 'fallacious'.[35]

As opinion began to solidify around the eastern route, figures as diverse as Sir Charles Wilson at the Intelligence Department in Cairo, Lord John Hay, Commander-in-Chief of the Mediterranean Fleet, and Major-General Sir John Adye, Governor of Gibraltar, voiced their endorsement. The last, an old friend of Gordon's, recommended 'an English Regiment & a few guns'.[36] Stephenson completed a report at Hartington's request, echoing the prevailing wisdom that an approach from the Red Sea was 'the best route for an expedition to Khartoum in the event of one being undertaken'.[37] Even Gladstone conceded that 'Suakim & Berber route has utterly beaten Nile route for a larger expedition', although there was the inevitable caveat: 'But the question of a small expedition has hardly yet been touched, while some believe Gordon is or will be free, & there need be no expedition at all.'[38] The Prime Minister was still clinging to a futile hope that his fragmenting policy of non-intervention could be salvaged.

A Sawākīn-Berber railway?

Then an influential voice at the Admiralty proposed a radical adjustment: a railway line running all or part of the way from Sawākīn to Berber. Sir Cooper Key, the First Naval Lord, noted that 'the construction of a railway ... had been considered, and it appeared feasible to complete it by the 1st of November. Then the troops could be assembled at Suakim and proceed rapidly to Berber.'[39] The water problem would be addressed by a system of iron pipes, pumping either well-water or the product of mechanical condensers at Sawākīn through a succession of fortified posts along the railway track. Even if the line were built only as far as the steepest ridge of hills, a distance of just thirty miles but a climb of some 3,000 feet, a fortified bridgehead could be constructed there and used as a base for a camel-mounted advance on Berber.

The plan further envisaged a coordinated attack from the north, catching Berber in a pincer movement. The second strike would be led by Major Horatio Kitchener[40] of the Royal Engineers, currently on secondment to the Intelligence Department in Cairo, where he was described by Baring as 'young, energetic, ardently and exclusively devoted to his profession, and, as the honourable scars on his face testified, experienced in Soudanese warfare'.[41] The assignment, as one biographer has noted, 'put Kitchener into the lead. It made him the eyes and ears of the Sirdar [Wood], and enabled him to act as the herald of any expedition which might be despatched to rescue Gordon or to conquer the Sudan'.[42]

Sir Cooper Key was not the first to propose the construction of a railway line in Sudan. Khedive Ismā'īl had initiated an extension of the Egyptian railway network as far as Khartoum 'to bring the Soudan trade down the Nile through Egypt' but it was abandoned in 1877, shortly before Gordon's first tenure as Governor-General of Sudan, on financial grounds.[43] Gordon's own idea at the time was to lay partial extensions, bridging the impassable Nile cataracts with short stretches of railway, an idea he was still doggedly pursuing in his journal as late as 19 September 1884.[44]

Then, in June 1883, amid a welter of Cairo gossip that a railway would be the best way 'to pacify the lawless tribes, and develop the natural resources of the Soudan', a khedivial commission of inquiry was instructed to investigate the possibilities of a Sudan railway.[45] The commission was composed of seven experienced and well-connected officers and civil engineers, including the Minister of War, 'Umar Luṭfī, the former Governor-General of Sudan, 'Abd-al-Qādir Ḥilmi, and three more veterans of Sudan service: 'Uthmān Rifqi, Alexander Mason and Colonel Charles Watson. Two French engineers based in Egypt, Rousseau and Rigollet, whose presence ensured a diplomatic balance between British and French strategic interests, completed the list of signatories to the commission's report. Rejecting, primarily on grounds of expense, both the original 'north-south' plan to extend the Egyptian line from Assyut and an alternative option of a route from Sawākīn to Khartoum via Kassala and the Blue Nile, the Commission reported on 24 June 1883, firmly endorsing the Sawākīn-Berber plan and insisting that it presented 'no serious engineering difficulties':

> It must be remembered, too, that the saving which would be effected in the transport of troops and military stores would be very considerable. It is probable that if the railway were now in existence the revolt in the Sûdan which now gives so much trouble and causes such vast expense might either not have occurred at all or have been suppressed at an earlier date. The Commission have no hesitation in recommending that . . . the work be commenced as soon as possible . . . [and] desire to record their

opinion that the construction of the railway . . . is essential for the well-being of the Sûdan.[46]

But despite this vigorous expression of approval, no further action was taken. Augustus Wylde thought the route was vetoed in Cairo by 'all who had speculated in land along the line down the Nile Valley, for it would entirely put an end to any future chance of their property becoming valuable'.[47] Another, less cynical, rationale ran along the lines that, as Egypt had no navy, 'the Khedive did not wish to put the key to the Sudan in the hands of the sultan, or of England, or Italy; nor did he wish the commerce of the Sudan to be diverted from the Nile valley'.[48] Indeed, the 'north-south' route was revived soon after. In November 1883, just six months after the Commission had ruled it out as prohibitively expensive, the travel company Thomas Cook & Son advised its branches that the Egyptian Minister of Public Works had 'made a report to the Council of Ministers, in which he recommends the construction of a railway from Wadi-Halfa to Khartoum'.[49]

Advocates of the Sawākīn-Berber line, however, were not defeated. On 23 February 1884, a correspondent identified only as 'X', who appears remarkably well informed on the logistical and military implications of such a construction project, wrote to *The Times* to assert that 'it would not only materially assist General Gordon in his heroic mission, but it would also be a measure which he considered not long since as indispensable for the well-being of the Soudan'.[50] Baker, too, approved. His opinion, argued in consideration of 'a general plan of agricultural development for the Soudan', was that a better terminus would be somewhere between Shendi and Khartoum, i.e. upstream from the last serious cataract at a point 'where the river is navigable throughout the Blue and the White Niles, which would enable the produce of the interior to be transported by vessels from the Equatorial regions without the slightest hindrance'.[51]

But the freshest and most informed advice was provided by Captain Henry Baggallay, who had surveyed the eastern districts of Sudan in the early 1870s while on the staff of the civil engineer John Fowler in Egypt. Baggallay had also acquired valuable experience pushing lines through difficult terrain in the Rockies and the Sierra Nevada mountains in America, as well as in India's Deccan plateau during his years with the Southern Mahratta Railway.[52] On 23 May 1884, Baggallay submitted two detailed memoranda to Northbrook, who cross-referred them with Fowler's maps and promptly shared them with Hartington at the War Office, Childers at the Treasury and, fatally, Wolseley.

In his cover note, Baggallay set out the reasons for his belief that the Sawākīn-Berber route was not just the best chance to rescue Gordon but 'the only practical one' – even if, 'having regard to the climate, the necessity of moving troops with the party and the scarcity of water I do not think more than 5 miles per day could with certainty be accomplished'.[53] His detailed proposal envisaged a thirty-mile section to a 'cool and healthy camp' at the summit of the nearest range. From there, the line would drop gradually to Berber, a distance of 250 miles but with a descent of only 1500 feet.

An essential element of the Baggallay plan was the transport of boats on the line so constructed to Berber. 'During the Indian Famine in 1876,' he noted, 'I moved four large boats a hundred miles in trucks over a rough piece of unfinished railway passing through the dry beds of rivers where there were no bridges and found them all right at the end of the journey.' Troop reinforcements could similarly be brought up by train regardless of season, while the evacuation from Khartoum could resume, 'as the carrying power of the railway will be practically unlimited.'[54]

Baggallay reinforced his case with a second memorandum providing comprehensive technical details. Two hundred men, he calculated, working under seven foremen, would be required to lay the tracks, 'unloading carts & spacing sleepers on line', hammering in the spikes using an iron template 'to secure accurate gauge' and straightening the rails according to a precisely laid out method. Spelling out the ideal traffic flow to maximise efficiency and minimise blockages, he prescribed the locations for double sidings ('one for full wagons and the other for empties'), storage depots and camps: 'The main camp will always be at the station next to the end of the track. . . . It will consist of a number of house cars built in two stories, the men will sleep on the top story and the bottom part will be used for workshops, stores &c. In addition a number of tents will be pitched.'

Another 200 men at least 'under about 6 gangers' would be required to 'clear the line, level any obstacles, cut down bushes, and roughly prepare the surface' in front of the track-layers – as well as tidying up behind them by gravelling the railbed as neatly as possible. And 200 more again would be required at Sawākīn and at the primary 'depot stations' between the Red Sea and Berber. 'The water found on the line,' he predicted accurately, 'will probably be unfit for drinking purposes so water trains will be run. They will fill tanks placed at each depot station and the empty portable tanks at the camp will be exchanged for full ones.' His final summary left nothing to chance, factoring in a total of twenty-four foremen, ninety drivers, firemen and 'rope runners', sixty blacksmiths and carpenters, as well as nine locomotive fitters. It was as precisely worked out a plan as any campaign general could have wished for.[55]

It now seems unimaginable that Baggallay's impressive case can have been rejected, especially if delivery of the project had been entrusted to the Indian authorities. After all, the Raj had engineers, rolling stock and track to spare.[56] Even assuming military encounters with the Mahdī's forces and the hazard of line sabotage, taking Baggallay's pragmatically pessimistic estimate of five miles per day, Berber could be reached within two months. That trumped even the estimate of one subsequent correspondent to the Allahabad *Pioneer* (evidence of how widely the debate over the line spread) that Indian personnel using Indian resources could, once on the ground with equipment, get the job done in three.[57]

Had the plan been implemented within even a month of its conception, Stephenson could have had substantial forces within striking range of Khartoum by August, before Gordon despatched Stewart from the besieged city and began writing his celebrated journal. At first it seemed that even the most reluctant critic had been swayed. Even Gladstone was persuaded, although his fear that the railway might amount to the consolidation of an unwanted occupation was undiminished.

> Clear as is the case for the Railway from Suakim as against a large expedition by the Nile, in every other view it is attended with the most formidable difficulties of a moral & political kind . . . It is I think very doubtful whether, from the practical point of view, the "turning of the first sod" of a Soudan Railway will not be the substitution for an Egyptian domination there of an English domination over the whole or a part, more immaterial, more costly, more destructive, & altogether without foundation in public right.[58]

Money, of course, was a factor. Laying Baggallay's memoranda before the cabinet on 24 May 1884, Hartington spelled out the financial options: laying track over the entire distance from coast to river would take 130 days and cost 1¼ million pounds. A more modest stretch of track, pushing fifty miles into the interior, carried a more appealing price tag: just £310,000. But he warned that the deployment of six or seven thousand soldiers would add another million pounds, without taking Admiralty costs into consideration.[59] Still, the 'short track' option was attractively cheap; indeed, the £300,000 could be set aside from existing budgets discreetly and without the need for a Commons debate, whereas the full Sawākīn-Berber track cost enough to require parliamentary approval.[60]

Further discussion in cabinet on 10 June 1884 included news that Baggallay's design had been endorsed by Clarke, who himself had valuable experience of laying track in the Australian outback, terrain not dissimilar to the Sudanese hinterland. Clarke's cost estimate was £1,250,000, a figure that included 'the erection of defensible stations along the route'.[61] A personal friend of Childers, Clarke was a well-placed lobbyist. Clarke also knew Gladstone well enough to argue the railway's case 'on the supposition that we had no direct but only indirect interests in the Soudan'.[62] Four days later, the cabinet finally gave way and, as Northbrook recalled early the following year, authorisation was given for construction to begin.

> On June 14, I think it was, certain preparations were made for the construction of a railway from Suakin. Engineers were sent there and a certain amount of plant, with the view of being prepared to enter upon the construction of a railroad as soon as the weather would enable troops to be sent to that place. Piers were made so as to facilitate the disembarkation of the materials for the railroad.[63]

This looked like grounds for optimism, but the scheme was never completed. A company of Royal Engineers was despatched to build jetties and clear quayside space for a railhead. Rolling stock and associated hardware was also shipped to Sawākīn, including 'a number of passenger trucks, each to carry twelve soldiers and a brakesman on a platform in rear . . . lightly built, with tilt covers, and open at the sides, but with stout blinds of oiled canvas on rollers, for use if necessary'.[64] Yet even when construction was underway, observers at Sawākīn expressed concern that the sheer volume of material hastily despatched from Britain exceeded the capacity of the port's modest facilities, forcing a cluster of cargo vessels to wait at anchor off the coast.

Augustus Wylde watched with gloom as the rail crews inched out into the scrubland towards the first range of hills. He observed a depressing catalogue of administrative and physical problems: confusion between civilian and military authorities; confusion over the 'perfect babel of languages spoken by the workmen and coolies'; confusion over unloading at the dock, where 'one day it was too much rail and not enough sleeper, and *vice versa*'; and the exhaustion of the 'covering parties of troops' endeavouring to keep cool while watching the rail-gangs at work. Were the accounts ever to be salvaged from bureaucratic obscurity, Wylde concluded, 'it will be found that the twenty miles put down runs as nearly as possible into £50,000 per mile'.[65]

Wolseley and the Nile route

The failure of the railway was, in the short term at least, Wolseley's victory. It was also the product of a busy campaign of subversion. There was some irony in this, as Wolseley himself was not unappreciative of the military advantages created by an efficient railway system and had, eleven years earlier, researched the subject himself in some detail.[66] Still, in the early spring of 1884, he had tenaciously followed up his February memorandum about intervention in eastern Sudan with another plan, this time specifically requested by Hartington at the War Office, still a 'dissentient' figure within government.

This new 'general report' of 8 April, fully six weeks before the Baggallay memoranda, stated that any force must be 'exclusively British', as 'it is very doubtful if even the very best of our Indian regiments would stand the charges of the Arabs, such as those which our troops had recently to encounter near Suakin'.[67] And analysing the routes to Berber, from Massawa, Sawākīn or Wādī-Ḥalfāʾ, Wolseley declared that the third option was the best:

> Remembering the great superiority of river over land transport, the ease with which stores of all sorts are carried in boats, the great distances, comparatively speaking, that can be traversed daily in boats, and the vast saving in expense, I have no hesitation whatever in saying that the river route from Wadi Halfa to Khartoum is infinitely preferable to any other.[68]

Recalling that 8 April memorandum when working on his memoirs, Wolseley filled out the elements he had envisaged as making up the force, including cavalry, camel-mounted infantry, horse-drawn artillery, engineers and ancillary personnel.[69] This substantial expedition would have to be moved from Cairo to Assyūt by rail and then by river to Aswan, Korosko, Wādī-Ḥalfā', Dongola, Kūrti, Abū-Ḥamad, Berber and finally Khartoum. The Nile 'secured a constant supply of good drinking water,' he argued, 'and it reduced the difficulties of transport to a minimum, as each boat would carry an ample supply of food and ammunition for the men in it'.[70] And on the return journey, with much of that food eaten and ammunition expended, the boats 'would have room sufficient . . . for such of the women and children as it might be desirable to bring away with General Gordon. The English Troops, thus employed, should, according to my calculation, be back again on board ship at Alexandria about the 1st March 1885.'[71]

The Wolseley memorandum was received with great enthusiasm by the likes of Hartington and Dilke, who saw themselves as part of a small but morally uncompromised alliance advocating swift action to assist Gordon. Hartington was quick to follow up, referring Gladstone to Wolseley's 'rough sketch of an expedition' and warning him of the strict natural timetable that would dictate any implementation of the Nile route: 'The movement could not take place before the Nile rises in a month or six weeks; but preparations would have to be made almost immediately.'[72]

But with so few well-placed champions, Wolseley's blatant bid for a career-capping triumph struggled for credibility, especially in the face of the Baggallay memoranda that followed so soon after. Adrian Preston has convincingly cast the Wolseley plan as 'repeating on a vastly increased scale his earliest but largely forgotten triumph, the Red River Expedition [in Canada]. Like that earlier bloodless operation, this would be a gigantic ferrying service, a contest against time and nature rather than against men, and therefore a test of Wolseley's logistical skill.'[73] But the Sawākīn-Berber option had to be discredited first.

In Wolseley's version, then, the railway project is labelled variously a 'most costly undertaking', 'preposterous', 'silly', 'wild', 'absurdly ridiculous', 'absolutely senseless' and an 'enormous and useless waste of tax-payers' money'.[74] Using such language at Westminster, Wolseley set about undermining the majority opinion by denigrating its two most visible champions. Sir Andrew Clarke, he wrote in his campaign journal, was a 'goose', 'inexperienced and impracticable'.[75] The Duke of Cambridge is similarly denounced as an armchair general 'who knows nothing of war'. The Nile route was 'too startling, or as some would term it, of too radical a nature for a Prince educated as he had been in orthodox, old-fashioned notions'.[76]

Despite such efforts, Wolseley was nettled to see his own memorandum disregarded while Baggallay's gathered momentum. After two inconclusive cabinet discussions, on 21 and 23 April 1884, he wrote home to his wife to complain that, after being 'sent for in hot haste to go to Downing Street', he was 'tired and very much put out owing to the line about to be taken by the Government on the Soudan question'.[77] Chafing at the government's reluctance to sanction his plan – any plan – he badgered the dissident Hartington with a succession of letters that echoed almost exactly the War Minister's own views.

Remember, we can command many things, but all the gold of England will not affect the rise and fall of the Nile, or the duration of the hot and cold seasons in Egypt. Time is a most important element in the question, and indeed it will be an indelible disgrace if we allow the most generous, patriotic, and gallant of our public servants to die of want or fall into the hands of a cruel enemy because we would not hold out our hands to save him. At any rate I don't want to share the responsibility of leaving Charlie Gordon to his fate, and it is for this reason that I recommend immediate and active preparation for operations that may be forced upon us by and by.[78]

What Wolseley was not told was that tentative, even covert movement was underway in Egypt, despite the absence of a formal 'green light' and presumably at Hartington's unilateral behest. On 10 May 1884, Stephenson wrote, 'the military authorities in Cairo were ordered to purchase camels, and troops were to be held in readiness for a forward march in the autumn'.[79] With an eye to verifying the viability of the Wolseley/Baker route, Captain Tynte Hammill of the Royal Navy was sent at the end of May to survey the cataracts and produce detailed maps.[80] Hammill's report was described by Colonel Butler, the officer charged by Wolseley with building the rowing-boats in which his expeditionary force would be transported, as 'by far the ablest description of the river I had ever seen'.[81]

But the early summer passed and still no order came, for either route. On the Sawākīn-Berber front, Northbrook subsequently explained that the summer climate at Sawākīn posed a threat to the troops even more critical than the despatch of British troops posed a threat to policy. Soldiers were certainly needed, he told parliament, 'to give security for the undertaking [but] . . . during the months of May, June, and July, Suakin is probably the very worst place on the whole of that part of the Red Sea'.[82]

With the railway project floundering and the Nile alternative only tentatively researched, Gladstone was able to focus on domestic priorities. Weeks passed without a mention of Sudan. For all intents and purposes, Gordon had dropped out of view. Wolseley's frustration boiled over during a chance meeting with Lady Salisbury during the summer: when asked 'hopefully about the plans and preparations with which he must be busy', he responded tetchily: 'I have nothing to tell you. There are *no* plans and *no* preparations.'[83]

Two key factors triggered the breakdown of the Prime Minister's resistance. Opposition within the previously torpid cabinet finally became too strong to resist and, as Ronald Robinson has put it, the danger of Gordon's situation became 'obvious enough to be detached from the wider question of Britain's future in Egypt'.[84] Still, as late as 25 July 1884, the full cabinet convened for yet another discussion of the proposed expedition. It had been clear for some time that the cabinet was split into three factions: one that rejected an expedition outright and insisted on the withdrawal of Gordon and Stewart; another that advocated not just a punitive rescue expedition but a consequent period of occu-

pation or even a protectorate; and a third that argued for the minimum expeditionary force necessary to achieve the extraction of Gordon and his garrison
before conducting a dignified withdrawal.

Cabinet divisions on such foreign policy issues were but a part of ongoing
political rivalries, with some ministers nursing ambitions to force Gladstone into
retirement and remove his devoted acolyte, Granville, too. According to one
plan, Hartington would take over at 10 Downing Street, Dilke at the Foreign
Office and Childers move to the War Office. By early 1885, it has been argued,
these ambitions had consolidated into 'an extensive and secret plot among
senior ministers . . . to oust him [Gladstone] and share out his inheritance. There
was also personal harassment of Gladstone as an old, tired, and ill man'.[85]

At this 25 July meeting, there was a considerable majority in favour of at least
a partial advance, but even that majority did not have the clout to force a positive outcome. 'The issue was narrowed down to that of sending some sort of
British force to or towards Dongola,' Dilke reported afterwards; 'and this was
supported by Hartington, the Chancellor, Derby, Northbrook, Spencer,
Carlingford, Dodson, Chamberlain, and me, while on the other side were only Mr.
Gladstone, Harcourt, and Kimberley. Lord Granville said nothing. By the stout-
ness of their resistance the three for the moment prevailed over the nine.'[86] But
the dam was cracking. On 29 July 1884, the Lord Chancellor, Lord Selborne, circulated a long memorandum making precisely the points made by Wolseley,
Baring, Stewart, Burnaby and many others, albeit in appropriately legalistic
terminology. His point was based on the premise that the government acknowledged its responsibility for the safety of its own agent.

> The question remains, whether he has done anything which, fairly and
> reasonably considered, ought to exonerate us from that responsibility?
> For my own part, I see no ground for such an opinion, if anyone entertains
> it. . . . I am as much averse as any man possibly can be to sending out an
> unnecessary and a more or less costly expedition . . . But I am still more
> averse to acting towards a public servant, in whose reputation and safety
> all England . . . is interested . . . as if we had no real sense of the responsi-
> bilities which we have publicly acknowledged.[87]

Selborne was initially rebuffed by Gladstone, who again insisted that, with
some accounts claiming that Gordon was 'master of the situation' in Khartoum,
there was still a need to convert 'speculation into certainty'. Returning to his
theme of an undesirable change in policy, he noted that 'the intervention of a
British force . . . would wholly alter the character of the situation, involving us
as is probable in a religious war, and nearly certain to end in a permanent establishment in, and responsibility for the Soudan'.[88]

Selborne's dry reasoning was soon eclipsed by Hartington's rising anger. A
fortnight earlier, the Secretary for War had formally threatened to resign from
the cabinet. Writing to Granville, who had proven a worthless ally, he lamented

his off-hand treatment by Gladstone: 'At the last cabinet when it was mentioned, summoned, as I hoped, to decide on it, I got five minutes at the fag end, and was as usual put off. Another fortnight has passed, and the end of the session is approaching. I cannot be responsible for the military policy in Egypt under such conditions.'[89]

By this time, the Baggallay railway plan had been gathering dust for two months. The combination of Wolseley's machinations, the projected expense and Gladstone's refusal to endorse any project had given the politicians fatal pause. So in the end, Wolseley achieved his victory over the 'railway lobby' simply by virtue of raising enough doubt in the minds of politicians who were already inclined to prevarication, ultimately rendering the Sawākīn-Berber option impossible to achieve in time.

There still remained obstacles, not least raising funds for the Wolseley plan. The sum of £300,000, barely seed money in the context of an expedition on the scale Wolseley was planning, was secured with just days to go before the summer recess. The Vote of Credit on 5 August 1884 was carried by 174 votes to fourteen and the Nile option had the green light.[90] This sum was quickly consumed. As early as 15 September, Hartington told Dilke that 'he had already spent "£750,000 out of the £300,000" for the Gordon expedition'.[91]

By January 1885, when the annual Army and Navy Estimates came up for approval, Gladstone noted a startling figure for army expenditure: £19,355,000 instead of £15,930,000. While the Sudan expedition cannot be assumed to have accounted for all that £3½ million overspend, Gladstone, in a letter to Childers at the Treasury, expressed the hope that 'a shorter time than 6 months after April 1 may probably suffice to bring the troops home from the Soudan'.[92] And when the naval figures came in, projecting a £1¾ million overspend – of which operations off the Red Sea coast, as well as those in support of Wolseley's Nile expedition, may be assumed to have contributed a considerable amount – the Prime Minister told Childers that the costs were 'somewhat appalling'.[93]

The Gordon Relief Expedition

The universal assumption of the military in Cairo was that General Stephenson would lead the expedition. Indeed, the day after the vote in London, Hartington formally notified Stephenson of the cabinet's decision to send a force at least as far as Dongola and briefed him on Wolseley's idiosyncratic proposal involving small whaling boats. The Duke of Cambridge himself followed up on 14 August 1884, writing to tell Stephenson how glad he was 'to think that the whole conduct of this difficult operation is intended to be carried out under your directions'.[94] Stephenson was pleased to be on the move in support of Gordon but not at all in favour of Wolseley's proposed methods. 'Can move to Wady Halfa,' he retorted, 'four battalions, 2,200 bayonets; two squadrons, 200 sabres; one battery – horse or field artillery; two batteries, mountain; and mounted infantry. Small boats proposed not suitable. Can procure large amount of water transport, locally.'[95]

But Stephenson underestimated Wolseley's influence and was already being outflanked by the wily general. Colonel William Butler, based at Plymouth, had circulated at Wolseley's behest a detailed memorandum, entitled 'Notes on the Advantages of the Use of Small Boats for the Ascent of the Nile'.[96] And even as the transport plan sketched out in the memorandum received cabinet sanction on 12 August, Wolseley was agitating to lead the expedition himself. The appointment was only achieved after the declared opposition of the Queen, largely based on the influence of the Duke of Cambridge, was overcome. But on 26 August 1884, Wolseley finally 'received the intimation that the Queen had given her consent to my having command of the Khartoum Relief Force. The mode of announcing the fact in the following day's newspapers had been settled in the War Office that afternoon.'[97]

Three days later, Hartington notified Stephenson of his usurpation: 'It was unfair on you and on your staff,' he wrote, 'to ask you to take the responsibility of the execution of a plan the details of which had perhaps not been sufficiently explained to you, but in which evidently you felt no confidence'.[98] Stephenson was 'annoyed and distressed . . . that it should be thought possible that he would not carry out any plans finally decided on as faithfully as if they had been his own' and, not surprisingly, considered resigning his Egyptian command.[99] He was prevailed upon to stay by sympathetic colleagues who found his sudden subordination 'very hard lines', the result of dirty work by 'a snob and a self-interested man':

> It requires explanation why Stephenson was refused the 3000 troops he asked for while Wolseley has about 7000 given to him. . . . People say he is trying to bolster up the expedition into a big business so as to reap extra credit himself and get an Earldom, and that his employment of every man in the service almost who has a handle [title] to his name is only part and parcel of the same selfish game and innate snobbishness.[100]

And so Wolseley sailed for Cairo, with his government's full blessing and almost limitless financial resources on demand. His formal instructions would follow later, subject to further fine-tuning by the cabinet.[101] After the months of chafing, rapid action might now have been expected. Instead, the brakes were applied. 'For two months he languished in Cairo,' Preston has remarked, 'building up a force that seemed grossly inconsistent with the specific and non-punitive objectives it was his mission to fulfil.'[102] Another problem was the time taken to construct the heavy timber boats. 'It will be remembered,' noted Colonel Charles Watson, Surveyor-General of the Egyptian Army, 'that it was on the 11th August that General Stephenson said he could send a force at once to Dongola, but it was not until the 1st November that the first of the small boats, having passed the cataract at Wady Halfa, started for Dongola.'[103]

Wolseley's own correspondence reveals the deliberate nature of this tempo. On the second anniversary of his triumph at al-Ṭall al-Kabīr, he wrote to his wife from his luxurious quarters in the Qaṣr al-Nūsa in Cairo, reflecting on the greater fame to come: 'If I am equally blessed, I ought to be shaking hands with Gordon near Khartoum, about the 31st January next. Remember that Khartoum by the Nile is over *1700* miles from Cairo.'[104] That calculation, adrift by just three days, was extraordinarily accurate, especially given the military setbacks that were to impede the advance of his expeditionary force.

In later years, however, Wolseley felt the need to revise his estimate. 'According to my calculation,' he wrote in the notes for his uncompleted memoirs, 'I believed that if the Force of 6,500 men proposed by me for this enterprise, were concentrated at Wady Halfa by the 1st September, we should reach Berber on the 20th October: and, assuming we had a stiff fight between that place and Shendy, we ought to reach Khartoum by the 10th November following.'[105] Yet even this retrospective re-evaluation of likely progress was dishonest. No systematic movement of troops even began until early September.

Even at this late stage, Gladstone did not regard the expedition as a *fait accompli*. 'We have reached a point at which I cannot dispute the propriety of putting Wolseley in a condition to proceed if necessary,' he wrote to Hartington on 13 September, 'and I rely fully on what you lately told me about Wolseley's desire to avoid if it be possible, the advance for which nevertheless he requires to have the means at his command.'[106] It beggars belief that Gladstone could have been so blind to Wolseley's ambition.

As for Gordon, the Prime Minister had lost patience. Faced with a series of smuggled messages of increasingly hysterical and self-contradictory nature, Gladstone wrote to Granville on 19 September to say that the cabinet was 'in danger of becoming simply ridiculous in our communications with him. . . . Our two *main* telegrams of April & May might be referred to as the basis of our policy.[107] . . . He is to conform . . . or else understand that he will cease in any manner to represent the British Government':

> I paraphrase him thus. 'Send troops to Khartoum, that they may hold it while I go all over the Soudan to fetch out (or otherwise) the Egyptian garrisons. That is contrary I know to your policy, but probably you have altered it in deference to me. Let me know whether this is so.'
>
> Ought he not to be informed at the earliest moment that no troops will be sent to Khartoum for any such purpose, and that he is to act upon our policy as committed to him, or not to be any longer officer of ours?[108]

The Wolseley plan was far from comprehensively thought through and improvisation began urgently. According to Sir Cooper Key, Wolseley blithely assigned responsibility for the first stages on the navigable Nile to the Admiralty. Troops, armaments and stores would be transported from Alexandria to Boulāq, Cairo's main river port. After travelling south by rail as far as Assyūt, they would again take to the water via Aswan to Wādī-Ḥalfāʾ, where the Royal Navy's responsibility would end.

Short of sufficient vessels, however, Key turned to an unlikely ally: the British travel agency, Thomas Cook & Son, which had consolidated its business in Egypt to such an extent that it enjoyed a monopoly of the passenger-steamer traffic on the Nile. 'Mr. Cook,' Key recalled in later years, 'would contract to carry 4000 troops from Assiout to Wady Halfa in one trip. There were two stern-wheel steamers building by Messrs. Yarrow that would be available, and might be sent up in sections to any point where it was desired to launch them, with workmen to put them together; this could be done in about three weeks, and they could be worked by native crews.'[109]

Liaising with Lieutenant-Colonel John Ardagh, the 'Commandant of Base' at Cairo, Thomas Cook & Son took on the immense physical challenge of delivering Wolseley's army as far as Wādī-Ḥalfāʾ. The commitment compromised regular tourist business for more than eighteen months and, starting in September 1884, the company was forced to apologise for its inability to 'announce any arrangements for the coming season'.[110] Four months later, Cook's branches were advised that 'the exigencies of the military department require us to hold the whole of the steamers ready for whatever military movements we may still be called upon to carry out' and as late as November 1885, the tourist business was still suffering because the company's Nile steamers required 'considerable overhauling and repairing before we are justified in again using them for the passenger business'.[111]

John Cook, son of the company founder, supervised the military contract in person. His account makes clear the extent to which Wolseley and his acolytes glossed over the challenges of reaching even Egypt's southern frontier, let alone Khartoum. Most accounts by contemporary military commanders were self-serving in the extreme, especially in light of the mission's dismal failure, but Cook laid out with devastating clarity the scale of the operation, the continuing delays and Wolseley's creeping augmentation of his force.

> The instructions we received were to provide for about 6,000 men, with six to eight thousand tons of stores, which we had to convey from Assiout, the termination of the Upper Egyptian Railway, to Wadi Halfa, the foot of the Second Cataract. We were also to convey the 400 special row-boats by railway from Alexandria to Assiout, and thence by steamers to Wadi Halfa. The Admiralty calculated that we should require about 12,000 tons of coal to work that expedition. We received our written orders as late as 2nd September, and we were bold enough to contract that the last of the 400 whaler should be at the terminal point by the first week in November. We had, however, ordered about 20,000 tons of coal to be in readiness.
>
> Instead of the numbers of men mentioned, we have conveyed about 11,000 English and 7,000 Egyptian troops, and nearly 40,000 tons of stores, and have consumed nearly 24,000 tons of coal, and have conveyed a total of about 40,000 tons of coal up the river, so that we still have about 16,000 tons ready for any contingency. . . . We do not know whether anyone can

realise what is meant by carrying out such a work.

At present we have only approximate figures, but we think we may say that, to convey the 40,000 tons of coal we had 28 large steamers between the Tyne and Alexandria; we have had something like 6,000 railway trucks in use between Alexandria and Boulac or Assiout, and for the military stores over 7,000 railway trucks in use. Instead of 400 row-boats we had 800 to convey, and that meant the use of 400 railway trucks of the special dimensions of 34 feet in length. Then for the river work we had 27 steamers employed almost day and night, and no fewer than 650 sailing boats, varying from 70 to 200 tons' capacity. To work these we had a little army of our own of about 5,000 men and boys, consisting of the fellaheen [rural labourers] of Lower Egypt.

It will thus be seen that our work in connection with the Expedition has been in some respects unique . . . and it is satisfactory to note that we completed the transport to the Second Cataract almost to the hour we undertook to do it, notwithstanding all the difficulties we had to contend against.[112]

This massive operation dwarfed the modest railway undertaking outlined by Baggallay. In the time that Thomas Cook & Son achieved their marathon transportation to Wādī-Ḥalfā', the railway line from Sawākīn could have been finished and Berber besieged. While the Nile route was clearly a serious misjudgement, worse was to come. The infrastructure put in place to reach Wādī-Ḥalfā' was no use beyond that point and the exhausted soldiers were forced to take to Wolseley's cherished whalers. Military personnel in Cairo were dismayed by Wolseley's insistence on these Canadian-style rowing-boats over local sailing vessels. 'It might be mentioned,' noted Watson, 'that half of the Royal Sussex Regiment, which was sent up to Dongola in September in native boats, took *thirteen days* to travel from Sarras to Dongola, a distance of 210 miles, whereas two months later on the troops in the small boats took about *five weeks* to cover the same distance.'[113]

Again, it is the account of John Cook that cuts closest to the quick, transcending the self-aggrandising histrionics of the military. Addressing the Royal Geographical Society on 5 January 1885, when the expedition was fully four months old but yet Wolseley's forward units were still hundreds of miles from Khartoum, Cook gave his audience a vivid description of the hardships endured in crossing the Nile cataracts. In terms of intelligence-gathering, Captain Hammill's reconnoitering of the route the previous May turned out to be worthless because the water had dropped so significantly. As a result, four or five additional stretches of dense rocky cataract had emerged between what the maps showed as the Second and Third Cataracts. On five separate occasions, Cook's own twenty-four-foot boat took 170 additional troops to manhandle through the obstacles. The vessels constantly had their timber hulls smashed on the black rocks. But Cook did not forget the sturdy courage of the rank-and-file.

The soldiers had had no previous experience whatever in river work. But they worked most freely and willingly under trying circumstances, and pushed along whistling and singing to keep their spirits up . . . Of course they suffered the first few days, especially from blisters, having to walk on parched granite rocks tugging at their boats, which were moved along some days only one or two miles, while for five consecutive days his glass registered 90° in the shade, and was scarcely below 80° at night.[114]

One final point is worth making about the Relief Expedition, clarifying its commander's authority relative to Gordon. Given the confusion over Gordon's conflicting roles and rapid accretion of executive authority during his Cairo stop-over of January 1884, it was only pragmatic of Wolseley to ensure that his own authority exceeded that of the Governor-General in Khartoum, irrespective of the uniform he wore on a given day. This was a wise precaution, as Gordon was certainly planning to use his khedivial rank to assert his independence of the expedition's commanding officer.

On 29 November 1884, for example, Gordon wrote in his journal: 'I have a strong conviction, that neither Baring or Lord W. have taken the precaution of bringing a Firman from Towfik Pacha, giving them a legal status superior to mine in the Soudan, if this conviction is the case (and the fiction of Towfik being Supreme Ruler is kept up), then it is, for me, to name the Govr-Genl . . . I have a perfect right to vacate the Gov^t & to appoint whomsoever I like, subject to the ultimate approval of Towfik Pacha. . . . The great question [is] "Is *any officer Civil or Military of Expedition possessed of a Firman of Towfik?*"'[115]

Wolseley therefore ensured that his formal instructions from the British government, dated 21 September 1884, specifically stated: 'Supreme political and civilian power will be conferred upon you in respect of the affairs of the Nile valley south of Aswan. General Gordon and Colonel Stewart are placed under your orders.'[116] He then buttressed this with a proclamation from Khedive Ṭawfīq, in which the Egyptian proxy government matched their British masters in placing Gordon under Wolseley's authority:

Lord Wolseley has been appointed by H.M. Government to command the British expedition to the Sudan, and full powers and necessary instructions have been given to him by H.M. Government. On the arrival of H.L. [His Lordship] in the Soudan it is necessary that you should obey his orders in order that he may accomplish his mission with success, which is our desire.[117]

CHAPTER 7

Gladstone's policy 'victory'

How many times have we written asking for reinforcements, calling your serious attention to the Soudan? No answer at all has come to us as to what has been decided in the matter, and the hearts of men have become weary of this delay. While you are eating, drinking, and resting on good beds, we and those with us, both soldiers and servants, are watching by night and day, endeavouring to quell the movements of this false Mahdi.... The reason why I have now sent Colonel Stewart is because you have been silent all this while and have neglected us, and lost time without doing any good.

Decoded letter from Gordon, 18 September 1884[1]

The death in action of General Muḥammad ʿAlī Ḥussein during the sortie of 5 September 1884 confirmed Gordon's inability to conduct more than a passive defence of the city's rudimentary ramparts. It was also one of the key factors motivating his decision to send Lieutenant-Colonel Hamill-Stewart downriver. It is not clear whether Gordon directly ordered Stewart to go on this risky and ultimately fatal mission; certainly his own self-exculpatory journal entries on the subject insist that he refused to issue such a command.[2] But as Gerald Graham later put it, the decision was 'too much like that of a captain of a sinking ship to be reassuring'.[3]

Late on 9 September, under cover of darkness, Gordon took his greatest gamble and despatched his ADC north in a last-ditch attempt to shame the cabinet in London into action. The last word from Stewart was a letter sent to Gordon on 14 September from a small island four miles south of Berber. As well as providing an exciting description of the journey so far, during which the steamers had been fired upon from Shendi and other towns held by the Mahdī, the letter makes it clear that Stewart bears no grudge against Gordon: 'You may depend upon it that I shall do everything in my power to assist you. Thanking you for the very great kindness with which you have over-looked my short-comings, and praying that the blessing of the Almighty may abide with you'.[4]

The Stewart mission was a desperate measure at a desperate time. Further compounding his gamble, Gordon sent the entire written record of the siege, an incontrovertible argument for the immediate rescue of a city under extreme duress. The mission has also been retrospectively justified in terms of short-term military advantage. 'Speculation is idle,' wrote Sir Charles Wilson the following year, 'but it should not be forgotten that if Stewart had passed the [4th, 5th and 6th] cataracts he would have met Kitchener at Debbeh on the 19th September, that the Sussex Regiment reached Dongola on the 20th, and that there was then no force north of Khartúm that could have opposed the march of 500 British troops.'[5]

The venture was certainly one that Gordon had been considering for months. As early as June, a telegram to Egerton reporting rumours of an advance by Mahdist forces under Muḥammad 'Uthmān al-Mīrghanī from Kassala clearly implies that Stewart would soon be in Cairo to 'tell you all details'.[6] More recently, the mission had been reinvented as one in which Stewart would retake Berber by force before pushing on for Dongola and eventually Cairo. On 23 August 1884, with misplaced optimism, Gordon wrote to Cairo to state: 'I hope shortly to take Berber. I have already sent Stewart Pasha, the English Consul, and the French Consul, with regular troops and Bashi-Bazouks, for that purpose.'[7] While Baring attempted to channel an urgent veto via Kitchener, Gladstone pondered Gordon's 'wild telegram' before commenting to Granville on 19 September that it 'beats every thing I have ever seen. I called him at the outset inspired and mad, but the madness is now uppermost.'[8]

The declaration about the seizure of Berber may have been pure fantasy, but it reveals at least that the passenger manifest was considered some time before Stewart's eventual departure. So, on 9 September, the European contingent, amplified by the addition of 19 Greek nationals, boarded the 'Abbās, a small steamer whose shallow draught maximised the prospects of traversing the cataracts. To help force a passage through the Mahdī's blockade, Maḥmūd Tal'āt was ordered to captain the Safīa and 'Alī Reza the Manṣūra as escorts at least as far as Berber. Muḥammad Nusshi, another senior officer of Gordon's Nile fleet, later recalled that, as this was expected to be the last chance to establish contact with Egypt before the arrival of any relief expedition, 'a circular note was spread through the town, telling whoever wanted to send letters to Cairo or Dongola to bring them to the Post Office'.[9]

Whatever the merits of the assignment, the journey was to be the death of Stewart and his fellow passengers. The escorts turned back to Khartoum at Berber, leaving the 'Abbās to continue alone. On 17 September 1884, perhaps just forty-eight hours from a successful rendezvous with Kitchener, the 'Abbās grounded. Lured by Suleiman wad Gamr, clan leader of the Manāṣīr, into what appeared to be a safe refuge outside the known range of Berber-based patrols, Stewart's party was set upon and slaughtered to a man.[10] The scale of Gordon's error in sending Khartoum's written record was also made terribly clear when the Mahdī himself sent a long letter on 22 October, detailing the haul that had fallen into his hands.[11]

Stewart's death deprived the British Army of one of its finest intelligence officers. Gordon himself was unaware even that Stewart's vessel had fallen into enemy hands until 14 October, when Aḥmad Muṣṭafa al-Amīn, commander of the Mahdī's troops on the west bank of the White Nile, notified him by letter. And as for Stewart's death, confirmation did not come until 3 November, when Gordon received a note from Kitchener at al-Dabba.[12] 'I cannot understand it,' he wrote to his sister Augusta; 'Very grieved for the relations of Stewart & Power & Herbin.'[13]

Gordon's Khartoum journals: style and substance

Stewart's departure left Gordon with the additional duty of continuing the official campaign journal. It is clear from the first entry that the chore became therapy, as night after night the isolated general poured out his thoughts in an incontinent and sometimes malevolent torrent. When he first picked up his pen on 10 September 1884, it was 236 days since he and Stewart had left London. Reading the journals with close attention, one is faced with striking evidence of Gordon's troubled personality. Indeed, in the six volumes that were transmitted to al-Metamma can be discerned in sharp close-up the manic/depressive cycle that had brought such turbulence to his previous life and informed the episodic nature of his military career. Still, the detail of deployment and counter-deployment, in words and maps, the minute-by-minute accounts of skirmishing steamers and incoming artillery rounds all presented a true and exciting picture of combat in the raw. A typical sample may be found in his hastily scribbled and frequently updated entry for 12 November 1884:

> 10.30 AM, for half an hour, firing lulled, but then recommenced, and is still going on. The Ismailia was struck with a shell, but I hear, is not seriously damaged. The "Husseinyeh" is aground. (I feel much the want of my other steamers, at Metemma [the vessels that carried prior volumes of the journals from Khartoum]).
>
> 11.15 AM Firing has lulled, it was very heavy for the last ¾ hrs, from "Ismailia" & Arabs, it is now desultory, and is dying away. "Husseinyeh" still aground. Ismailia at anchor. What a six hours of anxiety for me, when I saw the shells strike the water near the steamers from Arabs, imagine my feelings!
>
> We have 831 £ in specie [Latin, 'in its actual form'; i.e. coins] & 42800 £ in paper! [i.e. Gordon's siege banknotes] and there is 14600 £ *in paper* out in town! I call this state of Finance not bad after more than 8 months blockade, the troops are owed ½ month's pay, & even that can be scarcely called owed them, for I have given them stores & beyond the regulations, [several words deleted and illegible]. Noon Firing ceased, I am glad to say, I have lived *years* in these last *hours*! Had I lost the "Ismailia", I should have

lost the Husseinyeh! (aground) & then Omdaraman [Omdurman]! & the North Fort! & then the town! 1 P.M. Arabs firing on the steamers with their two guns, Husseinyeh *still aground*, that is the reason of it. Firing 1.30 P.M. now has ceased. "Ismailia" struck by 3 shell, had 1 man killed, 15 wounded on board of her, she did really very well.[14]

A military log, of course, was never intended as literature and when it comes to Gordon's prose style there is little to excite. By far the most plentiful quotations and allusions, unsurprisingly given the general's record for piety and his recent year-long sojourn in the Holy Land, come from the Bible. In the first volume especially, covering 10 to 23 September, Gordon indulges in lengthy philosophical and spiritual examination, scrutinising selected verses from the Bible and occasionally the Qur'ān, musing aloud on matters which have nothing to do with the function of the campaign journal.[15] Such passages, however, diminish rapidly and almost completely in succeeding volumes as the siege progresses and Gordon's focus is divided between immediate military matters on the one hand and paranoid imaginings on the other.[16]

Despite his years of Sudan service, however, Gordon was surprisingly incompetent at recording Arabic names correctly. Thus, for example, the Mahdī's great commander ʿAbd-al-Rahman wad al-Nujūmi is named 'Walad-a-Goun', while Muḥammad ʿUthmān Abū-Qarja becomes 'Abou Gugkiz' and al-Nūr Muḥammad ʿAnqara is rendered as 'Nuchranza'.[17]

More significant for Gordon's future readers, be they politicians or the wider public, were his biting caricatures of England's aristocratic elite. What truly astonished contemporary readers was that a serving officer of the Queen could subject Her Majesty's ministers to such a sustained tirade of abuse. Most of Gordon's more protracted lampoons were wholly unfair and, in libelling the men characterised as determined to see his mission fail, probably actionable. One amusing imagined exchange pitted Granville against Salisbury, with Gordon only thinly obscuring the protagonists' identities.[18]

> L . . . d G . . . e, in answer to questions put by M . . . s of S . . . . . y replied that the noble M . . . . s seemed to take a special delight in asking questions, which he knew, he, (L . . . d G . . . . e) could not answer. He could say he had given a deal of time & attention to the affairs of the Soudan, but he frankly acknowledged that the names of places & people were so mixed up, that it was impossible to get a true view of the case (a laugh). The noble M . . . s asked what the policy of HMG was, it was as if he asked the policy of a log floating down stream, it was going to the sea, as every one who had an ounce of brains, could see, well! that was the policy of HMG, it was a decided policy & a straight forward one, to drift along, & take advantage of every circumstance. His L . . . p concluded in deprecating the frequent questioning, on subjects, which, as His L . . . p had said, he knew nothing about, and further did not care to know anything about.[19]

As Gordon's friend and army colleague, Colonel Butler, correctly observed, 'the Journal is a complete laying bare of the man's mind'.[20] But the mind thus laid bare, in increasingly powerful, if poignant, terms, is a mind unravelling. Gordon's imaginary exchanges go well beyond satire into the realms of paranoia and delusion. In the untidy pages of the original manuscript, written, in the terminal stages of the siege, on the backs of Egyptian Telegraph Service forms and bound in improvised cardboard covers, we find a man endlessly rehearsing arguments for and against retreat, surrender, a British rescue mission, resignation of his commission, an Ottoman mercenary expedition paid for by American millionaires, even suicide.

Following the departure of Stewart and Power, Gordon was a man profoundly alone. None of his subordinates spoke English and he spoke little beyond basic Arabic. Any contact with his Europhile Cairene officers was in French. And once the telegraph lines into Khartoum from north and east were cut, the only contact with Cairo and London was by smuggled message. Months went by without any substantial information from outside and the dilatory pace at which the Relief Expedition was first debated and then mounted meant that the blizzard of proposals and counter-proposals in the journal volumes accumulating at Metemma went unseen by Wolseley until too late. Gordon, meanwhile, succumbing to growing paranoia, expanded wildly on his theme that Granville, of all people, had staked everything on an early victory by the Mahdī. This vignette, expunged from the published edition, finds Granville perusing the papers at home.

"Well! It is better here, than in that stifling London, with those inquisitive fellows pestering one's life out day after day." (Takes up Times) "Wha-a-at!" (reads) "Positive information from Dongola, Kartoum holds out! Leader on situation calling on Govt. to take steps." (yells for) "Sanderson! [Granville's private secretary] Sanderson!" (who enters) "What is this I see in Times." "What do you say, all the papers full of it, strong article in "Standard" reflecting on Govt." "Why, he said distinctly, he could only hold out six months, and that was in March." (counts the months) "August" why he ought to have given in! What is to be done! They will be howling for an expedition. What did we tell him in June? Oh yes; to make contacts with Arab tribes, and we would pay all expenses." (Sanderson smiles) "You need not laugh, it is no laughing matter; that abominable Mahdi! Why on earth does he not guard his roads better. What is to be done?" "Ask him more questions! eh! and trust to time." "Well, not bad idea. Telegraph out and say, "Govt cannot act till they know exact state of affairs, as to garrisons &c. Telegraph Gl......e [Gladstone], if he is cutting down trees, he will act with greater vigour: oh yes! certainly, send for Wolseley at once, say Soudan spectre has reappeared."[21]

Enduring personal obsessions

Gordon did not imagine that such extraordinary digressions from the military essentials of a campaign journal would ever be published. Indeed, each of his original volumes contains many sections, some as long as eleven pages of manuscript, struck through in pen or pencil as an indication that they were to be 'pruned out'. But he did expect at least parts of the journal to be made public as some form of official document.

Indeed, it was with an eye to the eventual inclusion of his journal's salient parts in a government dossier that he included a specific advisory note to Wolseley about the different treatment of public and private material when he despatched Volume 6 by steamer to Metemma. 'Since departure 10 Sept of Lt. Col. Stewart CMG,' he wrote, 'I have kept a daily journal of all events at Kartoum, which contains also my private opinions on certain facts, which perhaps it is just as well you should know confidentially. You can, of course, make extracts of all official matter, and will naturally leave my private opinions out in the case of publication.'[22]

This assumption that the diary's most controversial elements would be deemed of value by senior officers and, possibly, a wider readership, demonstrated considerable vanity on the part of a man who professed to have little interest in material reward or celebrity. Yet the journals represented Gordon's best chance to win vindication for his own philosophical and military arguments. On a personal basis, those arguments centred on a moral opposition to Gladstone's own unshakeable determination on foreign non-interference. It was Gordon's position that personal morality and national honour should preclude the possibility of abandoning allies, let alone subordinates, in the face of enemy attack.

More practically relevant in the imperial context, Gordon also argued that the withdrawal policy would not only drive all Sudanese into the arms of the Mahdī, but also embolden like-minded Muslims to mount similar uprisings in Egypt, the Ottoman possessions and even in British India. 'It cannot be too strongly impressed on the public,' he argued on 17 September, 'that it is not the Mahdi's forces which are to be feared, but the rising of the populations by his emissaries.'[23] Few overtly contradicted this argument, although Sir Alfred Lyall, then Chief Commissioner of Oudh in British India, had earlier written: 'The Mahdi's fortunes do not interest India. The talk in some of the papers about the necessity of smashing him, in order to avert the risk of some general Mahomedan uprising, is futile and imaginative.'[24]

This, therefore, obligated a middle path between Gladstone's stubborn policy of 'minimum engagement, zero responsibility' on the one hand and aggressive, Conservative-style imperial expansion on the other. Gordon's solution was that the least interventionist solution was to use Turkey as a counter to the Mahdī. On this point, Gordon revealed a profound lack of empathy with the Sudanese and a continuing failure to comprehend the nature of either the Mahdī or the uprising he led, just as he had in his pre-mission analysis of the situation in Sudan and in his absurd proposal to buy off the Mahdī with the offer of the Sultanate of Kordofan.

The widespread cross-community support for the Mahdī's rebellion had its roots in decades of hatred for the Ottoman/Egyptian occupation, derided collectively by Sudanese as *al-Turkīa*, the 'Era of the Turks'. Gordon failed to see any irony in proposing to combat a rebellion against those 'Turks' by sending in . . . the Turks! But the opportunity to address military and civilian supporters through the journals prompted endlessly reworked justifications for Gordon's proposal of an indigenous administration under al-Zubeir Raḥma Manṣūr. Subsidising al-Zubeir with Turkish military backing, he argued, would be far cheaper than a full-scale British military mission.[25] In fact, Gordon had written to Sultan Abdülhamit II in April, asking for 3,000 Turkish troops to head off the spreading menace posed by the Mahdī:

> Your Majesty as head of the Mussulmin [sic] Faith must know far better than I do, that the False Prophet threatens Your Majesty's spiritual authority, and that if he is allowed to capture Kartoum and the other towns which now hold out, he will by his emissaries, raise the Hedjaz, Syria, Palestine and Damascus. . . . If the beleaguered towns [in Sudan] fall, Your Majesty may be sure that all the Hedjaz will rise, for the False Prophet's prestige will be then immense. We can hold out for five months, and I believe if Your Majesty sends these men these men will not have to fire a shot, the rebels will dissolve as ice before fire.[26]

Similar letters were dashed off to the Emperors of Austria-Hungary, Germany and Russia, the King of Italy and to Pope Leo XIII. To these dignitaries, Gordon presented a variation on his fund-raising scheme: 'Is it possible for Your Majesties to relax your laws,' he wrote, 'and let your subjects volunteer to come to our succour, and could not Your Majesties allow volunteer subscription to cover the expenses. The questions is one of civilization agst the worse form of ascetic fanaticism, headed by an impious adventurer, who is condemned by the very religion, he claims to belong to.'[27]

As for Wolseley's relief force, Gordon's running commentary on its function serves not least to draw attention to its dismally slow progress. Confirmation that such an expedition was at least underway came to Khartoum only on 18 September 1884, when spies from Shendi reported 'the arrival of troops at Dongola, and their advance towards Berber'.[28] Gordon was categorical in refusing to accept that its primary function was to rescue him.

> I altogether *decline* the imputation that the projected expedition has come to *relieve me*. It has come to SAVE OUR NATIONAL HONOUR, *in extricating the garrisons, &c., from a position our action in Egypt has placed these garrisons: I was a relief expedition No 1, they are relief expedition* NO. 2. As for myself, I

could make good my retreat at any moment if I wished. Now realise, what would happen, if the 1st *Relief expedition* was to bolt, & the steamers fell into hands of the Mahdi, the 2nd *Relief Expedition* (for the honour of England, engaged in extricating garrisons) would be somewhat hampered. We the 1st and 2nd Expeditions are equally engaged for honour of England. This is fair logic. *I came up to extricate garrisons, and failed.* [Wolseley] *comes up to extricate garrisons* & (I hope) *succeeds.* [Wolseley] *does not come up to extricate me.* The extrication of the garrisons was supposed to affect our national honour. . . . I am not the "*rescued lamb*", and I will not be.[29]

Cross-referring Gordon's journal entries, each written in an increasingly fraught atmosphere of isolation, deprivation and violence, with those in Wolseley's own campaign diary makes for a riveting juxtaposition of desperation and complacency. The day Gordon assumed responsibility for the Khartoum log, the first batch of special boats for Wolseley's relief expedition had left Britain. Wolseley himself had only arrived in Cairo the previous day.[30] By 18 September, when Gordon first heard about the Relief Expedition, its commander was still in Cairo, enjoying dinner with the Khedive and a firework show afterwards.[31] Wolseley did not head south until the evening of 27 September, travelling by rail to Assyūt.[32]

On 4 October, Gordon notched up another day of siege in his journal: 'Today is the 206th day, we have been more or less shut up. Delightful life!'[33] Wolseley, meanwhile, had made it only as far as Korosko, a point from which a desert crossing direct to Abū-Ḥamad and thence to Berber was still an option and where he found Kitchener's small detachment of roving scouts.[34] Seventeen days later Gordon embarked on the fifth volume of his journal, scribbling grimly on the flimsy unlined paper that the Mahdī had at last reached Omdurman.[35] The British expeditionary force, meanwhile, was stuck at Wādī-Ḥalfāʾ, 'struggling with difficulties of transport, lack of coal, and administrative hitches'.[36] Despite his refusal to be 'the rescued lamb', Gordon's journal is peppered with obsessive calculations as to the likely arrival date of the rescue force:

> I calculate that the advance force of troops arrived at Wadi Halfa on 22 Sept, that they took 20 days from there to Debba, so that on 12 Oct, they were at Debba (Stewart (D.V.) arrived Debba on the 28th Sept.) and I calculate they could not be at Metemma – Shendy, before 10 Nov[r] which will give them 29 days for 150 Miles, thence it is 5 days here for a steamer so that 15 Nov[r] ought to see them, or their advance guard.[37]

These estimates, possibly based on Gordon's own hectic pace of travel through inhospitable terrain, were far too optimistic. That very day, Wolseley was still at the 2nd Cataract, known locally as the *Bāb al-Kabīr* or 'great gate', arguing with the Royal Navy over its 'management of our boats' and with Thomas Cook & Son over coal supplies, while Butler struggled to manhandle the whalers over the immense black boulders of the rapids.[38] Wolseley would not reach Dongola until 3 November, Ambukol on 12 December, al-Dabba on 15 December and Kūrti – still 285 miles from Khartoum by the Nile route – 'in the evening of the 16th December 1884', two days after Gordon's final surviving diary entry.[39]

> Dec[r] 14. Arabs fired 2 shells at Palace this morning. 546 ardebs [2736 bushels] Dhoora! in store, also 83525 okes [233,670 lb.] of Biscuit! 10.30 A.M. The steamers are down at Omdaraman, engaging the Arabs, consequently I am on *tenter hooks*! 11.20 A.M. Steamers returned, the "Bordeen" was struck by a shell, in her battery, we had only one man wounded. [Remainder of line deleted]
>
>   We are going to send down "Bordeen" tomorrow, with this journal. If I was in command of the 200 men of Expeditionary Force, which are all that are necessary for movement, I should stop just below Halfyeh & attack Arabs at that place before I came on here to Kartoum. I should then communicate with North Fort, and act according to circumstances. NOW MARK THIS, if Expeditionary Force, and I ask for no more than 200 men does not come in 10 days, *the town may fall*, and I have done my best for the honour of our country. Good bye. C. G. Gordon.[40]

Could Khartoum could have been relieved had Wolseley been removed from command and a more direct route taken? On 3 October 1884, *The Times* reported in an editorial 'a statement so startling that, notwithstanding the unimpeachable source from which it proceeds, we give it with considerable reserve. The statement of our Correspondent is that LORD WOLSELEY has been summoned to return to London before the end of the present month, and that the command of the Nile expedition will be assumed, on LORD WOLSELEY's departure, by GENERAL STEPHENSON. . . . But the recall of LORD WOLSELEY would clearly mean a material change of policy, and the step, however it may be explained, would therefore be regarded by the country with very grave anxiety.'[41]

The report was picked up in later editions the same day by almost every newspaper in Britain and Ireland. Word travelled fast and on 4 October, Wolseley, by now at Korosko, wrote to his wife to describe how he had received 'a telegram from the *Central News* saying the *Times* states I have been recalled, and asking if it be true. What a curious rumour!'[42] That same day, an official denial was issued by the military command in Cairo.[43] Parliament was not in session at the time but by 30 October, a week after the House of Commons resumed business, Gladstone was able to express his government's 'perfect confidence in his [Wolseley's] ability and skill'.[44]

Still, even if the politicians had not wavered, the Queen was deeply dissatisfied with the general's progress and did not hesitate to tell him so. Wolseley's subsequent letter to his wife Louise reveals not just his anger at the monarch's intervention, but his still complacent attitude to the mission in hand.

I am brimfull [sic] of wrath at a letter from the Q which I enclose. She could scarcely have written a General in the field a nastier letter: so ungracious, so ungenerous. . . . As she is the Queen, I cannot argue with her, so I mean to stop writing to her. She owes me a great deal, I owe her nothing. Every reward I have received has been drawn from Her at the point of the bayonet. I expect Sir C. Wilson with two steamers & about 100 soldiers & 50 of the Rl. Navy to reach Khartoum next Tuesday the 20th instant, and that Wilson will get back to Matammeh or *before* on evening of 27th or morning of 28th. On the news he brings will depend all my future movements.[45]

Wolseley's survival may have prompted Gladstone's opponents to look for a more radical policy reversal in the shape of a reassertion of British military strength in eastern Sudan. The rationale here was twofold: a flanking manoeuvre to draw away the Mahdī's forces, who might otherwise be massed to resist Wolseley's advance; and the provision of a shorter exit route to Sawākīn. As always, *The Times* was swift to comment scathingly on the Gladstonian record in foreign affairs. On 5 January 1885, with Wolseley still labouring upriver, an editorial called on Gladstone to resign, as 'our interests, not in Egypt alone, but throughout the whole of the Imperial system, are suffering from a dangerous paralysis of will. If MR. GLADSTONE and LORD GRANVILLE . . . are fatally crippled, for decision and action, by personal engagements, at a crisis so vital, they must be prepared – hard though the saying may be – to make way for others who are not similarly incapacitated.'[46]

Hamilton, who knew the way things worked, noted the unfairness of Granville being made the scapegoat: 'The policy is Mr. G.'s; and he would be the last to palm off the responsibility for it on a colleague. The prevalent idea is that Mr. G. won't trouble himself about foreign matters like Egypt; whereas it is Egypt, and nothing but Egypt, which occupies his thoughts.'[47] But Gladstone was frequently absent and when the cabinet met on 7 January 1885 to debate intensifying British military involvement through a new push from Sawākīn, 'it was,' as Kimberley noted, 'left to Hartington to exercise his discretion after consulting Wolseley'.[48]

Gladstone, at home at Hawarden Hall, was horrified. 'We have already performed once, of course with loss, & with frightful slaughter of most gallant Arabs in two bloody battles, this operation of 'pacifying' the Eastern Soudan, & I am very loath to have another such pacification, & quite unable to see how it is to be better or more effective. . . . what I think we ought to know is *whether Wolseley upon his own responsibility deems a new expedition through Suakim against Osman Digna requisite for the efficiency & success of his own expedition against Khartoum.*'[49] On the specific point of retaining possession of Sawākīn itself indefinitely, Gladstone categorically restated standing policy: any British deployment 'will be sent as in no way to fetter the Cabinet with reference to ulterior occupation'.[50] It was another brief policy wobble, but Gladstone had reasserted control and with his explicit disapproval the initiative died on the vine.

It was Augustus Wylde, writing in Sawākīn in 1887, who observed that 'no pen
or brush will ever be able to relate or depict the last horrors at Khartoum'.[51]
Without Gordon's final volume of journal, describing forty-two miserable days
between 15 December 1884 and 25 January 1885, Wylde's is an accurate summary
of the information gap in English. Arabic sources, however, are available.
Bordeini Bey, a grain merchant in Khartoum, produced a vivid account, in which
he described the surrender on 5 January 1885 of the small garrison under
Farajallah Rāghib at Fort Omdurman, the desperate scouring of Khartoum's
warehouses for any remaining grain, the collection of all available ammunition
and powder in the stone-built Catholic church near the Governor-General's
mansion and Gordon's preparation of a small steamer, the *Muḥammad ʿAlī*, as an
escape vessel for the city's leading officials (though not for himself).[52]

Bordeini's account culminated in the 'heavy despair' of what was to be for
many residents their last day alive: 'It was a gloomy day, that last day in
Khartoum; hundreds lay dead and dying in the streets from starvation, and there
were none to bury them'.[53] Kitchener, too, was privy to intelligence from Arabic-
speaking sources who revealed that famine in the city had prompted Gordon to
send more than half the civilian population out of Khartoum during the first
week of January 1885, there to await the Mahdī's mercy:

> The state of the garrison was then desperate from want of food; all the
> donkeys, dogs, cats, rats, &c., had been eaten; a small ration of grain was
> issued daily to the troops, and a sort of bread was made from pounded
> palm tree fibres. . . . Gordon continually visited the posts, and personally
> encouraged the soldiers to stand firm; it was said during this period that
> he never slept.[54]

After so many months of determined resistance, Gordon launched his last
desperate military sortie on 18 January 1884. With his troops hugely outnum-
bered, short of ammunition and incapacitated by hunger, failure was inevitable
and triggered a bitter row five days later between Gordon and his senior
Egyptian staff officers, General Faraj al-Zeini, Colonel Ḥassan al-Bahnasāwī and
Bakhīt Butraki, the latter commanding the still–loyal Shaiqīa militiamen known
as 'Bashi-bazouks'. That same day, 23 January, the civilian City Council met to
discuss surrender. It must have been the power of Gordon's personality, coupled
with a glimmer of hope that the British rescue force might yet arrive in time,
that persuaded the fearful and starving dignitaries of Khartoum to agree to hold
out further. Gordon's spies had alerted him three days earlier to the steady
advance of the Relief Expedition.[55] But few could have doubted that the end was
near.

When the end did come, during the night of 25-26 January, Gordon himself
was 'slightly ill' and his famished troops had either abandoned their posts on the
broken walls to search for food in town or, weakened by malnutrition, maintained position on the fortifications but in no condition to resist the advance of

the Mahdī's army under cover of the early morning darkness. One anomalous but interesting account current in Omdurman in the immediate aftermath of the fall of Khartoum, relayed by a Hausa pilgrim from West Africa named only as Abūbakar, claims that Gordon was captured alive but grievously wounded and describes the Mahdī's anger at the general's subsequent murder.

> The Pasha, he said he would not run away till he was captured. He was struck with a gun; he was pierced with a sword and a spear; he was struck with a stone. The Mahdi had said, 'He must not be killed, he must be brought before me; men do not kill a king in war'. When the Pasha said he would not go to the place of the Mahdi, all the Mahdi's men struck him. The Mahdi, when he heard it, said, 'Let his head be brought'. It was cut off, his body was thrown into the river. When his head was brought to the Mahdi he said, 'Close his eyes'. He said, 'You have done a wicked thing; why did you kill him?' He was angry; he rose up, he returned to his camp in the evening.[56]

Personal and political recriminations

News of the fall of Khartoum reached Wolseley at Kūrti at 7.30pm on 4 February 1884. 'Knocked out of tune', as he put it in a morose journal entry, he reflected that he had 'no longer any "mission" to accomplish, and I am sure the British Govt. would not think of a campaign for the conquest of the Soudan or for "smashing up" the Mahdi'.[57] Of the Gladstone government, the general's instinct was likely to be accurate, but the feeling of the wider country was another matter.

Relayed via headquarters in Cairo, the news reached the heart of government in London early on 5 February. At 3am, the young Liberal MP Reginald Brett was delegated to bear the bad news to Granville, but was 'wholly unable to find the old gentleman' and sought out Hamilton instead.[58] Gladstone himself learned the news from Hartington, his host at Holker Hall, shortly before noon and promptly wired his fellow ministers to meet in cabinet the following day.[59] 'The circumstances are sad & trying,' he noted in his journal that night: 'it is one of the least points about them, that they may put an end to this Govt.'[60]

There were few who did not blame Gladstone in person for the loss of Gordon. Among his defenders was the Liberal pamphleteer Hirst Hollowell, who argued that, since Gordon's 'continuance and ultimately his death in Khartoum were due to his repudiation of Government advice . . . it would be sheer idolatry of a great name to say that Gordon was not mistaken, insubordinate, and violent in his Soudan policy of 1884'.[61] 'We see the same want of subordination,' added Charles Coe, another contemporary pamphleteer, 'the same determined self-will; we see the same Oriental way of dealing with Oriental peoples.'[62] Such trenchant criticisms make the discreet ridicule dished out later by Lytton Strachey, lampooning Gordon for his outdated values, irrational beliefs, relentless vigour and excessive brandy consumption, seem mild indeed.[63]

But the feelings of the majority were summed up by the young Beatrix Potter in her diary: 'O, if some lunatic had shot old Gladstone twelve months since. It is too dreadful to believe, what will foreigners say? Surely our cowardly Cabinet who are responsible for it will go down?'[64] Baring agreed, arguing later that 'there can scarcely be a doubt that if the decision to send an expedition to General Gordon's relief had been taken in April or May, instead of in August, the objects of the expedition would have been obtained.'[65] Demetrius Boulger, by contrast, blamed Baring himself for the earlier delay, when he had vetoed Gordon's appointment for several crucial weeks:

> He knew that Gordon was a difficult, let it be granted an impossible colleague; that he would do things in his own way in defiance of diplomatic timidity and official rigidity; and that, instead of there being in the Egyptian firmament the one planet Baring, there would be only the single sun of Gordon. . . . It was his opposition alone that retarded Gordon's departure by seven weeks . . . and that delay, I repeat it solemnly, cost Gordon his life. Whoever else was to blame afterwards, the first against whom a verdict of Guilty must be entered, without any hope of reprieve at the bar of history, was Sir Evelyn Baring.[66]

Wolseley, who also had a reputation to rehabilitate, agreed that 'time was so unpardonably squandered'.[67] Specifically and vindictively, he did his best to make Wilson the scapegoat for a two-delay at Metemma, where he rested his battle-weary troops. Wilson, he wrote later, 'had never been in action until he was inside the Square at the Battle of Abu Klea, and I don't think his Maker had bestowed upon him the nerve required by the man whose duty it was to reach Khartoum in time to save Gordon'.[68] The only military resignation was that of Sir Evelyn Wood as Sirdar of the Egyptian army. But Wood had suffered from ill-health during the Nile campaign, spent far too much of his own money maintaining the lifestyle expected of a senior officer and, even while there was still hope of rescuing Gordon, he had informed Baring that he would not retain his command of the Egyptian army 'on any terms'.[69]

Queen Victoria herself was explicit: 'Dreadful news after breakfast! . . . It is too fearful. The Government is alone to blame, by refusing to send the expedition till it was too late. Telegraphed en clair to Mr. Gladstone, Lord Granville, and Lord Hartington, expressing how dreadfully shocked I was at the news, all the more so when one felt it might have been prevented.'[70] The overwrought tone of the monarch's letter to Augusta, one of Gordon's surviving sisters, typifies the national mood:

> To think of your dear, noble, heroic Brother, who served his country and his Queen so truly, so heroically, with a self-sacrifice so edifying to the World, not having been rescued. That the promises of support were not fulfilled – which I so frequently and constantly pressed on those who asked

him to go – is to me grief inexpressible! Indeed, it has made me ill! My heart
bleeds for you, his Sister, who have gone through so many anxieties on his
account, and who loved the dear Brother as he deserved to be. . . . Would
you express to your other Sisters and your eldest Brother [Sir Henry] my
true sympathy, and what I do so keenly feel, the stain left upon England
for your dear Brother's cruel, though heroic, fate![71]

Such highly personalised recriminations reverberated through the political
scene, driven by trenchant commentary in the opposition press.[72] 'The shock
caused by the news of the fall of Khartoum,' thundered *The Times*, 'has no parallel
in the experience of the present generation. No words of ours can adequately
express the mingled feelings of dismay, consternation, and indignant disgust
universally evoked by this lamentable result of a long course of disregard of the
elementary maxims of statesmanship.'[73] The *Morning Post* anticipated both heads
rolling at Westminster and vigorous military action in Sudan itself: 'This
catastrophe is so stupendous and its consequences are so far-reaching that . . .
we can hardly believe it possible that the present Administration will remain in
office a week after Parliament meets. . . . We cannot turn our back upon the
MAHDI and his hordes without sacrificing Egypt and shaking to its foundations
our Indian Empire. Having entered on this struggle, we must go on with it, and
having gone to the Soudan we can only quit it as victors.'[74]

Indeed, it is striking that Gladstone was as roundly abused by Radicals as by
Conservatives, though for different reasons. 'The wrong man has unfortunately
been killed in the Soudan,' opined *Reynold's Newspaper* in late February, 'and
legislation for the British people is to be postponed in favour of a debate in which
the Government of Mr. Gladstone are to be censured for doing too much, or too
little, or both . . . Our unemployed people are asked to starve, and to look
contented at the spectacle of millions being wasted . . . for no practical purpose
except the safe reestablishment of an effete, demoralized, and demoralizing
government in Egypt.'[75] At the other end of the spectrum, the National Union of
Conservative and Constitutional Associations published a pamphlet, 'Gordon
and the Government', which listed among the crimes of the Gladstone cabinet:
the ban on Gordon visiting the Mahdī; the ban on him travelling south of
Khartoum; the refusal to send the relief expedition until it was too late; the
refusal to attempt to use Graham's troops to open the route from Sawākīn to
Berber; and the refusal to send al-Zubeir Raḥma. The pamphlet concluded
rhetorically, 'Upon Whose Head Lies His Blood?'[76] In the absence of any personal
response from the Prime Minister, we are forced to turn to his amanuensis,
Edward Hamilton, for a clear but private statement of what could not be said in
public:

The real charge against the government is not the hesitation to embark on
this perilous undertaking, though they might have been more prompt and
active with their *preparations*; but their weakness in not turning a deaf ear

to the sentimental cry for interference in the Soudan with which we had no direct concern whatever, and in not resisting the clamour for employing a lunatic on the most delicate of missions.[77]

In terms of immediate political impact, the early spring of 1884 saw much the same level of vituperative parliamentary argument as had the previous year. The key question was the viability of the Gladstone administration. After all, it was Sir Randolph Churchill who had warned in the Commons on 25 March 1884 that 'if the matter were left to chance, and General Gordon were sacrificed, owing to the neglect, and indifference, and callousness, and heartlessness of the Government, then they would not keep their seats for twenty-four hours after the news was known'.[78] Gladstone's own determination to continue as Prime Minister appears to have taken a serious knock. Dilke reported that on 19 February 1885, exactly a fortnight after news of the fall of Khartoum reached London, Gladstone was 'anxious to be turned out on the vote of censure' tabled by Northcote for 23 February.[79] Northcote's motion read as follows:

> ... that the course pursued by Her Majesty's Government in respect to the affairs of Egypt and the Soudan, has involved a great sacrifice of valuable lives and a heavy expenditure without any beneficial result, and has rendered it imperatively necessary in the interests of the British Empire and of the Egyptian people, that Her Majesty's Government should distinctly recognise, and take decided measures to fulfil, the special responsibility now incumbent on them, to assure a good and stable Government to Egypt and to those portions of the Soudan which are necessary to its security.[80]

The debate was savage, with the government under heavy fire from right and left. George Goschen and W.E. Forster, Liberal imperialists both, satirised the futility of any campaign aimed at 'smashing' the Mahdī before retreating and echoed the Conservative taunt that expediency had dictated a policy 'that they intend to go to Khartoum to please the Whigs, and that they intend to retire from Khartoum to please the Radicals'.[81]

By contrast, Radicals condemned any future military action as a betrayal of the original Gladstonian principle of non-intervention. Outside parliament, too, leftists were on fiery form. On 5 February 1885, the day the news of the fall of Khartoum reached London, the Radical MP Leonard Courtney insisted at Torpoint that the Sudanese were merely fighting for their own liberty: 'If I stood alone, I would protest against the notion of waging war against the Mahdi . . . simply for the purpose of showing our might'.[82] His colleague John Morley, speaking in Glasgow, made prescient remarks about the duration of a British occupation of Sudan: 'The advocates of revenge and war would first say that honour demanded the flying of the British flag in Khartoum. That done, honour would again demand that the flag flew there for ever'.[83]

Gladstone's political survival, after four nights of long and acrimonious argument, was little short of miraculous. 'The division was taken at four in the morning [on 28 February],' recorded Morley, 'and the result was that the government which had come in with morning radiance five years ago, was worn down to an attenuated majority of fourteen [288-302].'[84] This meagre victory, however, was overshadowed by defeat in the Lords on the same motion by the heavy margin of 189-68.[85] Still, the Tories were in no position to mount an effective counter-attack. Northcote, after failing so visibly to inflict a fatal wound, was himself fatally wounded as the leader of a party revealed to be lacking 'an effective and acceptable power structure': indeed, it has since been argued that it took the Mahdī to transform the Conservatives, 'after much travail, into an effectively-led party' under Salisbury.[86]

Despite the Commons reprieve, the gloom affecting Gladstone was spreading. Matters were not helped by the on-going bitter arguments within the cabinet over Egypt proper. With so much acrimony over Egyptian finances, the future of the British occupation and administration, as well as the question of diplomatic co-operation with France, the Sudan disaster came at a bad time.[87] After parting briefly to rest, the cabinet reconvened a few hours after the vote. According to Dilke's account, those in favour of resignation were listed as 'S. [Selborne], G. [Granville], Sp. [Spencer], D. [Derby], Hn. [Hartington], N. [Northbrook], Ch. [Childers]'. Those against were listed as 'Gl. [Gladstone], C. [Carlingford], Hc. [Harcourt], Cha. [Chamberlain], Dil. [Dilke], L. [Shaw-Lefevre], K. [Kimberley], T. [Trevelyan]'.[88] Catching up on his own journal the following week, Kimberley recalled 'a most extraordinary discussion in the Cabinet lasting 4 hours & ¾ . . . [with] evident differences of opinion'. Gladstone, rallying fast after the close call in the Commons, used his casting vote to oppose resignation. Kimberley concluded, 'I am persuaded we were right'.[89]

Retreat and abandonment of Sudan

The death of Gordon and the brief but violent surge of popular anger nearly wrested Sudan policy from Gladstone's control at last. On 13 March 1885, memorial services for Gordon were held in St Paul's, Westminster Abbey, at Canterbury, Durham, Winchester and further afield.[90] Several respected individuals were also quick to express anxiety about the potential effect of the Mahdī's success in British India. 'The fall of Khartum and the fate of Gordon must have a bad effect on India and the East,' argued Sir Richard Temple in *Contemporary Review*, 'unless the reverse shall be retrieved, and . . . from this point of view the recapture of that place is extremely desirable; so desirable indeed, that it becomes hard to draw the line between urgent expediency and necessity.'[91] Dilke's account reveals a frantic decision-making process: 'Courtney and Morley [both Radical MPs] had insisted in private letters that we should only rescue, and not attack the rebels, and the Times agreed with them – unless we intended to stay in the country and establish a Government. Wolseley's policy would be represented as one of "smash and retire".'[92]

Extraordinarily, Gladstone at first allowed Hartington to dominate proceedings. A cabinet session on 7 February 1885 concluded by endorsing a strong message to Wolseley, in which the general was given full discretion over the timing and location of any future attack on the Mahdī's forces: 'Your military policy is to be based on the necessity . . . that the power of the Mahdi at Khartoum must be overthrown'.[93] Two days later, Hartington wired Wolseley with news of reinforcements proposed for Sawākīn, in order to reopen the eastern front: '6 battalions, besides battalion and marines now there; 4 squadrons of cavalry, 2 batteries artillery, 2 companies Engineers . . . This will make total of about 9,000 all ranks.'[94]

Also on the eastern front, the Sawākīn-Berber railway was suddenly revived, with Sir Andrew Clarke put in charge of initial arrangements for both railway plant and water supply. Overseen by Lord Haliburton at the War Office's supply department, construction of a 'railway of English narrow gauge' was contracted out to Lucas & Aird, while Edwards & Tweedle were signed up to assemble the 'large condensers . . . and miles of water-pipes to run alongside the railway'.[95] 'The Soudan campaign' rejoiced The Times, 'will, perhaps, be remembered in connexion with a great engineering work calculated to confer great and lasting advantages upon the country. When the railway line touches Berber, the Soudan difficulties will assume an altogether different aspect.'[96]

Beyond the immediate strategic imperative, there were plenty of advocates ready to resume campaigning for the railway. A correspondent only identified as 'M' opined in the Morning Post that, even if it had to be built in the face of 'the whole power of the Mahdi flushed with victory . . . when we did "scuttle out" of the country, instead of a few hawsers rotting on the cataract rocks being the sole record of our ill-advised expedition, we should at least leave behind us something that would be useful for those into whose hands the destiny of the Soudan falls'.[97]

So had Gladstone capitulated? A list of talking-points for a meeting on 10 February with the Turkish and Egyptian ambassadors, Constantine Musurus and Ḥassan Fahmī, makes it clear that, on central policy, he had not.

> Original policy: evacuation of the Soudan by Egypt, and its restoration to freedom. Approved by Khedive & Egyptian Govt. Has undergone no change. But events have occurred to prevent its immediate execution. . . . The nature of the military object was changed. The recent decisions are military decisions.

A. It became necessary for General [Wolseley] to know whether he was or was not to proceed on intention of ours to overthrow the Mahdi's power at Khartoum . . .

B. We decided in the affirmative. Consequences, required by the General from us: 1. Action agst. Osman Digna, required to open the road to Berber. 2. Decision to commence construction of a railway. 3. Intention . . . to overthrow the power of the Mahdi at Khartoum. . . . All of which will of course be matter for the consideration of Parlt.[98]

The prospect of an intensified campaign against the Mahdī placed an immense weight on Wolseley's shoulders. Indeed, Hartington conceded to him that, while 'we desire to check the Mahdi's advance in the provinces of the Soudan which he has not yet conquered by any means in our power', the challenge of retaking even Berber in the face of both the Sudanese summer and the full strength of the Mahdī's armies, 'released by the fall of Khartoum', necessitated a radical reassessment of military priorities.[99]

But Hartington was already out of tune with rapidly changing sentiment. His own party was in uproar over the renewed Sudan mandate.[100] Gordon himself had been far from alone in wondering whether, 'should the town fall . . . it will be worth the while of Her Majesty's Government to continue its expedition'.[101] And even Wolseley knew that his depleted force had no immediate prospect of success against the Mahdī, though his ego refused to concede either that he had erred in any way or that his government might not support him with reinforcements on his terms. But he did concede that the British Army had 'no party' in northern Sudan in its favour: 'They look upon us with hatred as infidels and invaders who have come here for our own selfish ends, and who intend, if we succeed, to place in power some foreign ruler, who will tax and oppress them as the Egyptian Pashas did.'[102]

Perhaps most importantly, public attention waned remarkably swiftly. Northbrook's account reflects the government's shame and weariness – and the rapid ebbing of any collective appetite for military reprisals.

The feeling . . . against the continuance of fighting in the Soudan is getting very strong. Neither Egyptian nor Soudan expeditions have been popular among the working classes, but now the unpopularity is rapidly spreading to the 'upper ten' [ten-thousand establishment elite] and even to the Tories. There was never a greater mistake made than that Salisbury should have pronounced for a prolonged occupation of the Soudan. . . . This went very far beyond anything we had ever engaged to do, and I am inclined to think beyond what it is in our power to do.[103]

Wolseley's career ambitions, however, had not dimmed, even after the disastrous failure of his expedition. Backed by Victoria and by Baring in Cairo, he demanded to be named Gordon's successor as Governor-General of Sudan or, in

Gladstone's own words, 'made formally, as he is now substantially, master *in the region to which his present military action extends*'.[104] As well as being arrogant, this demand reversed Wolseley's prior proposal that Khedive Ṭawfīq's brother, Prince Ḥassan, be made 'High Commissioner with the English army, with power over all mudirs [provincial governors] and other civil authorities in the Soudan'.[105]

Gladstone was quite clear that the demand should not be entertained. His arguments were relayed to the Queen by Sir Henry Ponsonby: 'Mr. Gladstone objects to it because the tone is that of a Turkish Pasha pardoning a revolted province, and no hint is given that the Soudan will be disunited from Egypt. . . . Besides which he objects to there being any Governor-General of the Soudan.'[106] Gladstone's objections were shared in various forms by the whole cabinet. Shortly before the decision was taken to veto the appointment, Dilke described the collective animosity among ministers towards Wolseley, who, it was felt, had misrepresented the situation in Sudan.

> Northbrook and I, soon joined by Harcourt and Chamberlain, were in favour of stopping our impossible campaign. I argued that when we decided to destroy the power of the Mahdi, it was on Wolseley's telling us that he hoped possibly to take Khartoum at once. For some weeks after that he intended to take Berber. Then he had told us that he at least could occupy Abu Hamed. Now he was in full retreat . . . The Chancellor wrote on a slip of paper for me: 'We seem to be fighting three enemies at once. (1) The Mahdi; (2) certain of our people here; (3) Wolseley.[107]

Such feelings were almost universal. 'The country is rapidly becoming luke-warm about the Soudan,' noted Hamilton on 9 March 1885: 'They are waking up to the purposelessness of the undertaking.'[108] A pamphlet by Edward Beesley, President of the London Positivist Society, pithily titled *Retirement from the Soudan*, summed up the general feeling. 'There can . . . be no greater mistake,' Beesley wrote, 'than to suppose that the mass of the English people have made up their minds to support the prolongation of the War in the Soudan. As long as it was a question of rescuing Gordon, few cared to incur the odium of appearing to grudge the sacrifices involved in a campaign for that purpose . . . but that pretext for an insensate and criminal war no longer remains.'[109]

One by one, Beesley knocked down what he called the 'pretexts' for war – the responsibility of the Mahdī himself for the death of Gordon; the danger of a Sudanese invasion of Egypt; the danger of a widespread Islamic uprising, especially in India; the obligation to leave a better government in Khartoum – before addressing perhaps the most important point affecting Victorian public morale. As to the 'loss of prestige consequent on retirement', he wrote, 'we have suffered no reverse at the hands of the Mahdi. On the contrary, we have defeated his armies five times with heavy slaughter. Our military superiority over semi-civilised races has never been more strikingly demonstrated.'[110]

All that was now needed was an excuse for withdrawal that would permit the reassertion of the old policy on the old terms. The 'Pendjeh Incident', an imperial scare story far away on the fringes of British India, provided it.* On 8 April, Gladstone wrote to Hartington, observing that 'the contingency of war cannot be wholly shut out of view'.[111] Serious as it was in geo-political terms, the incident served as a handy excuse to end military involvement in Sudan. As Kimberley put it, 'a sort of compromise has been made':

> Parliament is to be informed that the expedition is suspended only in order that our troops may be available for service, if required, "elsewhere". For all that the Soudan campaign is a thing of the past: and happily. No good reason can now be given for an advance in the Soudan, unless we intend permanently to occupy the country: and that would be madness. It is urgently necessary to extricate ourselves from a situation which exposes us to affronts from all sides.[112]

Hartington, previously Wolseley's best ally within cabinet, cravenly wrote to the general to inform him that his elevation to Governor-General was not 'expedient' because 'the position with Russia in Affghanistan [sic] is so critical'.[113] Gladstone was quick to reclaim the ideological high ground: 'I am not prepared to go on [in Sudan] upon any terms, Russia or no Russia'.[114] And the potential for two simultaneous and demanding conflicts helped persuade even the Queen that curtailing Wolseley's ambitions in Sudan was the best remaining option – although she still noted bitterly that 'after the loss of all the blood and treasure which have been spent . . . the abandonment of this policy, without the attainment of any definite results, [is] painful in the extreme'.[115]

Still the Gladstone administration staggered on. A formula was found that persuaded Hartington not to resign. The Sawākīn-Berber railway was again halted. Wolseley was recalled to London and General Stephenson resumed his ranking seniority, instructed to defend the southern frontier of Egypt and pursue the Mahdī's fighters only if deemed advisable in the context of purely Egyptian security. An official memorandum clarified the role of the British Army on the Nile as 'neither for vengeance . . . nor for conquest . . . [but] for the safety of Egypt'.[116] Two years and five months after the initial formulation of Gladstone's Sudan policy – minimum engagement, zero responsibility – Hartington's decisive message to Wolseley on 20 April 1885 made it clear that, after a long and turbulent road, that policy was now achieved.

---

* On 30 March 1885, Russian imperial forces under General Komarov attacked the Afghan army, inflicting heavy losses and seizing territory. Lord Dufferin, previously so prominent in Cairo, was instrumental in averting war and, following his diplomatic triumph, a boundary commission established Afghanistan's northern frontier, thus creating an effective buffer state between Russia and the Raj.

Government will announce on Tuesday that it is necessary to hold all military resources of Empire, including forces in the Soudan, available for service wherever required. They will not, therefore, make provision for further offensive operations in Soudan, or for military preparations for early advance on Khartoum, beyond ... river steam-boats contracted for, and completion of Wady Halfa Railway. . . . With cessation of active operations on Nile, any considerable extension of the Suakin-Berber Railway must be suspended; but, as Suakin must be held for the present, it may be necessary to occupy one or more stations in the neighbourhood . . . Government will retain garrison in Egypt and defend frontier.[117]

CHAPTER 8

Gladstone's defeat and the seeds of future policy

Sorrow and rage was in every heart. Sorrow for the gallant soul we had striven with might & main to save and rage at the Ministry whose folly had prevented the effort to reach Khartoum from being undertaken earlier. Well, he is gone from amongst us, and I shall never know his like again: indeed many Generations may come & go without producing a Charlie Gordon.

Lord Wolseley, 5 March 1885[1]

The Khartoum journals: politics and personalities

When Wolseley despatched Gordon's journals to Baring in Cairo in February 1885, along with a substantial quantity of correspondence in English and Arabic, two emotions were uppermost in his mind. He was personally distraught that, after such a marathon campaign, he had been just two days too late. And he was certain that Gordon's jottings were worth publishing in full. But the swift transfer of the diaries from Baring to London presented the War Office with a tricky problem. What should be done with a bombshell of a document whose existence was at this stage known to only a few, but whose content could add to the already widespread opprobrium felt for the Gladstone cabinet for its failure to reach Khartoum in time?

Damaging as it was to the Gladstone ministry, there was no law to support suppression of the entire text. There would be no Official Secrets Act until 1889 and there were no legal constraints upon what material written by a serving army officer like Gordon could or could not be published, especially when the author was already dead.[2] Besides, Sudan had already been abandoned and the Gladstone government was busy preparing for a general election that winter. The argument that the journals jeopardised British interests in Egypt or elsewhere was impossible to sustain, even if publication might help demonise Gladstone personally and rally electoral support to the opposition Conservatives.

The delicate job of negotiating between Sir Henry Gordon and the War Office civil servants, whose instinct was for suppression or comprehensive censorship, fell to Hamilton. Utterly loyal to Gladstone and no admirer of Gordon, he had two urgent questions to address: should criticism of government personalities and policies be excised or should it be published 'warts and all'? and who should have ownership of the journal itself, the family to which Gordon belonged or the state to which he had pledged his service and in whose name he had written the diary? To mitigate their loss, Gordon's family had already been awarded a 'large and unconventional' grant of £20,000 by order of parliament.[3] Now, according to Sir Ralph Thompson, Permanent Under-Secretary at the War Office, 'the question of the final custody of the original Diary Lord Hartington will settle when he has read it and formed an estimate of its character.'[4]

On 18 March 1885, nearly two months after Gordon's death, the decision was taken at the War Office first to send a sample section, a photographic copy of Volume 6 of the journal, to Sir Henry, 'with a request that he would strike out such portions as he thought should not be made public; the question of final custody being reserved.'[5] Sir Henry was outraged and declined even to read a word of the journal sent in this form: 'After my service of close upon half a century,' he replied tersely, 'I think the War Office might have trusted my honour and have sent me the original diary, which my sisters and myself were most anxious to see.'[6] Not all his sisters: Augusta Gordon, the loyal spinster who received letters of condolence from Queen Victoria, wrote later, on publication of the journals: 'I cannot read them. The whole past is so dreadful, without adding to the pain by knowing what he went through.'[7]

The journals were first discussed by the full cabinet on 20 March, with Gladstone commenting to colleagues that Sir Henry had 'brought to me his wrath.'[8] After the meeting, Gladstone wrote a mollifying reply, noting delicately that other political issues had left him 'in ignorance of some particulars as to General Gordon's Journal.'[9] In fact, Gladstone was profoundly shocked by a comprehensive reading of the same partial excerpt, Volume 6. In an outraged letter to Lord Hartington, he noted: 'General Gordon, not content with charging mere error on us . . . insinuates against us (so I read him) the most abominable charges, & conveys plainly enough that we waited for & counted upon his ruin as the desired means of extricating ourselves from embarrassment. How much more of this poisoned stuff the other five Fascicles contain I know not.'[10] Hamilton recorded not just the extent of the Prime Minister's anger, but the political implications of censorship.

Mr. G. feels it is impossible under the circumstances for the Government to undertake the office of pruning. This is quite clear. Mr. G. thinks that the journal if published would lend itself to be so greatly distorted that it would 'kill' the government. I am not sure myself whether the publication of it en bloc would not do more harm to the memory and fame of Gordon than to the government. It is clearly the production of a totally disordered mind . . . [and] shows an utter want of dignity or magnanimity, which even the extraordinarily trying circumstances can not excuse. It has lowered the man greatly in Mr. G.'s estimation. Mr. G. says he could not have used the words of panegyric which he did use in the House of Commons in reference to Gordon, had he first seen this journal.[11]

Despite the Prime Minister's strong feelings, exploratory talks between the War Office and Sir Henry Gordon continued. Pressure for a speedy resolution of the problem was increased when details of the journal's controversial content were blurted out over dinner by Chamberlain, 'a most indefensible piece of indiscretion', repetition of which was forestalled by 'some precautionary injunctions' from Hartington.[12] Mollified by the correspondence from Downing Street, Sir Henry was persuaded to make some initial edits, first to Volume 6 and then Volume 2. But these appear to have been less than satisfactory to Thompson, who took it upon himself to make further revisions of a much more draconian nature. On 17 April he wrote to Sir Henry Gordon to say that 'he had excluded all criticisms & suggestions about the policy of the Govt (irrespectively of their hostile character), and also all allusions to Govt officials; but he reminded Sir H.G. that it was still open to him to publish the whole diary.'[13]

Thus the onus of responsibility shifted to Sir Henry, who was left 'in a regular fix' over the choice of a government-approved edit or a full 'warts and all' version. He was, of course, only too aware that 'the eliminations made by Sir R.T. would deprive the publication of all interest'; his considered conclusion, therefore, was 'to accept the alternative of publishing the Journal as a whole . . . [omitting] certain names of friends of Genl Gordon as well as supposed Ministerial conversations.'[14] This appears to have satisfied the War Office and, on 23 April 1885, Hartington noted that, failing a satisfactorily comprehensive revision, the government would be best served by allowing Gordon's character to emerge unedited. 'I should be inclined to wash our hands of it altogether,' he wrote; 'unless published in a strictly revised form, it should be published complete; i.e. with all its eccentricities and extravagances.'[15] That position was approved by the cabinet on 28 April: 'Gordon. As far as we have a desire it is for the publication of the whole, but do not attempt to interfere with his [i.e. Sir Henry's] discretion'.[16]

To edit the mass of scrawled papers, Sir Henry selected Egmont Hake, a distant relative of the late general (his paternal grandmother was Gordon's aunt) and the author of a recent and favourable account of Gordon's Chinese adventures in the 1860s.[17] Sir Henry appears not have known that Hake was a zealous member of the Conservative Party, who declared himself 'glad to undertake any post in the interests of Conservatism . . . [and] devote what abilities I possess to the Cause.'[18] This loyalty certainly presented a conflict of interest when it came to editing a volume containing so much trenchant criticism of the incumbent Liberal administration, in an election year to boot.

On 21 May 1885, shortly before publication, Wilfrid Blunt, a celebrity of salon society widely known to be highly critical of the government's policies in Egypt and Sudan, recorded in his diary that 'Mr. Egmont Hake called to-day to consult me on various points connected with the "Gordon Diaries" he is publishing. He admits that Gordon made great mistakes at Khartoum, both as to men and things'.[19] Far from focusing on those mistakes, however, Hake chose to dwell in his introduction and footnotes on the sins of the government. Given the cabinet-endorsed decision to opt for an unexpurgated edition, Hake had little say in the question of disregarding Gordon's repeated injunction to 'prune out' his manuscript. Indeed, had Gordon's proposed elisions been cut, the total length of the six volumes would have been reduced by more than twenty-thousand words.

As for Gordon's error-strewn transliterations, they were problems that his editor, with no access at all to Sudan or Sudanese, was unequipped to correct. Hake did try belatedly to get expert help from Blunt, writing on 16 May 1885 to request his 'knowledge of Egypt and Egyptian affairs . . . to get at the history and position of the people whom General Gordon names.'[20] Hake was indeed invited to visit Blunt to discuss the manuscript, but there is no evidence that specialist knowledge was brought to bear. Perhaps with publication just forty days off, it was too late to make large-scale alterations. In any case, with Gordon's own errors compounded by Hake's incorrect readings of the general's hasty scrawl, the published journals were left riddled with errors, including the name of Gordon's own Egyptian aide-de-camp, Ibrāhīm Fawzī, who becomes in print 'Ibrahim Tongi'.

Hake was compelled to censor some of Gordon's more gratuitously offensive or downright libellous remarks, especially accusations of conspiracy, ineptitude, cowardice and corruption. His edition also tastefully omitted the names of specific establishment personalities who figured prominently in Gordon's increasingly deranged imaginary conversations, in which they were usually pictured as conniving to effect the capture of Khartoum and the frustration of Gordon's rescue mission. There were thirty-five instances of such censorship, a modest constraint imposed by Sir Henry, who was paid the astronomical advance of 5,000 guineas against an anticipated first edition print-run of 13,000 copies. Hake was paid £500, while the anonymous translator of the Arabic documents received £155.[21]

The copies of the Diaries . . . are complete copies thereof as corrected by General Gordon himself with the exception of a few passages amounting to about eight or ten pages in the whole not considered by Sir Henry William Gordon to contain matters of general interest and also with the exception of names of living individuals who in his opinion might feel injured or wounded by the publication of their names, the publishers being nevertheless at liberty to print the name of any person named in the diaries with his or her consent.[22]

Deletions thus forced on Hake included frequent references to members of the aristocracy, prominent government officials and officers involved in the Relief Expedition: Granville, Sanderson and Connaught at the Foreign Office; Dufferin, Malet, Baring and Egerton in Cairo; even Kitchener on the Nile and Chermside at Sawākīn, loyal soldiers working to effect Gordon's release from the siege. Some embarrassment was thus averted, though Granville and Baring in particular could justifiably have complained about feeling 'injured or wounded' by heavily critical material that the censor did not remove. Indeed, Major Charles Watson, a former protégé of Gordon's, wrote to his mother from Cairo shortly after the publication of the journals to comment on Hake's uneven editing: 'I think it is a pity that they have cut out a great deal of what he [Gordon] said about the Government, while leaving in his remarks about Baring. Now, Baring really wanted to help him, and the Government would not let him.'[23]

But while Baring was savaged, criticism of the highest officers of state was censored. Late in the siege, Gordon squarely pinned the blame for the deaths of soldiers under his command on 'the wretched policy of Mr Gladstone': the phrase was excised.[24] In the middle of an immensely long entry for 17 September, he wrote: 'I have seen Lords Clarendon, Derby, Granville, Layard, Dilke, Bourke at different times, & when one left their august presences, one marvelled at the Foreign Policy of Gt Britain being in such hands': all the names were removed.[25] Similarly, a powerful sentence denouncing Gladstone's core policy as 'selfish and inhuman' was also deleted.[26]

Some personal references were judged to be just too frank. Learning of the deaths of Stewart, Power and their fellow passengers on the 'Abbās, Gordon reflected with his usual bluntness on their characters: 'Power was headstrong, & wilful, and did not calmly weigh things. Herbin [the French consul] was the sharpest of the three, but was not very disposed to assert his opinion'.[27] By the time of publication, Stewart and Power were both established as romantic heroes in England: uncomplimentary comments about Power and the suggestion that Stewart had been less clever than a Frenchman were both intolerable.

Occasionally, Gordon's insults were simply racist. Ismā'īl 'Ayūb, his prede-cessor as Governor-General, while acknowledged as a competent administrator, is derided as 'a coward', who 'would not keep his fingers from pinching and stealing.'[28] Guiseppe Cuzzi, Gordon's agent at Berber who fell into the Mahdī's hands and was compelled to convert to Islam, is denounced as 'a vile traitor, like all Italians I ever met.'[29] A British financier, Henry Oppenheim, comes in for gratuitously personal attack: 'One of the greatest sinners in the way of getting Egypt into financial difficulties (whence all this trouble) is *Oppenheim, a wretched suttler*, who, in Crimea, used to sell cheeses at £2 each, and other things at the most exorbitant prices, *a regular Jew*.'[30] The words italicised here were omitted by Hake. Longer cuts included some of Gordon's more deranged imaginary exchanges, among them a typically contemptuous depiction of two professional Foreign Office civil servants, 'diplomatists' whom Gordon prided himself on offending as often as possible, talking about the defenders of Khartoum.

> 'Bother them! They have got in more Dhoora [grain meal], that is another two months they will hold out. What that Mahdi is about, I cannot make out. Why does he not put all his guns on the river, and stop the route; eh what.' 'We will have to go to Kartoum! Why it will cost millions, what a wretched business!' 'What! Send Zebehr? our conscience recoils from that, it is elastic but not equal to that, it is a pact with the Devil, what do you say.' ... 'I say, do you not think there is any way of getting hold of him, in a quiet way, &c. &c. It is positively throwing good money after bad, to send Lord W. [Wolseley] up after *him*.'[31]

Such examples of bigotry and vindictiveness may have been cut because they undermined Gordon's reputation for an almost saintly fair-mindedness. But many, including Baring in Cairo, believed that concealing Gordon's less edifying personal characteristics was a mistake. In his 1902 memoir, he wrote that the inclusion of 'a good deal of violent and very foolish abuse ... would have enabled the public to judge more accurately of the value of General Gordon's criticisms, than was possible when only an expurgated edition was issued'.[32] Baring's clear imputation, that Gordon uncensored would have revealed Gordon unhinged, outraged the late general's nephew, who wrote to Wilfrid Blunt that such sentiments left 'a nasty taste in the mouth.'[33]

Hake's national lecture tour

Political machinations over the 'Khartoum Journals' became still more devious in the aftermath of publication, a time when Egmont Hake's true political colours, informing his agreement to undertake the editing commission, became much clearer. By the end of the summer, Hake had embarked on a series of nationwide speaking engagements, ostensibly part of a routine promotional tour. Friends such as Blunt, however, knew that Hake was working directly for the opposition at Westminster. On 30 July, after lunching with Wilfrid Meynell, editor of the *Weekly Register*, Blunt wrote in his diary: 'Meynell tells me that Lord Salisbury has engaged Hake to lecture in all the large towns in England preparatory to the elections. Lord Salisbury* is to pay the expenses.'[34]

In fact, Blunt's gossipy luncheons may not have been as precisely well-informed as he liked to believe. The Hake tour was financed not by Salisbury, but by his eldest son, Lord Cranborne. Being a Conservative parliamentary candidate

---

* Robert Cecil, 3rd Marquis of Salisbury, became Prime Minister briefly from 23 June 1885-28 January 1886, then again from 25 July 1886-11 August 1892 and from 25 June 1895-11 July 1902.

in the 1885 election was certainly motive enough for Hake's patron to ensure that as much anti-Gladstone material as possible reached the public. Cranborne's widow, Lady Alice, later recalled both the tour and its cost:

> He was only about twenty-four when the death of Gordon and the surrender of the Soudan took place. It affected him so deeply that he and his sister determined that the whole story should be known, and they engaged a well-known lecturer to visit the chief centres of population in England. . . . When the bill came in it was far beyond what they had counted on, but they met it alone.[35]

The lecture tour lasted several months, and attracted audiences as large as 7,000 people on a single night. It was orchestrated by the Conservatives' new chief election agent, Richard Middleton. The tour was a triumph of what Hake called 'the work of conversion' and by December he was able to write to Cranborne to congratulate him on winning a seat at Darwen in Lancashire.* Hake also reported that, of the many letters he had been sent 'relative to the lectures . . . you will be glad to hear that not a few of these are from new members [of parliament] who insist on crediting me with a share in their election'.[36]

But concealing both the identity of the tour's financial backer and its political sub-text had been a constant preoccupation. As early as 31 August, Middleton met Hake to discuss the tour and reported to Cranborne: 'It appears the Liberals are enquiring [about] the object of Mr. Hake's lecture. The answer that has been given is not quite satisfactory.'[37] Hake touched on the same issue in a jubilant letter to his benefactor in mid-September in which he boasted about a succession of sell-out appearances: paid reserved ticketing, he suggested, would supply 'a raison d'etre for the lecturing tour & would damp speculation, which must spring up, as to how the expenses are paid & as to where the enterprise takes its origin'.

> I may say that the result, as far as holding the audience and convincing them goes, was an absolute success. It was easy to see that the lecture carried with it the most violent radicals & I was informed by men on the platform that it supplied a new element of thought and contention. . . . The Guildhall at Worcester was packed & the standing-room crowded, but among those present were a good many women and children

* The election itself took place between 24 November and 18 December 1885, following both an extension of the franchise and a redistribution of seats. Gladstone's Liberal Party won the most seats (319), ahead of Lord Salisbury's Conservative Party (247) and Charles Stewart Parnell's Irish Nationalists (86); a splinter group called the Liberal Unionists, led by Lord Hartington (Gladstone's one-time Secretary of War) won 11, with the remaining seven seats divided between smaller parties.

[i.e. non-voters]. . . . Had it been possible for us to engage our own hall, the largest in every town, & had it been thought advisable to appeal to all parties, radicals, liberals & conservatives, on the political aspect of Gordon's Mission, the subject might be flashed over the country in a manner to produce a crisis in advance of the elections.[38]

Hake rarely declined an opportunity to speak as his scheduled tour was extended by invitations to speak at Wigan, Sheffield, Ripon and Scarborough. In Edinburgh, scene of some of Gladstone's finest oratorical moments, Hake deliberately schemed to produce 'a good counter-effect' during the Prime Minister's anticipated campaign visit.[39] In Glasgow on 2 October, a large audience assembled to hear Hake deliver an oration that expanded on the 'ten distinct requests' for help made by this 'representative of British honour', all rejected by the Gladstone government. At a time when 'the episode of General Gordon almost seemed to have lapsed into ancient history . . . Mr. Egmont Hake, at any rate, does not allow the national memory to slumber,' the *Glasgow Herald* commented approvingly; 'he startles while he recalls to it the step by which events reached their sad an inglorious consummation'.[40]

By November, Hake was banging the drum in the north-east of England. Under the headlines 'Indictment of the Late Government' and 'Gordon's Martyrdom and Liberal Dishonour', *The Hull Packet and East Riding Times* described Hake's contrast of Gordon's innate nobility and strategic vision with the perfidy of the government:

And so it transpired that they who refused to send 100 men had to send thousands (cries of 'Shame'). . . . They only did it ten months after when the people of England forced them to do it (prolonged cheering). What was the result? Disgrace, defeat, dishonour, simply because they would not listen to the one man who knew so much when they knew so little (applause). . . . Let it be written that our children, and our children's children, and their great grandchildren for a hundred generations might see that an English general, with the honour of the nation in his hand, was left to die like a dog in the sands, and charged with the full political and moral responsibility of the Liberal Government (long cries of 'Shame', and cheers).[41]

Reaction to the journals' publication

The reception accorded to the journals when the edited manuscript finally emerged on 25 June 1885 was almost enthusiastic. Among the few dissenting or cautionary voices was *Country Gentleman*, which appraised the purely literary merit of the journals as 'disappointing': 'It was not nearly up to my expectations . . . and if it be true that Mr. Kegan Paul and his partner . . . gave £5000 for the copyright, I fear they will rue their bargain. . . . The story is altogether incoherent. But I dare say that the journals have been injured in the editing'.[42] The *Birmingham Daily Post* gave its readers a tacit warning that the account was 'somewhat discursive', with 'no fine writing, no writing for effect' but that, the paper gallantly insisted, only served to highlight Gordon's 'generosity, his humility, his religious enthusiasm, his singularity of belief . . . his satirical humour, his strictness as a disciplinarian, and his delightfully English downrightness of speech.'[43] The *Daily News* found fault with the editorial process, commenting perceptively that Hake's footnotes were 'too often of that exploded [discredited] class which are less elucidations of the text than expressions of the writer's views and feelings.'[44]

The problem of representative selection defeated many reviewers, who found themselves simply overwhelmed by the sheer volume and force of Gordon's words, struggling to select quotations from across the thematic scope and ninety-six-day timescale of the journals. The *Graphic* lamented that 'it is difficult to speak adequately in the space at command', while *The Times* commented diplomatically that 'where every line is of almost thrilling interest, it is difficult to adjust with any nice degree of proportion the parts of the volume which are of the greatest intrinsic value or interest.'[45] To cope with this volume of material, some papers opted for a straightforward chronological sequence of extracts, without commentary, while others set out brief quotations under terse headlines to flesh out a thematic analysis of the journals.

Hake's retention of Gordon's repeated references to 'pruning down' deceived the reviewer in the *Exeter Flying Post*, who assumed that the injunction had indeed been heeded and that what he was reading was the result of such pruning. Selecting just six telling paragraphs to sum up a period 'crowded with incident', the *Post* noted that 'Mr. Hake has faithfully carried out this instruction, and . . . everything that was extraneous to the immediate subject dealt with or to the incident recorded, has been carefully eliminated by the General's representative.'[46] The *Daily News*, by contrast, had it at least partly right: the paper assumed correctly that Gordon's injunction had been overruled, though it was wrong both to assume that it had been done 'on the authority of Sir Henry Gordon' and to conclude that 'the reader . . . has little ground to complain of suppression'.[47]

Reviewers found much common ground, most conspicuously the poignancy of Gordon's mourning for Stewart and the other passengers aboard the *'Abbās*. Gordon's protracted arguments over the appointment of al-Zubeir Raḥma as his successor were also widely described, though rarely verbatim. Others picked out individual incidents to illustrate the general's humour, faith or courage, while many appreciated his well-drawn caricatures.

For many papers, however, the impact of the journals on domestic politics was inescapable. The *Cardiff Western Mail* highlighted 'His Judgement on Liberal Policy', while the *Aberdeen Weekly Journal* spoke of 'Grave Reflections on Gladstonian Policy in the Soudan'.[48] The *Belfast News-Letter* was more explicit. Under the headline 'Condemnation of the Late Government', the paper quoted Gordon's diatribe of 8 November 1884, culminating in the comment, 'There is one thing which is quite incomprehensible, if it is right to send up an Expedition now, why was it not right to send it up before?'[49] *The Glasgow Herald*, unaware of Hake's loyalty to the opposition Conservative Party, quoted from the editor's bitter and politically loaded introductory note: 'Gordon tells us plainly in his Journals how great is the evil done by the policy of Her Majesty's Government, and for how long that evil will live when the Government is dead.'[50]

Nor was it only the press that was absorbed with Gordon. Music hall audiences in the late 1880s joined in with gusto as the artistes on stage performed numbers such as G.H. MacDermott's *Too Late, Too Late*, the lyrics of which stressed Gordon's 'commitment to service, duty and the protection of native races.'[51] Other popular songs with identical themes included N.G. Travers's *Too Late!*, and Harry Windley's *Gordon (Hero of Khartoum)*: 'Gordon, Gordon, hear his pleading cry / Far over the pathless waste / Where he was left to die'.[52] Theatre-goers in London's West End, too, might swoon over the predicament of Grace Armytage and Priscilla Prym, prisoners of the despicable Mahdī reduced to praying for the relief of Gordon in *Khartoum!*, a 'new and entirely original spectacular military drama in nine tableaux.'[53]

At the other end of the social spectrum, in England's most prominent public schools, a generally mixed picture of pro- and anti-imperialism solidified after Gordon's death into an almost universal animosity towards Gladstone. At Harrow, Radley, Wellington and Haileybury, Gordon was accorded epitaphs crafted in Latin and Greek, while school debates were recorded as ending in 'near-unanimous anti-government votes.'[54]

Composers like Edward Elgar were deeply moved by the Gordon story. Though his 'Gordon Symphony' was never completed, Elgar transplanted many of its ideas and emotions into other works, not least *The Dream of Gerontius*. Details of Elgar's ongoing efforts were revealed to readers of *The Musical Times*, who learned that 'the extraordinary career of General Gordon – his military achievements, his unbounded energy, his self-sacrifice, his resolution, his deep religious fervour – offers to a composer of Mr Elgar's temperament a magnificent subject . . . that appeals to the sympathies of all true-hearted Englishmen.'[55]

In the literary arena, the reaction of contemporary writers to the fate of Gordon was equally emotional and often bitterly critical of the Gladstone government. Long sections of Geoffrey Drage's contemporary novel *Cyril*, a book largely about contemporary Russia, not Egypt or Sudan, are filled with dense and detailed analysis of Gordon's mission to Sudan. The author not only uses official papers by then in the public domain but quotes verbatim letters written by Gordon during the final stages of the siege of Khartoum.[56] The substance was a wholly irrelevant digression from the Russian narrative but it was hard to find a writer in contemporary England who remained immune to the popular swell of emotion that followed Gordon's death.

British poets found it much easier to convert the Gordon story into written form. One Cambridge undergraduate found a publisher for a sequence of 115 sonnets entitled *Khartoum and Thither*, narrating Gordon's triumphant arrival in

Khartoum and heroic defence of the city.[57] Another typical selection can be found in *Epitaphs on C.G. Gordon*, a stylish little anthology of thirty-one poems in Greek, Latin and English. The compiler was the editor of the *Journal of Education*, which had launched a competition with a prize of five guineas to compose a suitable epitaph for the hero of Khartoum. The entries poured in, all stressing heroism, selflessness and an almost messianic purpose.

> Not in his own cause Gordon drew the sword,
> Duty, not fame, his lode-star – at her call,
> Far in the East he tamed the Tartar horde,
> Held fate at bay from Khartoum's crumbling wall;
> The wide world mourned for him, twice glorified,
> He lived for others, and for others died.[58]

Many of these literary effusions were also highly politicised, having a measurable impact in their challenge to late Victorian imperialism. The most celebrated of these advocates of change was Blunt, whose strident anti-imperialist scourging echoed the impulse to overseas retrenchment that drove Gladstone. After failing to galvanise support in English society or politics for the ʿArābi revolution, let alone avert the 1882 British invasion, Blunt paid for his unpatriotic affiliation by being denounced as 'another ʿArābi in a frock coat' who should be shot alongside the colonel.[59] Left smarting and temporarily ostracised by society friends whose financial interests in Egypt were in jeopardy, the poet retaliated by predicting the eventual demise of British imperialism:

> Thou hast deserved men's hatred. They shall hate thee.
> Thou hast deserved men's fear. Their fear shall kill.
> Thou hast thy foot upon the weak. The weakest
> With his bruised head shall strike thee on the heel.[60]

Blunt and Gordon, despite their dramatically different lifestyles, maintained a regular exchange of letters in which they shared their loathing of 'the Parasite ring of Pashas' running Egypt.[61] The apparently affectionate tone of their correspondence, however, may have been misleading. Blunt adopted a remarkably blasé attitude to Gordon's death, enthusiastically welcoming the fall of Khartoum as 'unexpected and glorious news', an attitude that placed him in a tiny minority and endeared him to few in salon society.[62]

Another poet in whom sentiments of revulsion at the heavy hand of imperialism were translated into initially powerful but ultimately ambivalent verse was William Watson, who like Blunt owed a debt in his early years to the patronage of Dante Gabriel Rossetti.[63] In June 1885, coinciding almost exactly with the Hake edition of Gordon's Khartoum journals, Watson published in the *National Review* a series of fifteen sonnets collectively called *Ver Tenebrosum*, or 'The Gloomy Spring'.[64] A range of subjects are addressed, verse by verse: thus,

British glory 'well-nigh more resembles shame' (IX), while true patriotism is identified as a readiness to identify 'the unseemly blot' on England's 'whiteness' (VI). Government ministers are labelled 'purblind guides' (VII) and the 'Political Luminary' who gives Sonnet VIII its title – a figure assumed to be Gladstone – is denounced as 'Sire of huge sorrows . . . A man whose virtue, genius, grandeur, worth / Wrought deadlier ill than ages can undo'. Most immediately, however, the reader is struck by the venom of the opening sonnet, 'The Soudanese', a stark declaration of Watson's loathing of militarism in general and the British Army campaign against the Mahdī in particular.

> They wrong'd not us, nor sought 'gainst us to wage
> The bitter battle. On their God they cried
> For succour, deeming justice to abide
> In heaven, if banish'd from earth's vicinage.
> And when they rose with a gall'd lion's rage,
> We, on the captor's, keeper's, tamer's side,
> We, with the alien tyranny allied,
> We bade them back to their Egyptian cage.
> Scarce knew they who we were! A wind of blight
> From the mysterious far north-west we came,
> Our greatness now their veriest babes have learn'd,
> Where, in wild desert homes, by day, by night,
> Thousands that weep their warriors unreturn'd,
> O England, O my country, curse thy name!

The great Scottish writer, Robert Louis Stevenson, was similarly engaged by the Sudan crisis and its aftermath. By the summer of 1885, he was already well known as a light-hearted and occasionally cynical essayist, a literary columnist of some stature and the author of *Travels with a Donkey* and, most famously, *Treasure Island*. Less well known were his interests in politics both domestic and foreign. He wrote essays on unionism and the Irish Question and, in 1881, wrote in powerful terms about British involvement in the 'unmanly Transvaal war' in South Africa.[65]

Despite his perpetual struggle with health problems that brought him dangerously close to death on numerous occasions, Stevenson was able to monitor developments in Sudan closely. The fall of Khartoum, he commented to John Symonds shortly after the event, brought 'dark days of public dishonour'; as for Gordon's death, it was an outrage: 'England stands before the world dripping with blood and daubed with dishonour.'[66] Stevenson clearly separated Gordon the man from the political ministry whose agent he was. Unlike Blunt or Watson, however, Stevenson bottled up his anger and impotence. While applauding anyone who showed 'one spark of manly sensibility', for example those 'taking their names off the Gordon Memorial Committee rather than sit thereon with Gladstone', Stevenson had decided not even to write in protest to the Prime Minister: 'Why was I silent? I feel I have no right to blame anyone; but I won't write to the G.O.M.. I do really not see my way to any form of signature: unless 'your fellow criminal in the eyes of God', which might disquiet the proprieties.'[67]

Stevenson's suppressed resentment was later transferred, when in 1889 his poor health necessitated a transfer to the islands of Hawaii, to the cause of Samoa: a commitment to the independence of South Pacific islanders that was explicitly prompted by a sense of guilt at not having spoken out sufficiently in support of Gordon.

> I did not say then in the papers what I might have said before it was too late. I might not have been able to save Gordon, but at least I should feel I had done something. It was this thought that finally induced me to write my first letter to The Times about Samoa. I thought, I have lost one opportunity, I will not lose another.[68]

Art meets politics

On the left wing of British politics, the Gordon mission had provoked considerable antipathy. For many socialists and peace activists, already humiliated by their failure to muster the support of even Quaker MPs, let alone the wider population, to avert the invasion and occupation of Egypt in 1882, Gordon amounted to a 'stalking horse' for further imperialist meddling abroad. The International Arbitration and Peace Association organised a two-day conference in April 1884 to debate the Sudan crisis and Gordon's mission, but the outcome was weak and inconclusive, producing only a tepid resolution that armed interference in Egypt's internal affairs, a portfolio that ironically embraced Sudan, was 'unnecessary, impolitic and unjust'.[69]

Even after the fall of Khartoum, the movement was divided. In February 1885, hard on the news of Gordon's death, the Workmen's Peace Association, whose declared purpose was 'advocating the settlement of all international disputes by arbitration, and the establishment of a High Court of Nations for that purpose', gathered in London to call for a full military withdrawal from Sudan. But decades of Liberal loyalty were hard to reverse and confusion prevailed. As the Liberal MP Samuel Storey put it to his Memorial Hall audience: 'When a Tory Government went to war what violent opponents of war all the Liberals were (laughter) but where was the peace party now?'[70]

The Socialist League, by contrast, was cohesive, dynamic and effective at garnering favourable press coverage. The issue of Gordon and his Sudan deployment had played a large part in the establishment of the League in 1884, as William Morris and others parted company in acrimonious circumstances from Henry Hyndman, the authoritarian leader of the Social Democratic Federation. Hyndman had argued for a military rescue expedition to pluck Gordon from the siege of Khartoum, while Morris, ever suspicious of the authorities running

Egypt as a purely capitalist venture, on behalf of the bond-holders, took exactly the opposite view. One of his last actions as a member of the Federation was to propose and see passed a motion opposing any such expedition, even one mounted 'under the pretence of rescuing General Gordon'.[71]

Morris was passionately committed to the right of the Sudanese to self-determination and, when Gordon was killed in late January 1885, he stated quite starkly that Khartoum had 'fallen – into the hands of the people it belongs to', a position endorsed by the Socialist League.[72] On 16 February, the League despatched an internal resolution to a number of papers expressing its delight at the fall of Khartoum.[73] At a succession of meetings through the spring of 1885, Morris argued that 'the war in the Soudan was prompted by the capitalist class, with a view to the extension of their fields of exploitation' and that 'the victory gained by the Soudanese was a triumph of right over wrong won by a people struggling for their freedom.'[74]

Seen from this viewpoint, there was little to differentiate between Gordon and the Relief Expedition that had failed so narrowly to rescue him. Morris denounced the expedition as 'stealers and the spreaders of the blessings of shoddy civilisation', while five days earlier, the League had condemned the invasion of Sudan in a declaration published in the *Pall Mall Gazette*, the *Standard* and the *St James's Gazette*.[75] The resolution passed by the SL provisional Council stated that 'the invasion of the Soudan was undertaken with the covert intention of exploiting that country for the purposes of commercial greed; and that, therefore the check inflicted on the British invaders should be hailed by all supporters of the cause of the people as a triumph of right over wrong, of righteous self-defence over ruffianly brigandage'.[76] It was a position that culminated in the publication on 2 March 1885 of a four-page leaflet, the *Manifesto of the Socialist League on the Soudan War*, which urged the British people to 'protest against the wicked and infamous act of brigandage now being perpetrated for the interest solely of the "privileged" classes of this country . . . the foulest stream of well-planned hypocrisy and fraud that has ever disgraced the foreign policy even of this commercial age'.[77]

Nor was Gordon immune from the trenchant criticism of the left. 'It was quite necessary to attack the Gordon-worship which has been used as a stalking-horse for such wide spread murder,' Morris wrote in April 1885, concluding with a devastating critique of the late general's mission: 'He betrayed the trust reposed in him & used his military & administrative capacity for the purpose of bringing the Soudanese under the subjection of a vile tyranny. To make a hero of such a man is a direct attack on public morality.'[78]

Security, rivalry and vengeance

The socialist polemicist Annie Besant's 1885 pamphlet *Gordon Judged out of his own Mouth* was a devastatingly accurate personal critique in which she rehearsed Gordon's personal flaws with merciless accuracy. He was, she wrote, 'a straightforward, brave, soldier of fortune . . . trying to do his duty to the tyrant who hired him, while often disgusted by the acts entailed by that duty; fearless, hot-tempered, variable, inconsistent, often violent and unjust . . . possessed of arbitrary authority and often exercising it recklessly . . . sometimes grim, some-times mocking'. But Besant still believed that 'the rebuking voices' of England's working classes had effectively 'checked the statesmen and the pressmen who were using his name as the fiery cross to gather an army of revenge.'[79]

But the oratorical volume of the political left and the vilification of Gordon faded rapidly. Instead, his apotheosis followed hard on the heels of the condem-nation of Gladstone, who was neither knighted nor ennobled (although statues of Gladstone far outnumber those cast in honour of Gordon). By the mid-1890s, the power of the left had waned, while that of the Conservatives and fellow neo-imperialists grew strongly, encouraging those who, in Winston Churchill's words, dreamed of a 'bright or vague vision of Imperial power, of transconti-nental railways, of African Viceroys, of conquest and commerce.'[80] And, as Cynthia Behrman has noted, the general's survival in the 'mythology of culture' was lasting: 'There is nothing so heroic as a dead hero, especially one who has died in a dramatic and unnecessary way. . . . The fact that he was not reached in time led to a spasm of collective remorse and guilt, which led to a glorification of Gordon as a figure of tragedy, crucified for the sins of the nation.'[81]

Such sentiment contributed to the revival of Conservative political fortunes. Gladstone's newly apparent weakness, in large measure a consequence of the Gordon disaster, was dramatically exposed by the 1885 electoral setback and the ensuing 1886 general election ended Gladstone's domination of British politics for several years.[82] Conservative re-election led to a resurgence of imperialist sentiment within government and the consequent determination to retain, rather than evacuate, Egypt proper. Three factors played a crucial part: internal Egyptian reform, international colonial rivalry and security.

But where would the Conservatives focus their foreign policy? Salisbury's first instinct was to complete Gladstone's planned withdrawal from Egypt. Henry Drummond Wolff, the new British High Commissioner, conducted intensive regional diplomacy before proposing a dual British-Ottoman commission to oversee military and political reform in Egypt. But Baring had other plans. As Mowat has written, 'the reforms needed to make Egypt viable after a British withdrawal would take a considerable time . . . [and] British troops could not be withdrawn for many years to come.'[83]

But Baring's modified policy of *festina lente* on institutional reform was just one factor in persuading Salisbury of the merits of retaining Egypt. Much had changed in the years since the invasion of Egypt in September 1882, when the division of Africa among the European imperial powers had scarcely even begun, beyond King Leopold's far-sighted but cruelly inhumane investment in the Congo basin. In just three years, the incipient 'scramble' had already gone so far that for any aspirant colonial nation, as Britain became again with the election of Salisbury, the abandonment of any territory in which it had a commercial investment, military foothold or direct political control would be tantamount to announcing to France, Belgium, Italy, Germany and Portugal that it was theirs to fight over.

But it was security, the third strand of responsibility dictated by the retention of Egypt, that raised the weightiest issues pertaining to Sudan and eventually dictated forceful military intervention in the upper Nile districts.[84] Even setting aside imperial rivalries, the questions of the Nile water supply and the potential for Islamic unrest were priorities that the British authorities in Cairo made sure that the new cabinet in London maintained high on their foreign affairs agenda. In compiling the most impressive analysis to date of the 'water security' argument, Terje Tvedt has noted that 'several years before the decision to occupy the Sudan was officially taken', British specialists in hydrology and irrigation, frustrated by the loss to the Mahdī of the Nilometers at al-Roseires, Khartoum and Berber, were already discussing 'the necessity of controlling the Nile upstream.'[85]

Another security factor was the known hostility of the regime in Omdurman, now ruled by the Mahdī's successor, the Khalīfa ʿAbdullāhi. Anxieties were especially exacerbated after the attempted invasion of Egypt in 1889 by ʿAbd-al-Raḥman al-Nujūmi, a belligerent but poorly-planned initiative crushed by the British at the battle of Tūshka. It was Britain's good fortune that the Khalīfa's paranoia and determination to obliterate any potential rival for power led him to ensure the failure of the campaign by denying al-Nujūmi adequate supplies of food or ammunition.[86] Politicians like Sir Michael Hicks-Beach, the new Chancellor of the Exchequer, were convinced that 'Egypt could never be held to be permanently secured so long as a hostile power was in occupation of the Nile Valley up to Khartoum.'[87]

Still, there were many who believed that even an anti-European presence in Sudan was less dangerous to British interests in Egypt than a *rival* European presence. The clannishness, autocracy and disregard for public health or welfare prevailing in the Khalīfa's independent Sudan, where years of drought and serial smallpox epidemics were combined with renascent pre-Mahdīa tribal divisions, made the territory vulnerable to incursion from other colonial adventurers. By June 1894, Major Reginald Wingate, director of military intelligence in the Egyptian Army, was of the opinion that it was 'not the Khalifa's possible disintegration which will draw us into an expedition, it is the pressure of France and other European nations towards the Nile Valley which will force England to go to Khartoum.'[88]

In short, fear of France, Belgium and Italy was greater than fear of the Khalīfa and necessitated the creation of a buffer state to Egypt's south. King Leopold of the Belgians hoped to expand his African estates far beyond the Congo basin and was scheming to lease the entire southern Sudan as far north as Khartoum.[89] To the east, the Italians were engaged in a bitter three-way confrontation with the Abyssinian kingdom and the Khalīfa's forces. And the French were moving in the west, threatening to claim territory as far north as Fashoda on the White Nile, the site of an Egyptian garrison destroyed by the Mahdī. The French diplomatic position was that a non-military expedition would put Paris in a position to 'intervene usefully in settling the question of the Egyptian Sudan', in other words to make sure that at least Britain didn't get its hands on the territory.[90]

So the 'Fashoda Incident' of late 1898 was vindication for those who argued that, had Britain not advanced deep into Sudanese territory and destroyed the military power of the Khalīfa, the job would have been done by the French, who would then have consolidated imperial dominance over the Sahel, splitting British control of eastern Africa and threatening Egypt from the south. Such sentiments had made it a short logical progression to argue for the occupation of Sudan.

Some, like Wylde at Sawākin, made a moral argument for renewed British involvement: 'In God's name let us have a settlement of the question, and try to make some reparation for the amount of blood-guiltiness we have on our hands, and by our future behaviour strive to wash away the stain that disgraces the name of England in her dealings with the Soudan during the last few years.'[91] Baring in Cairo adopted a three-prong argument: morality, humanitarianism and revenge. Apparently able to shoulder the responsibility of Egyptian reform and still have time to monitor developments elsewhere, Baring argued strongly for more forceful intervention to the south. Seemingly forgetting his role in forcing the resignation of Muḥammad Sharīf's cabinet over the mandatory withdrawal from Sudan, he opined with breathtaking hypocrisy that 'a sense of shame was generally felt in Great Britain that under British auspices, Egyptian territory should have undergone such severe shrinkage'.[92] As early as 1891, Baring was citing the testimony of Fr Joseph Ohrwalder, a Kordofan missionary who escaped from the Khalīfa's detention in Omdurman, as evidence that nothing short of a full British occupation was desirable.

> Without doubt great discontent prevails. With the exception of the Baggara [al-Baqāra, the Khalīfa's tribe and military power-base], the whole population of the Soudan would welcome the re-establishment of Egyptian rule ... The stimulus of commercial interests, a desire to aid in the suppression of the slave trade, pity and commiseration for the inhabitants of the Soudan ... a well-founded opinion that, owing to its geographical situation, the Soudan cannot and should not be permanently separated from Egypt, and a very natural desire that the Egyptian Government should be reinstated ... are all so many elements tending in the same direction.[93]

This language directly echoed that used by senior British military commanders in Egypt, many of whom still felt in the mid-1890s the shame of their withdrawal from Sudan in the wake of Wolseley's failed Nile expedition. After all, had not Wolseley himself written to Qāsim al-Mūsa, the leader of the Shaiqīa, shortly after the fall of Khartoum: 'We mean to destroy the power of Mohammed Ahmed at Khartoum, no matter how long it may take us to do so; you know Gordon Pasha's countrymen are not likely to turn back from any enterprise they have begun until it has been fully accomplished'?[94]

This 'second chance' lobby found its most articulate and influential spokesman in Wingate, who was responsible for a literary trilogy that, in the uncompromising words of Peter Holt, 'should be regarded primarily as war-propaganda' through which 'the sensational presentation of events and personalities . . . helped to keep alive the emotions of 1885 until circumstances and opportunity made possible the reconquest of the Sudan.'[95] Common to all three of these propaganda volumes – Wingate's own *Mahdiism and the Egyptian Soudan*, Ohrwalder's *Ten Years Captivity in the Mahdi's Camp* and Rudolf Slatin's *Fire and Sword in the Sudan* – is the theme of destruction of a half-century of Egyptian-inspired civilising progress by the Mahdī's uprising.

More important than this retrospective denigration, however, is the challenge laid before the reader. Slatin concludes his account by expressing the hope 'that these, my experiences, may prove of some value when the time for action may arise, and when, if God wills, my services may be utilized in helping to abolish the rule of my tyrannical master and life-long enemy, the Khalifa Abdullahi, and re-establish in that country the Government authority I struggled with some measure of success, but, alas! vainly, to uphold.'[96] More explicitly, Ohrwalder (or Wingate) concludes his account with a rhetorical question: 'Mahdiism is founded on plunder and violence, and by plunder and violence it is carried on. . . . How long shall this condition of affairs continue? . . . How long shall Europe – and above all that nation which has first part in Egypt and the Soudan – which stands deservedly first in civilizing savage races, how long shall Europe and Great Britain watch unmoved the outrages of the Khalifa and the destruction of the Sudan people?'[97]

Wingate's publications harvested considerable press support. *The Times* greeted Ohrwalder as 'a thrilling tale of suffering and horrors, it has not been surpassed in recent years . . . The work gives us a clearer account of the origin and real character of the Mahdist movement than we have seen elsewhere.'[98] On 20 October 1892, favourable reviews appeared in several papers, including the *Graphic*, which noted that 'the horror of his narrative will carry his appeal deep into every English heart.'[99] So successful was Wingate's project that salon society was still buzzing over the grisly details at Christmas. An editorial in the *Morning Post* summarised prevailing attitudes about the ability of politicians to recognise when the time was ripe for forceful action: 'Englishmen in general can hardly look with much satisfaction upon the dealings of their country with the Soudan. . . . There may be much to be said against the advisability of interference . . . but when once the hand has been put to the plough the share must be driven through to the end. This is what we failed to recognise in Egypt ten years ago, and to this failure on our part may be traced the growth of the MAHDI's power and much of the anarchy that has since prevailed.'[100]

Slatin's offering also garnered plentiful reviews and, with British military action already underway on the Egypt/Sudan frontier, galvanised support for a renewed 'forward policy'. Wingate maximised official attention in advance of publication by citing Slatin as an impeccable source on French ambitions in the Bahr al-Ghazāl region. Aimed at promoting a 'maximum depth' invasion, his claims were absurdly overblown. No one in London, however, was privy to better information that would contradict the scary claims that 'the presence of foreigners unconcerned in the preservation of Egyptian interests ... would place them in such a predominating position as to render in a large measure valueless the occupation by Egypt of the remainder of the Egyptian Soudan.'[101] *The Times*, as always, led the way, gushing over Slatin's 'exciting and marvellous experiences' while praising the 'invaluable information towards the appreciation and solution of the great Soudan problem which the author does not conceal his conviction will still have to be settled for the security and legitimate satisfaction of the rulers of Egypt.'[102]

The invasion of Sudan

Thus the new policy of vengeance was cloaked with altruism. Nor was it only authors under the thumb of the military that contrasted 'Gordon's kindly paternal rule' with the 'prevailing anarchy, misery and misrule, the despairing outcry for help' in the Khalīfa's Sudan. Still, momentum for an invasion built up much more slowly among the political elite than among the military. Baring, for example, argued that an advance into Sudanese territory should wait until Egypt's military and financial capacities had been substantially reconstructed.[103] 'Before any reconquest could be entertained,' he explained, 'two conditions had to be fulfilled. In the first place, the Egyptian army would have to be made efficient. In the second place, not only had the solvency of the Egyptian Treasury to be assured, but funds had to be provided for the extraordinary expenditure which the assumption of an offensive policy would certainly involve.'[104] In this, he had the endorsement of Salisbury, who insisted that any military action be financially sustainable and risk-free.

Much has been written about the reconquest, one of the most dramatic incidents in Victorian Britain's imperial expansion. The central ideological principle, ever more publicly stated between 1890 and the first Dongola campaign in March 1896, was the reassertion of Nile Valley unity. This was a principle for which the Khedive Ṭawfīq and his civilian counsellors had been arguing since before the fall of Khartoum, on the grounds of both historic rights and water security. It was an idea that Winston Churchill endorsed in colourful terms:

> If the reader will look at a map of the Nile System, he cannot fail to be struck by its resemblance to a palm-tree. At the top the green and fertile area of the Delta spreads like the graceful leaves and foliage. The stem is

perhaps a little twisted, for the Nile makes a vast bend in flowing through the desert. South of Khartoum the likeness is again perfect, and the roots of the tree begin to stretch deeply into the Soudan. I can imagine no better illustration of the intimate and sympathetic connection between Egypt and the Southern Provinces.[105]

From 1892, when ʿAbbās Ḥilmī II inherited the Egyptian throne, such sentiments began to acquire even more explicitly nationalist overtones.[106] This did not sit well with the aspirations of the occupying power and there was more than a suggestion of the disingenuous in Britain's protestations of solidarity, even as the three architects of the invasion, Salisbury, Baring and Kitchener, plotted to use Egyptian money and Egyptian men to create what would become a de facto British entity. The hollowness of British solidarity is revealed by the fact that the railway constructed by Kitchener to transport the materiel essential for the invasion had a different gauge from the Egyptian main line.[107]

Baring later characterised his own contribution to this unique campaign, in which the Prime Minister in London allowed his proxy in Cairo to steer events, albeit with most day-to-day decisions abrogated to Kitchener, in modest terms, extolling the virtue of a hands-off civilian role. 'My own merits,' he wrote, 'such as they were, were of a purely negative character. . . . I abstained from mischievous activity, and I acted as check on the interference of others. I had full confidence in the abilities of the commander [and] encouraged him to pay no attention to those vexatious bureaucratic formalities with which, under the slang phrase of "red tape" our military system is overburdened.'[108]

Despite the 'fear factor' described above, Italian dominance in the Horn of Africa suited London's short-term strategic purposes and it was an Italian request for help, as the Khalīfa's troops gathered to retake the Italian-held town of Kassala, that irrevocably precipitated Britain's commitment in Sudan.[109] After the set-dressing provided by Wingate's propaganda machine, it was easy to muster support for a campaign against Gordon's killers. Baring, in short, was ready and Kitchener was given the green light to advance on Dongola on 12 March 1896.

Describing their motives for the invasion, British politicians in London and Cairo were diplomatically nimble. They portrayed it to the Khedive ʿAbbās Hilmi, who only learned of the plan after the army had received its marching orders, as the restoration of his lost dominions. To the French, the invasion was described as an Egyptian initiative to avert the Islamic threat on the southern border; and to the Sultan in Constantinople, still nominally the Khedive's overlord and prompted by the French to protest, as internal Egyptian business permissible under existing imperial sanctions.

For the likes of Kitchener, by now commanding the entire Egyptian Army, motivation was rather simpler. He was the archetypal servant and soldier of Empire. Hardened in Sudan's northern deserts during the failed 1884-5 relief expedition, he acquired fluent Arabic to liaise effectively with the northern tribes as an intelligence officer. Kitchener was married to the army, ambitious and obsessive about administrative efficiency, a man who never troubled to court popularity among superiors or junior officers. Like many fellow officers in Cairo, he itched to have a second chance against the men who had killed both his hero, Gordon, and his close friend, Lieutenant-Colonel Hamill-Stewart. What he hoped would be the extinction of Mahdism would serve as an additional by-product of victory.

The invasion was ruthlessly methodical, though neither inexorable, as is commonly believed, nor free of serious problems. It began smoothly enough, such minor Mahdist outposts as there were north of Berber falling with propor-tionally heavy casualties. Kitchener's force reached Akasha on 15 March 1896 and the Battle of Firket followed on 7 June. After a three-month delay caused by cholera and bad weather, the army pushed on up the Nile, reaching Kerma on 20 September and capturing Dongola itself without a fight three days later. By 26 September 1896, Kitchener was at Merowe: Dongola province was safely subdued to his rear, but there had been delays over logistics and money – and the cholera killed ten times as many soldiers as did the Sudanese.

The push south carried a still more dangerous risk: overstretch. So, with no one in London or Cairo hurrying his advance, Kitchener cautiously secured his line of communications and supply by constructing a railway across the Nubian Desert from Wādī-Ḥalfāʾ directly to Abū-Ḥamad, from which the Khalīfa's forces had first to be ejected. The first tracks were laid on 1 January 1897 and the railway reached Abū-Ḥamad on 31 October. Kitchener's 'flying column' inflicted heavy losses on the town's defenders in the second major engagement of the campaign, while his gunboat flotilla struggled up-river and rejoined the advance force at the end of August. Baring was all too aware of the risk of a large force cutting off Kitchener's retreat, a development that 'would, to say the least, have caused very serious embarrassment to . . . Kitchener.'[110] But by 31 August 1897, Kitchener was in control of Berber, the pivotal strategic point commanding not just the Nile route, but also access to the eastern desert route to Suakin that Gordon had so longed to see regained. Berber, like Dongola, surrendered without a fight after the local amīr, Zakī ʿUthmān, denied reinforcements by the Khalīfa, fell back on Shendi.

But then, wholly unexpectedly, Kitchener suffered a drastic loss of nerve, or at least a crisis of confidence in his own hybrid force. Fed up with reluctance of the politicians to fund what he thought necessary for military efficiency and physi-cally ill – indeed, his biographer says he was 'not far removed from a nervous collapse' – Kitchener submitted his resignation to Cairo on 18 October 1897, after nineteen months in the field and on the verge of his own final assault on the Khalīfa's capital at Omdurman.[111] His primary anxiety was a retaliatory attack by a substantial force under Maḥmūd Aḥmad from his fortified base at Metemma. Kitchener had no way of knowing that the amīr, faced with shortages of food and ammunition, desertions and internal power-struggles, was in no position to mount a serious counter-offensive during 1897 or 1898.[112] Kitchener feared that he would share the fate of Hicks and Gordon, becoming the third British general in command of Egyptian soldiers to be destroyed by the Sudanese.

So, at the beginning of November 1897 it seemed that the assault on Khartoum would have to be indefinitely postponed. Reinforcement by British units, however, made a material difference and made further delay at Berber intolerably wasteful. Although still profoundly anxious about the prospect of a massive retaliatory strike, Kitchener moved forward and when Maḥmūd Aḥmad's strike failed to emerge, his force, now spearheaded by the British Brigade, made short work of the limited opposition put up by the Khalīfa's troops on his renewed advance on Omdurman.

The remainder of the campaign featured two major engagements: the Battle of the Atbara on 8 April 1898 and the Battle of Omdurman on 2 September. The intervening summer period was spent in rest and recuperation while the river rose sufficiently to bring up supplies by armoured steamer. It is worth noting that the Anṣār failed to contest the passage of the Sabalūqa Gorge, although, anticipating opposition, Kitchener had sent part of his force via a large desert loop to circumnavigate the gorge's western heights.[113]

Months before Kitchener's final crushing victory over the Khalīfa's vast but outgunned armies among the Karari hills north of Omdurman, thought had been given to the administration of Sudan and the resolution formed 'to fly the British and Egyptian flags side by side', beginning with the capture of Khartoum.[114] The actual term 'condominium' had first been used by Gladstone as early as 28 June 1884 in a letter to Hartington in the context of the occupation of Egypt, not Sudan, by Britain.[115] But Baring, in self-satisfied tones, appropriated it as the resolution of what would otherwise be an 'insoluble dilemma':

> It occurred to me that the Sudan might be made neither English nor Egyptian, but Anglo-Egyptian. Sir Malcolm McIlwraith [a barrister specialising in Egyptian law] clothed this extremely illogical political conception in suitable legal phraseology. I must confess that I made the proposal with no very sanguine hopes that it would be accepted. Lord Salisbury, however . . . joyfully agreed to the creation of a hybrid State of a nature eminently calculated to shock the susceptibilities of international jurists.[116]

This hypothetical joint sovereignty might appear to have reflected a continuing political ambivalence about long-term involvement. In fact, legal niceties were never allowed to prejudice the way Sudan was actually administered, with the British making all the decisions and occupying the highest civil and military posts, while the Egyptians paid. This was the logical consequence of an occupation that was achieved with British troops in a primary role. In other words, Egypt's *a priori* right to tenure based on possession was extinguished. Writing soon after the establishment of the Condominium, Henry Traill expressed satisfaction that historical justice had been done, while Britain had secured lasting regional influence:

There is no Continental Government or people who fail to perceive that the restoration to Egypt of that vast tract of territory which was rent sixteen years ago from the dominions of the Khedive . . . has revealed new responsibilities which Great Britain alone can discharge. Nor can there be any one among them who doubts that, whatever efforts may be made either by diplomacy or by arms to dislodge her, she will never suffer herself to be driven from this post of duty by anything short of the overthrow of her naval supremacy and the collapse of her Empire.[117]

The newly ennobled Lord Kitchener of Khartoum remained in Gordon's former residence, a building-site within a larger building-site. He was the first Governor-General of the new order but just the latest in a long line of imposed foreign viceroys. During the fifty-six years of Condominium rule, Britain profited from its inheritance of some elements of modernity, dating in broadest terms back to the Egyptian invasion but more specifically to Ismāʿīl's drive to develop an efficient imperial infrastructure. The British did it all more systematically and fairly, replacing the Khalīfa's secular despotism with what Kitchener called 'an era of justice and kindly treatment'. But an occupation it remained, with the ghost of Gordon stalking the rubble-strewn streets.

Notes

Introduction

1. *Hansard*, Series 3, vol. 301 (13 August 1885-12 January 1886), cc. 31-2.
2. The well-educated son of a boat-builder from the Dongola region, Muḥammad Aḥmad had been appointed a *sheikh* and given the leadership of an important Sufi sect, the Sammānīa, based at Jazīra Aba on the White Nile.
3. Muḥammad Aḥmad al-Mahdī also described himself as *khalīfat rasūl Allah*, Successor to the Prophet Muḥammad. I have described the Sudanese side of this protracted struggle in Fergus Nicoll, *The Sword of the Prophet: The Mahdi of Sudan and the Death of General Gordon* (Stroud, Sutton Publishing, 2004).
4. The rulers of Egypt were thus given the title 'Governor' (*walī*). Ismāʿīl Ibrāhīm, who ruled from 18 January 1963 to 26 June 1879, when he was deposed by European creditors, was awarded a promotion to Khedive (from Persian *ḳadīv*, 'prince') by Sultan Abdülaziz in Constantinople; Richard Hill, *A Biographical Dictionary of the Sudan* (Oxford, Clarendon, 1967), pp. 68-9.
5. John Morley, *The Life of William Ewart Gladstone* (3 vols.) (London, Macmillan, 1903), vol. 2, p. 236. The clearest analysis of the ʿArābi phenomenon, using a wide range of Egyptian sources, is Juan Cole, *Colonialism and Revolution in the Middle East: Social and Cultural Origins of Egypt's ʿArābi Movement* (Princeton, PUP, 1993).
6. British Library (BL), Supplementary Gladstone Papers, Add. Ms. 56452, ff. 42-3, cited in Stephanie Laffer, 'Gordon's Ghosts: British Major-General Charles George Gordon and his Legacies' (Tallahassee, Florida State University PhD thesis, 2010), p. 43.
7. Granville Leveson-Gower, 2nd Earl Granville (1815-1891), served as Foreign Secretary from 1870-4 and 1880-5.
8. Letter dated 1888; *Lord Edmond Fitzmaurice, The Life of Granville George Leveson Gower: Second Earl Granville, K.G., 1815-1891 (2 vols.)* (London, Longmans, Green & Co., 1905), vol. 2, p. 401.

9. George Buckle (ed.) *The Letters of Queen Victoria: Second Series, 1879-1885* (3 vols.) (London: John Murray, 1928), vol. 3, p. 597.

10. Richard Shannon, *Gladstone: Heroic Minister 1865-1898* (London, Allen Lane, 1999), pp. 363-4.

11. Morley, *William Ewart Gladstone*, vol. 3, pp. 168-9.

12. Interview in *Belford's Magzine* (New York), September 1890.

13. The phase was first used by the Conservative MP Ellis Ashmead-Bartlett in the House of Commons on 15 March 1885; *Hansard*, vol. 285, cc. 1656-7. It was afterwards routinely adopted by all Gladstone's critics and by many objective historians, e.g. Alan Theobald, *The Mahdīya: A History of the Anglo-Egyptian Sudan, 1881-1899* (London, Longmans, 1951), p. 105.

14. Ronald Robinson and John Gallagher (with Alice Denny) (eds.), *Africa and the Victorians: The Official Mind of Imperialism* (London: Macmillan, 1961), p. 89.

15. Ibid., p. 115.

16. A.B. Cooke and John Vincent, *The Governing Passion: Cabinet Government and Party Politics in Britain, 1885-86* (Brighton: The Harvester Press, 1974), p. 32.

17. Morley, *Life of Gladstone*, vol. 3, p. 170.

18. *Hansard*, vol. 285, cc. 1656-7.

19. Annie Besant, *Gordon Judged out of his Own Mouth* (London, Freethought Publishing Co., 1885), p. 16.

20. Elizabeth Rundle Charles, *Three Martyrs of the Nineteenth Century: Studies from the Lives of Livingstone, Gordon, and Patteson* (London, Society for Promoting Christian Knowledge, 1885), p. 271.

21. Paul Auchterlonie, 'From the Eastern Question to the Death of General Gordon: Representations of the Middle East in the Victorian Periodical Press, 1876-1885', *British Journal of Middle Eastern Studies* 28/1 (2001), pp. 5-24.

22. Fergus Nicoll, 'Review: *Gordon, Victorian Hero* by C. Brad Faught', *Journal of the Society for Army Historical Research* (88/2010): 344-6.

23. Demetrius Boulger, *Life of Gordon* (2 vols.) (London, T. Fisher Unwin, 1896), vol. 2, p. 274.

24. Northbrook to Ripon, dated 13 February 1884; BL, Ripon Papers, Add. Ms. 43573, f. 85.

25. Stephen Gwynn, *The Life of the Rt. Hon. Sir Charles W. Dilke, Bart., M.P.* (2 vols., ed. Gertrude Tuckwell) (London: John Murray, 1917), vol. 2, p. 41.

26. Dudley Bahlman (ed.), *The Diary of Sir Edward Walter Hamilton, 1880-1885* (2 vols.) (Oxford, Clarendon Press, 1972), vol. 2, pp. 545 (23 January 1884) and 611 (6 June 1884).

27. Todd Gray Willy, 'The Agitation in Parliament and England over Charles George "Chinese" Gordon and his Mission to the Sudan: January 1884 to February 1885' (Iowa City: University of Iowa PhD thesis, 1962), p. 77.

28. A. Egmont Hake, *The Journals of Major-General C.G. Gordon, C.B., at Kartoum* (London: Kegan, Paul, Trench & Co., 1885).

29. Geoffrey Drage, *Cyril: A Romantic Novel* (London: W.H. Allen & Co., Ltd., 1889), p. 499.

30. Richard Hill, 'Review of Gerald Sparrow's Gordon: Mandarin and Pasha', in *Victorian Studies Dec. 1963* (Bloomington, Indiana University, 1963), pp. 210-12.

31. R Bertrand Russell, *Freedom and Organization (1814-1914)* (London, Allen & Unwin, 1934), p. 460.

32. Blunt letter to Gordon, dated March 1884, quoted in Elizabeth Longford, *A Pilgrimage of Passion: The Life of Wilfrid Scawen Blunt* (London, Weidenfeld & Nicolson, 1979), p. 209.

33. Joseph Ohrwalder, *Ten Years' Captivity in the Mahdī's Camp, 1882-1892* (London, Sampson Low Marston & Co., 1892); Rudolf Carl Slatin, *Fire and Sword in the Sudan: A Personal Narrative of Fighting and Serving the Dervishes, 1879-1895* (London, Edward Arnold, 1896).

34. Martin Daly, *The Sirdar: Sir Reginald Wingate and the British Empire in the Middle East* (Philadelphia, American Philosophical Society, 1997), pp. 45-7 and 70-8.

35. *The Monthly Packet* (56/1885), p. 182.

Chapter 1

1.   William Gladstone, 'England's Mission', in *The Nineteenth Century* 4 (1878), p. 570.

2.   Gladstone's re-election (Liberals 353 seats; Conservatives 238; Home Rulers 61) overturned six years of Tory rule under Benjamin Disraeli, who was subsequently raised to the House of Lords as Lord Beaconsfield.

3.   *The Times*, 27 March 1880, p. 9.

4.   Russell, *Freedom and Organization*, p. 460.

5.   R.C. Mowat, 'From Liberalism to Imperialism: The Case of Egypt 1875-1887', *The Historical Journal* 16/1 (1973), pp. 109-10.

6.   John Newsinger, 'Liberal Imperialism and the Occupation of Egypt in 1882', in *Race & Class* 49/3 (2008), pp. 55-7, presents a useful overview of the Midlothian campaign.

7.   William Gladstone, *Political Speeches in Scotland, March and April 1880* (2 vols.) (Edinburgh, Andrew Elliot, 1880), vol. 1, pp. 115-17.

8.   Gladstone, 'England's Mission', pp. 567 and 569.

9.   William Gladstone, 'Aggression on Egypt and Freedom in the East', *The Nineteenth Century* 2 (1877), pp. 149-66.

10. James S. Cotton and Edward J. Payne, *Colonies and Dependencies* (London, Macmillan & Co., 1883), p. 114.

11. Theodore Hoppen, *The Mid-Victorian Generation 1846-1886* (part of *The New Oxford History of England*) (Oxford, Clarendon, 1998), p. 656.

12. Prof. Sir John Seeley, *Expansion of England: Two Courses of Lectures* (London: Macmillan, 1883).

13. Richard Shannon, *Gladstone: Heroic Minister 1865-1898* (London, Allen Lane, 1999), p. 73.

14. Letter dated 18 February 1883; BL, Macmillan Archive, Add. Mss. 55074, ff. 43-4 and 47-8.

15. Seeley, *Expansion of England*, p. 51.

16. Ibid., pp. 220-2.

17. Khartoum Journal entry for 26 September 1884; BL, Gordon Papers, Add. Ms. 34475 (vol. 2), f. 29.

18. Henry Traill, *England, Egypt, and the Sudan* (London: Archibald Constable & Co., Ltd., 1900), p. 62.

19. Wilfrid Scawen Blunt, *Secret History of the English Occupation of Egypt: A Personal Narrative of Events* (New York, Knopf, 1922), pp. 180-1.

20. John Newsinger, 'Liberal Imperialism and the Occupation of Egypt in 1882', *Race & Class* 49/3 (2008), p. 56.

21. Robert Walling (ed.), *The Diaries of John Bright* (London, Cassell, 1930), pp. 487-8.

22. Morley, *William Ewart Gladstone*, vol. 2, p. 243.

23. Bright to Joseph Chamberlain, 4 January 1883, Birmingham University Library, Chamberlain Papers, 5/7/30, quoted in Eugenio Biagini, 'Exporting "Western and Beneficient Institutions": Gladstone and Empire, 1880-1885', *Gladstone Centenary Essays* (eds. David Bebbington and Roger Swift) (Liverpool, LUP, 2000), p. 206.

24. Bahlman, *Sir Edward Walter Hamilton*, vol. 1, p. 339.

25. William Butler, *Sir William Butler: An Autobiography* (London, Constable, 1913), p. 248.

26. John Darwin, *The Empire Project: The Rise and Fall of the British World System, 1830-1970* (Cambridge, CUP, 2009), pp. 72-5.

27. A.G. Hopkins, 'The Victorians and Africa: A Reconsideration of the Occupation of Egypt, 1882', *JAH* 27/2 (1986), p. 385.

28. Newsinger, 'Liberal Imperialism', p. 70.

29. Daly, *The Sirdar*, p. 13.

30. Kew, Granville Papers, PRO 30/29/127.

31. Agatha Ramm (ed.), *The Political Correspondence of Mr. Gladstone and Lord Granville, 1876-1886* (2 vols.) (Oxford, Clarendon Press, 1962), vol. 2, pp. 125 and 127.

32. Robinson and Gallagher, *Africa and the Victorians*, p. 21.

33. Robert T. Nightingale, *The Personnel of the British Foreign Office and Diplomatic Service, 1851-1929* (London, The Fabian Society, 1930), p. 3.

34. Kew, Granville Papers, PRO 30/29/126.

35. Colin Matthew (ed.), *The Gladstone Diaries: With Cabinet Minutes and Prime Ministerial Correspondence* (14 vols.) (Oxford, Clarendon, 1986), vol. 10, p. 361.

36. Ramm, *Political Correspondence*, vol. 1, pp. 451-6.

37. A firman (Persian: *farmān*, 'edict') was an official document issued under the seal of the Ottoman or Egyptian ruler.

38. Earl Cromer [Sir Evelyn Baring], *Modern Egypt* (2 vols.) (London: Macmillan, 1908), vol. 1, p. 301.

39. Sir Edward Malet (1837-1908), a highly experienced diplomat, was Sir Evelyn Baring's predecessor as British Agent in Cairo.

40. Nicoll, *Sword of the Prophet*, pp. 98-102 and 117-24; also Thomas Archer, *War in Egypt and the Soudan: An Episode in the History of the British Empire* (4 vols.) (London: Blackie & Son, 1886), vol. 3, pp. 5-7.

41. Malet to Granville, dated 26 October 1882; No. 58 in *Egypt No. 1 (1883) Further Correspondence Respecting the Affairs of Egypt.*

42. Malet to Granville, No. 65 (with Inclosure) in *Egypt No. 1 (1882).*

43. *Daily News*, 13 November 1882, p. 4.

44. Malet to Granville, dated 28 October 1882, No. 65 in *Egypt No. 1 (1883).*

45. Granville to Dufferin, No. 83 in ibid.

46. Arthur Ponsonby, *Henry Ponsonby: Queen Victoria's Private Secretary: His Life from His Letters* (London, Macmillan, 1942), p. 229.

47. *Hansard*, vol. 281 (2-19 July 1883), c. 1675.

48. Ibid., vol. 281, c. 1676.

49. Buckle, *Letters of Queen Victoria*, vol. 3, p. 455; Angus Hawkins and John Powell (eds.), *The Journal of John Wodehouse, First Earl of Kimberley, for 1862-1902* (London, Royal Historical Society, 1997), p. 498.

50. *Hansard*, vol. 281, c. 1676.

51. Frederick Temple Hamilton-Temple-Blackwood (1826-1902), 1st Lord Dufferin, was British Ambassador to Constantinople when he was seconded to Cairo as Special Commissioner, charged with drafting a new constitution to separate Egypt from Ottoman rule.

52. Ibid., vol. 276 (15 Feb-9 March 1883), c. 580.

53. *The Times*, 23 August 1881, p. 3.

54. Ibid., 20 December 1881, p. 5, and 20 February 1883, p. 5.

55. Dufferin to Granville, No. 44 in *Egypt No. 13 (1883) Correspondence Respecting the Affairs of Egypt.*

56. Baring to Granville, No. 38 in Egypt No. 1 (1884).

57. Granville to Hartington; No. 54 in ibid.

58. Letter dated 15 November, 1883; Matthew, Gladstone Diaries, vol. 11, p. 59.

59. Granville to Malet, 8 August 1883, No. 65 in *Egypt No. 22 (1883) Further Correspondence Respecting the Affairs of Egypt.*

60. Dufferin to Granville, 6 February 1883; No. 38 in *Egypt No. 6 (1883) Further Correspondence Respecting Reorganization in Egypt*; also Dufferin to Granville, 2 April 1883, No. 39 in *Egypt No. 13 (1883).*

61. Dufferin to Granville, 2 April 1883, No. 39 in ibid.

62. House of Commons, 12 February 1884; *Hansard*, vol. 284, c. 718.

63. Sir Samuel White Baker, 'The Soudan and its Future', *Contemporary Review* 45/65 (1884), pp. 77-80.

64. Buckle, *Letters of Queen Victoria*, vol. 3, p. 447.

65. Ibid., vol. 3, pp. 449-50.

66. Letter dated 2 November 1882; ibid., vol. 3, p. 357.

67. C. Brad Faught, *Gordon: Victorian Hero* (Washington, Potomac Books Inc., 2008).

68. Laffer, 'Gordon's Ghosts', pp. 19-24.

69. Gordon served as Governor of Equatoria from 1874-6 (under Gov.-Gen. Ismāʿīl Ayūb) and as Governor-General from 18 February 1877 to 8 December 1879.

70. Alice Moore-Harell, *Egypt's Africa Empire: Samuel Baker, Charles Gordon and the Creation of Equatoria* (Brighton, Sussex Academic Press, 2010). Gordon's own correspondence from the period was published as George Birkbeck Hill (ed.), *Colonel Gordon in Central Africa, 1874-79, from Letters and Documents* (London, T. de la Rue & co., 1881).

71. *The Morning Post*, 27 December 1883, p. 3.

72. Neal Ascherson, *The King Incorporated: Leopold II in the Age of Trusts* (London, Allen & Unwin, 1963), p. 123.

73. Lt.-Col. Seton Churchill, *General Gordon: A Christian Hero* (London: James Nisbet & Co., Ltd., 1904), pp. 182-3.

74. Charles Chenevix Trench, *Charley Gordon: An Eminent Victorian Reassessed* (London: Allen Lane, 1978), p. 179. See also the Army List, March 1882, p. 33, and November 1882, p. 58.

75. Letter from 'One who Knows the Facts', *Daily News*, 20 December 1882, p. 3.

76. John Flint, *Cecil Rhodes* (London, Hutchinson, 1974), pp. 56-7.

77. Quoted in Charles Chaillé Long, *The Three Prophets: Chinese Gordon, Mohammed-Ahmed (El Maahdi), Arabi Pasha* (New York, 1884), p. 40.

78. Ascherson, *The King Incorporated*, p. 124. See also R.P.P. Ceulemans, 'Les Tentatives de Léopold II pour Engager le Colonel Charles Gordon au Service de l'Association Internationale Africaine, 1880', *Zaïre 12 (1958)*, pp. 251-74.

79. Sir Edward Cook, *The Life of Florence Nightingale* (2 vols.) (London, Macmillan, 1913), vol. 2, pp. 328-9.

80. Wolseley, the hero of al-Ṭall al-Kabīr, was by this time Adjutant-General at the War Office, in charge of all administrative, organisational and personnel matter for the entire army.

81. Sir George Arthur (ed.), *The Letters of Lord and Lady Wolseley* (London, Heinemann, 1922), p. 122.

82. Kew, Foreign Office Papers, Foreign Office Papers, FO 78/3442; see also Makkī Shibeika, *British Policy in the Sudan 1882-1902* (London: Geoffrey Cumberledge, 1952), p. 146.

83. Memorandum dated 29 September 1882; Inclosure in Malet to Granville, 2 October 1882, No. 37 in *Egypt No. 1 (1884)*.

84. Verney to Granville, 17 November 1882; Kew, Granville Papers, PRO 30/29/168.

85. Dufferin to Granville, dated 18 November 1882, No. 27 in *Egypt No. 2 (1883) Correspondence Respecting Reorganization in Egypt*.

86. Ponsonby to Granville, 24 December 1882; Kew, G/D 29/138, cited in Shibeika, *British Policy*, p. 147. This letter is conspicuously absent from Buckle, *Letters of Queen Victoria*, vol. 3, pp. 384-7.

87. Tony Little, 'Gladstone, Granville and Ireland, 1885-6' (Lecture given at Gladstone Conference, Hawarden Castle, 2010), pp. 10-11.

88. Malet to Granville, 1 November 1882; Kew, Foreign Office Papers, FO 78/3442.

89. Granville memorandum on conversation with Gordon, 18 November 1882; Kew, G/D 29/168. This important meeting is a rare omission in Chenevix Trench, *Charley Gordon*, p. 180.

90. Northbrook to Granville, 23 November 1882, Kew G/D 29/138.

91. Wilfrid Blunt, *Gordon At Khartoum: Being a Personal Narrative of Events* (London, Stephen Swift & Co., 1911), pp. 12-13.

92. Boulger, *Life of Gordon*, p. 281.

93. Lt.-Col. Stewart, who had already been active in Egypt since the invasion, was accidentally demoted in Granville to Malet, No. 61 in *Egypt No. 1 (1883)*: ' . . . if it is safe you may send Captain Stewart to the Soudan to report on the state of that district'.

94. Ramm, *Political Correspondence*, vol. 1, pp. 453-4.

95. Sudan Archive, University of Durham (SAD), Stewart Papers, 896/3, pp. 3-8. The Durham archive contains (Stewart Papers, 896/3-6) Stewart's journal as well as his telegrams to Malet. Stewart began in December 1882 and began transmitting brief updates on the activities of the Mahdī and General ʿAbd-al-Qādir to Malet and Dufferin in Cairo, who in turn passed them on to London; Nos. 2, 8, 22, 40 and 45 in *Egypt No. 5 (1883) Further Correspondence Respecting the Affairs in Egypt* and Nos. 5, 9, 10, 13, 16, 19, 21, 24, 25, 26, 28, 29, 31, 38 and 43 in *Egypt No. 13 (1883) Correspondence Respecting the Affairs of Egypt*. Despite having to send these prolific updates, Stewart was able to complete his authoritative final report by 9 February 1883: *Egypt No. 11 (1883) Report on the Soudan by Lieutenant-Colonel Stewart*. See also W. Melville Pimblett, *Story of the Soudan War: From the Rise of the Revolt July, 1881, to the Fall of Khartoum and death of Gordon, Jan., 1885* (London, Remington & Co., 1885), pp. 18-21.

96. Nos. 2, 8, 22, 40 and 45 in *Egypt No. 5 (1883) Further Correspondence Respecting the Affairs in Egypt* and Nos. 5, 9, 10, 13, 16, 19, 21, 24, 25, 26, 28, 29, 31, 38 and 43 in *Egypt No. 13 (1883) Correspondence Respecting the Affairs of Egypt*.

Chapter 2

1. Major-General William W. Loring, *A Confederate Soldier in Egypt* (New York, Dodd, Mead & Co., 1884), pp. 272-3.

2. Martin Daly (ed.), *The Road to Shaykan: Letters of General William Hicks Pasha, Written During the Sennar and Kordofan Campaigns, 1883* (Durham, University of Durham, 1983).

3. Dufferin to Granville, 6 February 1883, No. 38 in *Egypt No. 6 (1883)*.

4. Granville to W. Chauncey Cartwright, dated 7 May 1883; No. 57 in ibid.

5. French original in Inclosure, Malet to Granville, 28 May 1883, No. 23 in *Egypt No. 22 (1883)* .

6. Robert Wilson, *The Life and Times of Queen Victoria* (4 vols.) (London: Cassell, 1901), vol. 4, p. 670.

7. *The Times*, 24 November 1883, p. 5.

8. De Coëtlogon was deputy to Governor-General ʿAlā al-Dīn Ṣiddīq, who was killed alongside Hicks; Hill, *Biographical Dictionary*, p. 111.

9. Baring to Granville, No. 96 in *Egypt No. 1 (1884)* .

10. Archer, *War in Egypt and the Soudan*, vol. 3, p. 42.

11. Northbrook to Ripon, dated 13 December 1883; BL, Ripon Papers, Add. Ms. 43573, ff. 56-7.

12. *Liberté*, 23 November 1883.

13. Augustus Wylde, *'83 to '87 in the Soudan: With an Account of Sir William Hewett's Mission to King John of Abyssinia* (2 vols.) (London, Remington & Co., 1888), vol. 1, pp. 5-6.

14. ʿUthmān Abū-Bakr Diqna was appointed leader of the eastern campaign on 8 May 1883 by personal order of the Mahdī. He harassed government garrisons and rallied regional clans to attack Egyptian and British forces in a series of battles on the Red Sea coast.

15. Ibid., vol. 1, p. 1.

16. William Gladstone, *The Bulgarian Horrors and the Question of the East* (London, John Murray, 1876), p. 2.

17. Bahlman, *Sir Edward Walter Hamilton*, vol. 2, p. 613.

18. Nicoll, *Sword of the Prophet*, pp. 160-3.

19. Bernard Mallet, *Thomas George, Earl of Northbrook, G.C.S.I.: A Memoir* (London, Longmans, Green & Co., 1908), p. 178.

20. Frank Power, *Letters from Khartoum: Written During the Siege* (London: Sampson, Low, Marston, Searle & Rivington, 1885), p. 53.

21. Bernard Holland, *The Life of Spencer Compton, Eighth Duke of Devonshire* [Lord Hartington] (2 vols.) (London: Longmans, Green & Co., 1911), vol. 1, p. 411.

22. Hartington to Granville, 23 November 1883; ibid., vol. 1, pp. 411-12.

23. Henry Patterson, *The Imâm Mahdi; or The Moslem Millennium, from the Koran and Authentic Traditions* (London: Hamilton, Adams & Co., 1884), p. 63.

24. *The Times*, 15 December 1883, p. 9.

25. Ibrāhīm Muḥammad ʿAlī ʿAbbās, 'The British Debate on the Containment of

the Sudanese Mahdist Revolution, November 1883-February 1885', *Adab* 2-3 (1975), p. 22.

26. Charles Issawi (ed.), *The Economic History of the Middle East 1800-1914* (Chicago, UCP, 1966), p. 19.

27. ʿAbbās, 'The British Debate', p. 20.

28. Dufferin to Baring, 10 December 1883; Kew, Cromer Papers, FO 633/7.

29. Derek Welsby, *Sudan's First Railway: The Gordon Relief Expedition and the Dongola Campaign* (London, Sudan Archaeological Research Society, 2011), pp. 1-2.

30. Robert Felkin, 'The Egyptian Soudan', *The Scottish Geographical Magazine* 1/6 (June 1885), pp. 235-6.

31. *The Times*, 9 January 1883, p. 3.

32. *Pall Mall Gazette*, 9 January 1884, p. 9.

33. Terje Tvedt, *The River Nile and its Economic, Political, Social and Cultural Role: An Annotated Bibliography* (Bergen: UBP, 2000), p. 26.

34. *The Times*, 7 December 1883, p. 7.

35. Sir Samuel Baker, 'Egypt's Proper Frontier', *The Nineteenth Century* 89 (July 1884), pp. 41-2.

36. Ibid., pp. 41-2.

37. Granville met Cross in London on 29 December 1883; Cross to Granville, dated 5 January 1884; Kew, Granville Papers, PRO 30/29/146.

38. Ramm, *Political Correspondence*, vol. 1, p. 456.

39. *Evening Standard*, 6 February 1884, p. 8.

40. Gladstone note following 22 November cabinet meeting; Matthew, *Gladstone Diaries*, vol. 11, p. 62.

41. Granville to Mururus Pasha, No. 143 in *Egypt No. 1 (1884)* .

42. Letter dated 27 November; Matthew, *Gladstone Diaries*, vol. 11, p. 66.

43. Firman of investiture dated 19 Shaʿbān 1296; Chaillé Long, *Three Prophets*, p. 230 fn.

44. Cromer, *Modern Egypt*, vol. 2, pp. 334-5.

45. Baring to Granville, No. 145 in *Egypt No. 1 (1884)*.

46. Granville to Baring, No. 151 in ibid.

47. Mallet, *Earl of Northbrook*, p. 175.

48. Victoria to Granville, in Buckle, *Letters of Queen Victoria*, vol. 3, p. 469.

49. Traill, *England, Egypt, and the Sudan*, pp. 67-8.

50. Cromer, *Modern Egypt*, p. 392 fn.

51. The court of the Sultan, and hence the Ottoman Empire more widely, was known as the 'Sublime Porte' after the 'Lofty Gate' (*bāb al-ʿālī*) of the Grand Vizier's residence and administrative headquarters near Topkapi Palace in Constantinople.

52. Letter dated 2 January 1884 (translated from French original), enclosed in Baring to Granville, Inclosure in No. 204 in *Egypt No. 1 (1884)* .

53. Cromer, *Modern Egypt*, vol. 1, p. 368.

54. Baring to Granville, No. 204 in *Egypt No. 1 (1884)*.

55. Baring to Granville, No. 109 in ibid. For brief biographies, see Harold Raugh, *The Victorians At War, 1815-1914: An Encyclopedia of British Military History* (New York, ABC-CLIO Ltd., 2004), pp. 42, 311-12 and 346-7.

56. Buckle, *Letters of Queen Victoria*, vol. 3, pp. 455-7.

57. Lt.-Gen. Sir Frederick Stephenson, *At Home and on the Battlefield: Letters from the Crimea, China and Egypt, 1854-1888* (London, John Murray, 1915), p. 311.

58. Baker to Baring, 17 January 1884; Kew, Cromer Papers, FO 633/7.

59. Gladstone's notes of the meeting; Matthew, *Gladstone Diaries*, vol. 11, p. 94.

60. Granville to Baring, 4 January 1884, No. 209 in *Egypt No. 1 (1884)*.

61. Cromer, *Modern Egypt*, vol. 1, p. 382; this note was subsequently published as No. 210 (also 4 January 1884) in *Egypt No. 1 (1884)*.

62. Afaf Lutfi al-Sayyid, *Egypt and Cromer: A Study in Anglo-Egyptian Relations* (London, John Murray, 1968), p. 58.

63. Henry Traill, *Lord Cromer: A Biography* (London, Bliss, Sands & Co., 1897), p. 90.

64. Wylde, *'83 to '87*, vol. 1, p. 85.

65. Baron Karl de Malortie, *Here There and Everywhere: Being the Second Part of "'Twixt Old Times and New"* (London, Ward & Downey, Ltd., 1895), p. 195.

66. ʿAbd-al-Moneim Muḥammad Omar, *The Soudan Question: Based on British Documents* (Cairo, Misr Press, 1952), pp. 31-2.

67. George Stronach and George Halkett, *The Egyptian Red Book* (Edinburgh, William Blackwood & Sons, 1885), p.6.

68. de Malortie, *Here There and Everywhere*, pp. 189-91.

69. Stephenson, *At Home and on the Battlefield*, p. 311.

70. Nūbār Nubārian (1825-99) had served every Egyptian ruler from Muḥammad ʿAlī, the original Ottoman *wāli*, to Ismāʿīl. When the British forced Ismāʿīl's removal by the Sultan in 1879, Nūbār began a five-year period in the political wilderness before Baring offered him the post of Prime Minister.

71. Matthew, *Gladstone Diaries*, vol. 11, p. 103.

72. Roger Owen, 'The Brismes Annual Lecture 2004: Biography and Empire: Lord Cromer (1841-1917) Then and Now', in *British Journal of Middle Eastern Studies* (32 (1), May 2005), p. 6.

73. Earl of Cromer [Sir Evelyn Baring], *Political and Literary Essays, 1908-1913* (3 vols.) (London, Macmillan, 1913-16), vol. 1, p. 12.

74. Baron Samuel Selig de Kusel, *An Englishman's Recollections of Egypt 1863-1887* (London: John Lane, 1915), pp. 252-3.

75. Sir Evelyn Wood, *From Midshipman to Field Marshal* (2 vols.) (London, Methuen, 1906), vol. 2, p. 180.

76. Letter to Sir Henry Ponsonby, dated 1 February 1884; Ponsonby, *Henry Ponsonby*, p. 228.

77. Roger Owen, 'The Influence of Lord Cromer's Indian Experience on British Policy in Egypt 1883-1907', in *St Antony's Papers*, No. 17 (London, 1965).
78. 'Abbās, 'The British Debate', p. 5.
79. Baring to Granville, 3 December 1883, No. 150 in *Egypt No. 1 (1884)* has a detailed breakdown of remaining Egyptian troops in Sudan.
80. Baring to Granville, No. 3 in *Egypt No. 2 (1884) Correspondence Respecting General Gordon's Mission to Egypt.*
81. *The Times*, 21 January 1884, p. 5.
82. Stephenson, *Battlefield*, p. 314.
83. John Bowen, 'The Conflict of East and West in Egypt. III: The Sûdan and the Mahdi', in *Political Science Quarterly* 1/4 (1886), p. 651.
84. *Hansard*, vol. 284 (5-25 February 1884), cc. 4-5 and 39.
85. Traill, *England, Egypt, and the Sudan*, p. 75.
86. Winston Churchill, *The River War: An Historical Account of the Reconquest of the Soudan* (2 vols.) (London: Longman, Green & Co., 1899), vol. 1, p. 38.

Chapter 3

1. Ponsonby, *Henry Ponsonby*, p. 227.
2. West Sussex Record Office (WSRO), Blunt Papers, Boxes 24 and 65, contain correspondence dated between January 1882 and August 1883.
3. Blunt, *Gordon At Khartoum*, p. 159.
4. *The Morning Post*, 27 December 1883, p. 3.
5. Churchill, *General Gordon*, p. 212.
6. Letter from Leopold's personal secretary, Colonel Maximilien Strauch, to Mackinnon, dated 3 October 1879, cited in Marcel Luwel, *Sir Francis de Winton: Administrateur Général du Congo, 1884-1886* (Tervuren, Musée Royal de l'Afrique Centrale, 1964), p. 6.
7. Henry Moreton Stanley, *In Darkest Africa: Or the Quest, Rescue and Retreat of Emin, Governor of Equatoria* (2 vols.) (London, Sampson Low, 1890), vol. 1, pp. 19-20.
8. Letter to *The Times*, 18 January 1884, p. 6.
9. Quoted in Queen Victoria's journal for 23 January 1884, in Buckle, *Letters of Queen Victoria*, vol. 3, p. 474.
10. Lt.-Gen. Sir Gerald Graham, *Last Words with Gordon* (London: Chapman & Hall, 1887), pp. 6-7.
11. Sir Samuel White Baker, 'Soudan and its Future', *The Contemporary Review* 45/65 (1884), pp. 69-70.
12. Charles J. Burnett, *What is it to be, Order or Chaos, Out of our Egyptian and North-Eastern Central African Crisis?* (London., n.p., 1884), p. 8.
13. Ibid., p. 6.
14. John Balfour Browne, *Essays, Critical and Political* (2 vols.) (London, Longmans, Green & Co., 1907), vol. 2, p. 59.

15. At least two accounts of Gordon's mission were subsequently published under the aegis of The Patriotic Association: Anon, *General Gordon and the British Ministry* (London, Allen, 1885), cited in Hilmy, *Literature of Egypt and the Soudan*, vol. 1, pp. 268-70, and Anon, *The Soudan, 1882 to 1897: A Memory and a Nemesis: The Story of Gordon and the Great Betrayal, with a History and Maps* (London, n.p. 1897).

16. *The Times*, 21 January 1884, p. 6.

17. Note-paper headed 'Xmas 1884', possibly a fragment of notes for Wolseley's uncompleted memoir; Hove Library, Wolseley Papers, M1/12/27, ff. viii-ix.

18. Ibid., SSL.10/1, ff. clvi and clviii.

19. See Nicoll, *Sword of the Prophet*, pp. 45-9 and 182-3, for analysis of Gordon's first administration in Khartoum.

20. *The Times*, 9 January 1883, p. 3, and 17 February 1883, p. 4.

21. Boulger, *Life of Gordon*, pp. 280-1.

22. Lt.-Col. Spencer Childers, *The Life and Correspondence of the Right Honourable Hugh C.E. Childers, 1827-1896* (2 vols.) (London, John Murray, 1901), vol. 1, pp. 176-7.

23. Col. Robert H. Vetch (ed.), *Life of Lieut.-General the Hon. Sir Andrew Clarke, G.C.M.G, C.B., C.I.E.* (London: John Murray, 1905), pp. 261-2.

24. Ramm, *Political Correspondence*, vol. 2 (1873-1886), p. 116.

25. Entry for 29 November 1883; Matthew, *Gladstone Diaries*, vol. 11, p. 67.

26. Granville to Baring, 1 December 1883, No. 1 in *Egypt No. 2 (1884)*.

27. Boulger, *Life of Gordon*, p. 282.

28. Roger Owen, *Lord Cromer: Victorian Imperialist, Edwardian Proconsul* (Oxford: OUP, 2004), p. 103.

29. Jean Bray, *The Mysterious Captain Brocklehurst: General Gordon's Unknown Aide* (Cheltenham, Reardon, 2006), p. 40.

30. Baring to Granville, 2 December 1883, No. 2 in *Egypt No. 2 (1884)* .

31. Letter to *The Times*, 1 January 1884, p. 4.

32. *Pall Mall Gazette*, 9 January 1884, p. 1.

33. Ibid., pp. 11-12.

34. Ibid., 9 January 1884, pp. 11-12.

35. Ibid., 9 January 1884, p. 12.

36. Todd Gray Willy, 'The Agitation in Parliament and England over Charles George "Chinese" Gordon and his Mission to the Sudan: January 1884 to February 1885' (Iowa City: University of Iowa PhD thesis, 1962), pp. 38-40.

37. Granville to Baring, 10 January 1884, No. 4 in *Egypt No. 2 (1884)* .

38. Granville to Victoria, dated 12 January 1884, in Buckle, *Letters of Queen Victoria*, vol. 3, p. 470.

39. Ramm, *Political Correspondence*, vol. 2, p. 149.

40. Anon [Sir Henry Gordon], 'The Position of General Gordon: A Conversation', *The Contemporary Review* 45/866 (1884), p. 867.

41. Interview with Wolseley in *The Strand Magazine: An Illustrated Monthly, Vol. 3: January-June* (London, 1892).
42. Field Marshal Viscount Garnet Wolseley, *The Story of a Soldier's Life* (2 vols.) (London, Archibald Constable & Co., 1903), vol. 1, pp. 147-8.
43. Holland, *Duke of Devonshire*, vol. 1, p. 415.
44. Letter dated 4 January 1884; BL, Gordon Papers (Bell Collection), Add. 52388, ff. 135-7.
45. Granville letter to Sir Henry Ponsonby, dated 15 January 1884, in Buckle, *Letters of Queen Victoria*, vol. 3, p. 471.
46. Also dated 15 January 1884; Ramm, *Political Correspondence*, vol. 2, p. 149.
47. Vetch, *Sir Andrew Clarke*, pp. 262-4.
48. Buckle, *Letters of Queen Victoria*, vol. 3, pp. 471-2; see also Shibeika, *British Policy*, pp. 149-50.
49. Gordon to Northbrook in BL, Ripon Papers, Add. Ms. 43573, f. 90.
50. BL, Gordon Papers (Bell Collection), Add. 52388, f. 139.
51. Letter from Brussels dated 3 January 1884; REM, Gordon Papers, File: 'Gordon Letters'. 5 February was the date of planned departure from Lisbon.
52. Boulger, *Life of Gordon*, pp. 256-7.
53. Henry Morton Stanley, *The Congo and the Founding of its Free State: A Story of Work and Exploration* (2 vols.) (London, Sampson Low, Marston, Searle & Rivington, 1886), vol. 2, pp. 226-7.
54. Pimblett, *Soudan War*, p. 112.
55. Letter from Gordon to Baker, dated 11 January 1884; *The Times*, 14 January 1884, p. 10.
56. Ramm, *Political Correspondence*, vol. 2, pp. 149-50.
57. Note dated 15 January 1884; Kew, Granville Papers, PRO 30/29/128.
58. Hove, Wolseley Papers, SSL.9/1, f. clviii.
59. Ibid., f. xi.
60. Ramm, *Political Correspondence Granville*, vol. 2, p. 150.
61. Baring to Granville, 16 January 1884, No. 8 in *Egypt No. 2 (1884)* .
62. Baring to Granville, No. 9 in ibid.
63. Kew, Cromer Papers, FO 633/4, f. 42.
64. Buckle, *Letters of Queen Victoria*, vol. 3, p. 473.
65. Gordon to Northbrook in BL, Ripon Papers, Add. Ms. 43573, f. 89.
66. Boulger, *Life of Gordon*, pp. 257-8.
67. Gwynn and Tuckwell, *Sir Charles Dilke*, vol. 2, pp. 32-4.
68. Fitzmaurice, *Granville George Leveson Gower*, vol. 2, p. 400.
69. Hawkins and Powell, *Earl of Kimberley*, p. 340.
70. Stronach and Halkett, *Egyptian Red Book*, p. 8.
71. Holland, *Duke of Devonshire*, vol. 1, p. 418.
72. Northbrook to Ripon, dated 18 January 1884; BL, Ripon Papers, Add. Ms. 43573, f. 76.
73. Mallet, *Earl of Northbrook*, p. 177.

74. Gwynn and Tuckwell, *Sir Charles Dilke*, vol. 2, pp. 29 and 31.

75. Gladstone letter to Granville, dated 19 January 1884, cited in Fitzmaurice, *Granville George Leveson Gower*, vol. 2, p. 383.

76. Bahlman, *Sir Edward Hamilton*, vol. 2, p. 545.

77. Letter dated 19 January 1884; Boulger, *Life of Gordon*, pp. 260.

78. Butler, *Sir William Butler*, pp. 268-9.

79. Col. Sir Charles Wilson, 'Gordon's Staff- Officer at Khartum', *Blackwood's Edinburgh Magazine* 161/977 (March 1897), p. 320.

80. Ibid., p. 321.

81. Willy, 'The Agitation in Parliament and England', p. 75.

82. Hove, Wolseley Papers, W/PLB.1, ff. 12-15 and NRA.1047, f. 102; see also Luwel, *Sir Francis de Winton*, pp. 24-5.

83. *The Times*, 19 January 1884, p. 3.

84. *Pall Mall Gazette*, 19 January 1884. See also Joseph Lehmann, *All Sir Garnet: A Life of Field Marshal Wolseley* (London, Jonathan Cape, 1964), pp. 343-4.

85. Lady Gwendoline Cecil, *Life of Robert, Marquess of Salisbury* (4 vols.) (London: Hodder & Stoughton, 1921), vol. 3, p. 98.

86. Buckle, *Letters of Queen Victoria*, vol. 3, p. 474.

87. Lawrence Fabunmi, *Sudan in Anglo-Egyptian Relations: A Case Study in Power Politics, 1800-1956* (London: Longmans, 1967), p. 35.

88. Letter from Charles Allen; *The Times*, 18 January 1884, p. 6.

89. Notes following cabinet meeting on 22 January 1884; Matthew, *Gladstone Diaries*, vol. 11, p. 103.

90. Granville to Gordon, 18 January 1884, No. 10 in *Egypt No. 2 (1884)* .

Chapter 4

1. de Malortie, *Here There and Everywhere*, p. 196.

2. Postcard to General Sir Dighton Probyn VC (1833-1924, then Comptroller of the Royal Household at Windsor); facsimile, SAD, Brocklehurst Papers, 630/6/5.

3. Memorandum dated 22 January 1884; BL, Gladstone Papers, Add. 44629, ff. 71-2.

4. Shibeika, *British Policy*, pp. 160-1.

5. Inclosure No. 1 in Baring to Granville, No. 199 in *Egypt No. 12 (1884) Further Correspondence Respecting the Affairs of Egypt.*

6. Anon., 'Position of General Gordon', p. 869.

7. Cross to Granville, dated 5 January 1884; Kew, Foreign Office Papers, FO 30/29/146.

8. Inclosure 1 in Baring to Granville, 1 February 1884, No. 15 in *Egypt No. 12 (1884)* .

9. Inclosure 2 in ibid.

10. Inclosure dated 25 January 1884 in Baring to Granville (28 January 1884) in

Egypt No. 6 (1884) Despatch from Her Britannic Majesty's Agent and Consul-General in Egypt, Inclosing Further Instructions to General Gordon.

11. BL, Ripon Papers, Add. Ms. 43573, f. 89.
12. Letter dated 22 January 1884; BL, Gordon Papers (Bell Collection), Add. 52388, ff. 142-4.
13. Nicoll, *Sword of the Prophet*, pp. 164-6.
14. SAD, Stewart Papers, 896/7, f. 1 (recto).
15. Wilson, 'Gordon's Staff-Officer', p. 323.
16. SAD, Brocklehurst Papers, 630/5/28-9.
17. Al-Zubeir Raḥmatallah Manṣūr was a powerful slave-trader who used his own private army to mount raids along the Bahr al-Ghazāl river and into Equatoria. His invasion of Darfur and the murder of Sultan Ibrāhīm Muḥammad al-Ḥussein made him de facto ruler of western Sudan but when he travelled to Egypt in 1875 to lobby for the favour of the Khedive Ismāʿīl, he was detained and held in Cairo, which was where he remained when Gordon arrived.
18. Rudolf Slatin, Governor of Darfur, had surrendered to the Mahdī's regional commander, Muḥammad Khālid Zugal, on 23 December 1883 and was at this time being held in the Mahdī's camp at al-Rahad, near al-ʿUbeiḍ in Kordofan.
19. SAD, Stewart Papers, 896/7, ff. 1-3.
20. Ibid., f. 10.
21. Private correspondence from Stewart, only surviving in Cromer, *Modern Egypt*, vol. 1, p. 467.
22. SAD, Stewart Papers, 896/7, f. 32.
23. *The Times*, 1 December 1883, p. 5.
24. Ibid., 6 December 1883, p. 8.
25. Ibid., 7 December 1883, p. 7.
26. Ibid., 10 January 1884, p. 5.
27. SAD, Stewart Papers, 896/7, f. 48.
28. BL, Power Papers, Add. Ms. 58069, f. 114.
29. *The Times*, 21 February 1884, p. 5.
30. No. 132, Baring to Granville, in *Egypt 12 (1884)* .
31. No. 133, Baring to Granville, in ibid.
32. *Hansard*, vol. 284, c. 1527.
33. Ibid., c. 1607.
34. Ibid., c. 1874.
35. *Hansard*, vol. 285 (26 February-15 March 1884), cc. 188-206.
36. Henry Jackson, *Black Ivory and White, or The Story of El Zubeir Pasha, Slaver and Sultan, as Told by Himself* (Oxford, B.H. Blackwell, 1913), p. 90.
37. de Kusel, *Recollections of Egypt*, p. 261.
38. Khedive Ismāʿīl's decree, in French, dated 16 February 1974 (2 Muharram 1291); National Records Office, Khartoum (NRO), CAIRINT 1/3/8.
39. Loring, *Confederate Soldier*, pp. 276-7.

40. *Account of the Actions of Zubeir Pasha*; NRO, INTEL 1/15/74.

41. 'The Mahdi's Movements', *The Times*, 5 January 1884, p. 12; see also Boulger, *Life of Gordon*, pp. 271-3.

42. Letter to Sir Henry Ponsonby, dated 1 February 1884; Ponsonby, *Henry Ponsonby*, pp. 227-8.

43. SAD, 110/5/1; translation by ʿUthmān al-Nuṣairi.

44. SAD, Stewart Papers, 896/7, f. 2.

45. Sturge to Granville, dated 10 March 1884, No. 224 in *Egypt No. 12 (1884)* .

46. Baring to Granville, 28 February 1884, No. 169 in ibid.

47. Matthew, *Gladstone Diaries*, vol. 11, p. 119.

48. Granville to Baring, 29 February 1884, No. 177 in *Egypt No. 12 (1884)* .

49. Granville to Baring, No. 210 in ibid.

50. Morley, *William Ewart Gladstone*, vol. 3, pp. 159-60.

51. Matthew, *Gladstone Diaries*, vol. 11, p. 125.

52. Gladstone minute on 'Cabinet meetings on the Soudan', BL, Supplementary Gladstone Papers, Add. Add. Ms. 56452, ff. 22 and 24.

53. Granville to Baring, No. 2 in *Egypt No. 13 (1884) Further Correspondence Respecting the Affairs of Egypt*.

54. Churchill, *The River War*, vol. 1, pp. 44-5.

55. de Malortie, *Here There and Everywhere*, p. 200.

56. de Kusel, *Recollections of Egypt*, pp. 266-7.

57. Diary entry for 18 April 1884; de Malortie, *Here There and Everywhere*, p. 203.

58. An allusion to the 'seven vials of the wrath of God'; Revelations 16:2.

59. BL, Gordon Papers, Add. Ms. 34479 (Vol. 6), f. 93.

60. Baring to Granville, 17 January 1884, No. 6 in *Egypt No. 12 (1884)* .

61. Archer, *War in Egypt and the Soudan*, vol. 3, p. 86-7.

62. SAD, Stewart Papers, 896/7, f. 74.

63. *The Times*, 6 May 1884, p. 5; also *La Liberté* (Paris), 7 May 1884, p. 1.

64. Inclosure in Baring to Granville, 28 September 1884, No. 164 in *Egypt No. 35 (1884) Further Correspondence Respecting the Affairs of Egypt*.

65. Henry Keown-Boyd, *Soldiers of the Nile: A Biographical History of the British Officers of the Egyptian Army* (Thornbury, Thornbury Publications, 1996), p. 66.

66. *Egypt No. 11 (1883)*, p. 13.

67. 'Colonel Duncan to the General Officer commanding the Troops in Upper Egypt', Inclosure dated 28 July 1884 in No. 126, Egerton to Granville, 8 September 1884, in *Egypt No. 35 (1884)* .

68. Churchill, *General Gordon*, pp. 232-3.

Chapter 5

1. 'Tamanieb'; *Punch*, 22 March 1884, p. 141.
2. Bahlman, *Sir Edward Walter Hamilton*, vol. 2, p. 545.
3. *The Times*, 16 February 1884, p. 5.
4. Ibid., 18 February 1884, p. 12.
5. Bray, *Brocklehurst*, pp. 64-9.
6. *The Times*, 21 January 1884, p. 7.
7. 2,490 at Khartoum; 1,513 at Berber and Dongola; around 1,800 at Sawākīn; 6,624 at Sinnār, Kassala and other eastern outposts; 4,863 at al-Fāshir; 3,718 on the White Nile; 886 on the Bahr al-Ghazāl; and 2,131 in Equatoria; Baring to Granville, dated 3 December 1883, No. 150 in *Egypt No. 1 (1884)* .
8. Private note to Northbrook, dated 4 March 1884; BL, Supplementary Gladstone Papers, Add. Ms. 56452, f. 18.
9. Ronald Robinson, 'Imperial Problems in British Politics, 1880-1895', *The Cambridge History of the British Empire* (eds.: J.H. Rose, A. P. Newton and E. A. Benians) (9 vols.) (Cambridge, CUP, 1929-61), vol. 7, p. 153.
10. See Mowat, 'Liberalism to Imperialism', p. 118.
11. Baring suggested that Gordon's successor receive 'an annual subsidy of about 50,000*l.* for the first five years, to depend upon his good behaviour'; Baring to Granville, 28 February 1884, No. 169 in *Egypt No. 12 (1884)* .
12. Baring returned to Britain from late April to September 1884, attending many important meetings and briefing the cabinet in person. His stand-in was Edwin Egerton, a diplomat seconded temporarily to Cairo from the British Embassy in Greece who communicated frequently with Gordon and became the butt of many of Gordon's jokes in his later journal.
13. BL, Supplementary Gladstone Papers, Add. Ms. 56452, f. 16.
14. Letter dated 8 March 1884; BL, Gladstone Papers, Add. Ms. 44131, f. 49.
15. Letter dated 21 May 1884; Stephenson, *Battlefield*, p. 320.
16. Granville to Baring, No. 4 in *Egypt No. 8 (1884)* .
17. BL, Gladstone Papers, Add. Ms. 44267, f. 41.
18. Matthew, *Gladstone Diaries*, vol. 11, p. 112.
19. Hewett had masterminded the seizure of the Suez Canal during the 1882 British occupation of Egypt.
20. Hawkins and Powell, *Earl of Kimberley*, p. 340.
21. Wylde, *'83 to '87* , vol. 1, p. 31.
22. Matthew, *Gladstone Diaries*, vol. 11, p. 122.
23. *New York Times*, 22 January 1884, p. 4.
24. Matthew, *Gladstone Diaries*, vol. 11, p. 115.
25. Col. Robert H. Vetch (ed.), *Life, Letters, and Diaries of Lieut.-General Sir Gerald Graham, V.C., C.B., R.E.: With Portraits, Plans and His Principal Despatches* (Edinburgh, William Blackwood & Sons, 1901), pp. 266-9.
26. Nicoll, *Sword of the Prophet*, pp. 247-8.
27. Hove, Wolseley Papers, SSL.9/1, f. xlii.

28. Archer, *War in Egypt and the Soudan*, vol. 2, p. 286. see also Andrew Haggard, *Under Crescent and Star* (London, William Blackwood, 1895), pp. 172-80, and Wylde, *'83 to '87*, vol. 1, pp. 141-68.

29. Haggard, *Under Crescent and Star*, pp. 182-3.

30. Frederic Villiers, 'My Friend Corporal Tonbar', in *The Canadian Magazine* 15 (1900), pp. 41-2.

31. Graham, *Last Words*, p. 52; see also Vetch, *Sir Gerald Graham*, pp. 276-9.

32. Holland, *Duke of Devonshire*, vol. 1, pp. 425-9.

33. Bahlman, *Sir Edward Walter Hamilton*, vol. 2, p. 555.

34. Buckle, *Letters of Queen Victoria*, vol. 3, p. 477.

35. Fitzmaurice, *Life of Granville*, vol. 2, pp. 324 and 330.

36. This first 'Vote of Censure' was formally tabled in the Commons by the Leader of the Opposition, Sir Stafford Northcote, and in the Lords by Lord Salisbury.

37. *Hansard*, vol. 284, cc. 684-762 (12 February), 896-979 (14 February), 1025-1114 (15 February), 1208-87 (18 February), 1353-1462 (19 February); see also Andrew Lang, *Life, Letters, and Diaries of Sir Stafford Northcote, First Earl of Iddesleigh* (Edinburgh, William Blackwood & Sons, 1891), p. 349.

38. Matthew, *Gladstone Diaries*, vol. 11, p. 112.

39. Northbrook to Ripon, dated 13 February 1884, BL, Ripon Papers, Add. Ms. 43573, ff. 82-3.

40. Hawkins and Powell, *Kimberley*, p. 340.

41. *Hansard*, vol. 285, c. 1653.

42. Ibid., cc. 1656-7.

43. Ibid., cc. 1656-7; Henry du Pré Labouchère was the Radical MP for Northampton.

44. Hawkins and Powell, *Earl of Kimberley*, p. 341.

45. *Hansard*, vol. 286 (17 March-7 April 1884), c. 1509; see also Lang, *Sir Stafford Northcote*, p. 349.

46. *Hansard*, vol. 286, cc. 1510-23.

47. Possibly Pietro Agati, an Italian who had been in Sudan since 1853; Hill, *Biographical Dictionary*, p. 28.

48. *Hansard*, vol. 287, c. 288.

49. Ibid., cc. 292-3.

50. Gwynn and Tuckwell, *Sir Charles Dilke*, vol. 2, p. 51.

51. *Hansard*, vol. 288 (12 May-10 June 1884), c. 31.

52. Gwynn and Tuckwell, *Sir Charles Dilke*, vol. 2, p. 51.

53. Matthew, *Gladstone Diaries*, vol. 11, p. 145.

54. *Hansard*, vol. 288, c. 302.

55. Matthew, *Gladstone Diaries*, vol. 11, p. 145.

56. Gwynn and Tuckwell, *Sir Charles Dilke*, vol. 2, p. 34.

57. Diary entry for 13 May 1884; Hawkins and Powell, *Earl of Kimberley*, p. 343.

58. Baring to Granville, No. 301 in *Egypt No. 12 (1884)* ; also verbatim in Cromer, *Modern Egypt*, vol. 1, pp. 540-2.

59. Granville to Baring, No. 1 in *Egypt No. 13 (1884)* .

60. Gwynn and Tuckwell, *Sir Charles Dilke*, vol. 2, p. 44.

61. Buckle, *Letters of Queen Victoria*, vol. 3, p. 485.

62. Ibid., vol. 3, pp. 486-7.

63. Ibid., vol. 3, p. 491-2.

64. Cabinet meeting of 29 March 1884; Matthew, *Gladstone Diaries*, vol. 11, p. 130.

65. Graham, *Last Words*, p. 52. This refers to Gordon's journal entry of 24 October 1884; BL, Gordon Papers, Add. Ms. 34478 (vol. 5), f. 23.

66. Traill, *England, Egypt, and the Sudan*, pp. 76-7.

67. Granville to Baring, No. 3 in *Egypt No. 13 (1884)* .

68. Nicoll, *Sword of the Prophet*, pp. 229-30.

69. Matthew, *Gladstone Diaries*, vol. 11, pp. 124-5; also Morley, *Life of Gladstone*, vol. 3, pp. 159-60.

70. Nicoll, *Sword of the Prophet*, pp. 195-6.

71. REM, Gordon Papers, 'Lady Watson's Scrapbook', f. 4.

72. Baring to Granville, 7 April 1884, No. 7 in *Egypt No. 13 (1884)* ; on Muḥammad al-Dikkeir 'al-Kheir' 'Abdallah Khojali, see Hill, *Biographical Dictionary*, pp. 260-1.

73. Inclosure in Baring to Granville, 19 March 1884, No. 279 in *Egypt No. 12 (1884)*.

74. Open letter quoted in Drage, *Cyril*, p. 383.

75. Gladstone's journal entry for 21 April 1884; Matthew, *Gladstone Diaries*, vol. 11, p. 137.

76. Granville to Egerton, No. 30 in *Egypt No. 13 (1884)* .

77. Egerton to Granville, Nos. 31 and 32 in ibid.

78. Egerton to Granville, No. 33 in ibid.

79. Egerton to Granville, No. 34 in ibid.

80. Granville to Egerton, No. 35 in ibid..

81. Matthew, *Gladstone Diaries*, vol. 11, p. 138.

82. Granville to Egerton, 17 May 1884, *Egypt No. 22 (1884) Further Correspondence Respecting the Affairs of Egypt*.

83. BL, Gordon Papers, Add. 34479 (vol. 6), f. 73. The process by which this message was deciphered is described in Fergus Nicoll, '3000 = Mahdi; 3260 = Gordon', *Sudan Studies* 35 (2005), pp. 2-17.

84. Granville to Egerton, 23 April 1884, No. 36 in *Egypt No. 13 (1884)* .

85. Matthew, *Gladstone Diaries*, vol. 11, p. 138.

86. Gwynn and Tuckwell, *Sir Charles Dilke*, vol. 2, p. 60.

87. BL, Gordon Papers, Add. Ms. 34474 (vol. 1), ff. 58-9.

88. *The Times*, 29 September 1884, p. 5.

89. Pimblett, *Soudan War*, pp. 225-6.

90. *The Times*, 17 April 1884, p. 5.

91. Ibid., p. 5.

92. Baring to Granville, 20 and 31 March 1884, Nos. 4 and 6 in *Egypt No. 13 (1884)*.

93. Inclosure in Baring to Granville, 28 September 1884, No. 164 in *Egypt No. 35 (1884)*.

94. Baring to Granville, 17 September 1884, No. 129 in ibid.

95. REM, Gordon Papers, CHARE 4801.156.

96. Message to Baring dated 31 March 1884; Baring to Granville, dated 9 April 1884, No. 12 in *Egypt No. 13 (1884)*.

97. Chenevix Trench, *Charley Gordon*, pp. 132-5.

98. Anon., 'Position of General Gordon', pp. 873-8.

99. *The Times*, 29 July 1884, p. 8.

100. Sālih al-Mak, a Shaiqīa company commander, was one of the unsung heroes of the Sudan wars. And effective and courageous officer, he put up stubborn resistance to the efforts of the Mahdī to subjugate the Jazīra region but was eventually captured near al-Massallamīa on the Blue Nile.

101. Nicoll, *Sword of the Prophet*, pp. 191-2.

102. SAD, Stewart Papers, 896/7, f. 103.

103. Letter dated 4 November 1884; Inclosure in Colonel Swaine to Baring, No. 93 in *Egypt No. 1 (1885) Further Correspondence Respecting the Affairs of Egypt*.

104. Guiseppe Cuzzi had been Gordon's agent at Berber and was captured when the city fell; he was compelled to convert to Islam and took the name Muḥammad Yūsuf. At Khartoum, he was forced to try to persuade Gordon to surrender.

105. SAD, Stewart Papers, 896/7, f. 104.

106. Cromer, *Modern Egypt*, vol. 1, p. 433.

107. SAD, Stewart Papers, 896/7, ff. 89-90.

108. Wilson, 'Gordon's Staff-Officer', p. 322.

109. SAD, Stewart Papers, 896/7, f. 85.

110. Quoted in Edward Hamilton's diary entry for 27 March 1885; Bahlman, *Sir Edward Walter Hamilton*, vol. 2, p. 824.

111. Arabic telegram dated 19 August 1884; Inclosure in No. 156 in *Egypt No. 35 (1884)* .

112. SAD, Stewart Papers, 896/7, f. 84.

113. Anon., *Mr. John M. Cook's Visit to the Soudan, in Connection with the Expedition of 1884-85* (London: n.p., 1885), pp. 25-6.

114. Baker, 'Soudan and its Future', pp. 77-8.

115. Hill, *Biographical Dictionary*, p. 250.

116. Nicoll, *Sword of the Prophet*, pp. 196-7.

117. Gordon's letter dated 23 August 1884, enclosed in Baring to Granville, 17 September 1884, No. 129 in *Egypt No. 34 (1884). Further Correspondence Respecting the Affairs of Egypt* [between 5 and 21 October 1884].

118. Donald Featherstone, *Khartoum 1885: General Gordon's Last Stand* (Oxford, Osprey, 1993), p. 68.

119. Bordeini's commentary on Muhammad Nusshi's report, 'Gordon in Khartoum'; NRO, INTEL 5/2/14, ff. 66-7.

Chapter 6

1. Stronach and Halkett, *Egyptian Red Book*, p.4.
2. Buckle, *Letters of Queen Victoria*, vol. 3, p. 494.
3. Sir Thomas Sanderson to Granville, 8 December 1885, cited in Fitzmaurice, *Life of Granville*, vol. 2, p. 389.
4. Letter to Hartington, dated 26 March 1884; Holland, *Duke of Devonshire*, vol. 1, p. 433.
5. REM, Gordon Papers, CHARE 4801.156.
6. *Hansard*, vol. 287, c. 138
7. Lytton Strachey, *Eminent Victorians* (London: Chatto & Windus, 1918), p. 271.
8. Laffer, 'Gordon's Ghosts', pp. 83-4.
9. Burnaby subsequently joined Wolseley's relief expedition and was killed at the Battle of Abū-Ṭulayh ('Abu Klea') on 17 January 1885. A plaque and two memorial windows representing Burnaby and other 'British warrior saints' can be found in the deconsecrated Anglican cathedral in Khartoum.
10. Janet Henderson Robb, *The Primrose League, 1883-1906* (New York, Columbia University Press, 1942), p. 184.
11. *The Times*, 6 May 1884, p. 10.
12. Anon., *Life of Gordon* (London, Walter Scott, n.d.), p. 321.
13. *The Times*, 10 May 1884, p. 10; see also Paul Laity, *The British Peace Movement, 1870-1914* (Oxford, Clarendon, 2001), p. 101.
14. *The Times*, 10 May 1884, p. 7.
15. Ibid., 6 May 1884, p. 11.
16. Diary entry for 24 April 1884; Bahlman, *Sir Edward Walter Hamilton*, vol. 2, pp. 601-2.
17. Strachey, *Eminent Victorians*, p. 271.
18. Matthew, *Gladstone Diaries*, vol. 11, p. 145.
19. *The Times*, 17 April 1884, p. 5; see also Stronach and Halkett, *Egyptian Red Book*, p. 14.
20. *Punch*, 3 May 1884, p. 214.
21. de Kusel, *Recollections of Egypt*, p. 264.
22. Roundell Palmer, Earl of Selborne, *Memorials: Part II. Personal and Political 1865-1895* (2 vols.) (London, Macmillan & Co., 1898), vol. 2, p. 144.
23. *Hansard*, vol. 287, c. 751.
24. Matthew, *Gladstone Diaries*, vol. 11, pp. 140-1; also Gwynn and Tuckwell, *Sir Charles Dilke*, vol. 2, p. 49.
25. Wylde, *'83 to '87*, vol. 2, p. 109.
26. Padraig Yeates, 'An Irishman's Diary', in *The Irish Times*, 24 August 2009.
27. *Hansard*, vol. 287, c. 1039.

28. Hove, Wolseley Papers, SSL.9/1, ff. lix-xv.

29. Memorandum dated 13 April 1884 by Capt. WH Hall, entitled 'Confidential observations on Sir Samuel Baker's suggested Relief of Berber and Khartoum from Cairo by the Nile Route'; Kew, Cabinet Papers, CAB 37/12.

30. Anon., 'Position of General Gordon', p. 872.

31. James Grant, 'Route March, with Camels, from Berber to Korosko in 1863', *Proceedings of the Royal Geographical Society* 6/6 (1884), pp. 326-35.

32. Bowen, 'Sûdan and the Mahdi', p. 662.

33. C.P. Stone, 'The Route from Suakin to Berber', *Science* 5/114 (1885), p. 290.

34. Letter from Stephenson to his sisters, dated 21 December 1883; Stephenson, *Battlefield*, pp. 310-11.

35. Haggard, *Under Crescent and Star*, pp. 188-91.

36. Gen. Sir John Adye, *Recollections of a Military Life* (New York, Macmillan & Co., 1895).

37. Letter dated 9 May 1884; Stephenson, *Battlefield*, pp. 319-20.

38. Gladstone letter to Dilke, 30 May 1884; BL, Dilke Papers, Add. Ms. 43875, f. 171; Gwynn and Tuckwell, *Sir Charles Dilke*, vol. 2, p. 53. As late as 22 July 1884, Gladstone wrote to Granville: 'The Nile is impossible for an expedition. Suakim and Berber the only route'; Fitzmaurice, *Life of Granville*, vol. 2, p. 393.

39. Vice-Adm. Philip H. Colomb, *Memoirs of Admiral the Right Honble. Sir Astley Cooper Key* (London, Methuen & Co., 1898), pp. 467-8.

40. Kitchener's main task during 1884-5 was as liaison with the tribes of the northern Nile. Because this work took him much further south than his British Army colleagues and because his Arabic rapidly became fluent, Kitchener, travelling from Korosko to Dongola to al-Dabba, was also put in charge of communications with Khartoum.

41. Cromer, *Modern Egypt*, vol. 2, pp. 86-7; see also Hill, *Biographical Dictionary*, pp. 203-5.

42. Philip Magnus, *Kitchener: Portrait of an Imperialist* (London, John Murray, 1958), pp. 42-7.

43. Archer, *War in Egypt and the Soudan*, vol. 1, pp. 184-6.

44. BL, Gordon Papers, Add. Ms. 34474 (vol. 1), f. 54.

45. Donald Mackenzie Wallace, *Egypt and the Egyptian Question* (London, Macmillan & Co., 1883), p. 49.

46. Wylde, *'83 to '87*, vol. 2, pp. 130-5.

47. Ibid., vol. 2, pp. 136-7.

48. Anon., 'From Suakin to Berber', *Science* 5/12 (1885), p. 254.

49. Thomas Cook Archive, Peterborough (TCA), *Excursionist*, 1 November 1883, p. 5.

50. *The Times*, 23 February 1884, p. 4.

51. Baker, 'Soudan and its Future', p. 71; see also Richard Hill, 'The Suakin-Berber Railway', *Sudan Notes and Records* (SNR) 20/1 (1937), p. 107.

52. BL, Gladstone Papers, Add. Ms. 44267, f. 62.

53. Norfolk County Library (NCL), Baggallay Papers, MC 84/398, 532.x.4 (1884), f. 1.

54. Ibid., ff. 2-4.

55. Memo entitled 'Labour and arrangements required to construct 5 Miles of Metric gauge line per diem on The Souakin Berber Railway'; NCL, Baggallay Papers, MC 84/398, 532.x.4 (1884).

56. Hill, 'Suakin-Berber Railway', p. 110.

57. William Galloway, *The Battle of Tofrek: Fought Near Suakin, March 22*nd, *1885* (London, W.H. Allen, 1887), pp. 382-5.

58. BL, Dilke Papers, Add. Ms. 43875, f. 164.

59. Matthew, *Gladstone Diaries*, vol. 11, p. 150.

60. Ibid., vol. 11, p. 156.

61. Hill, 'Suakin-Berber Railway', p. 108.

62. Vetch, *Sir Andrew Clarke*, pp. 265-7.

63. Northbrook's response to Lord Salisbury during the Vote of Censure, 26 February 1885; *Hansard*, vol. 294 (18 November 1884-3 March 1885), c. 1336; see also Adrian Preston (ed.), *In Relief of Gordon: Lord Wolseley's Campaign Journal of the Khartoum Relief Expedition 1884-1885* (London: Hutchinson, 1967), p. xxx.

64. Archer, *War in Egypt and the Soudan*, vol. 3, p. 194-5.

65. Wylde, *'83 to '87*, vol. 2, p. 142.

66. Col. Sir Garnet Wolseley, *The Use of Railroads in War: A Lecture Delivered at Aldershot, on the 20th January, 1873* (London, Edwin S. Boot, 1873).

67. BL, Dilke Papers, Add. Ms. 43923, f. 173.

68. Ibid., f. 175. See also Col. C.E. Callwell, *Small Wars: A Tactical Textbook for Imperial Soldiers* (London, Greenhill Books, 1990), pp. 67-70.

69. Hove, Wolseley Papers, SSL.9/1, ff. x.

70. Ibid., f. xxxix.

71. Ibid., f. x.

72. Letter to Gladstone, 11 April 1884; Holland, *Duke of Devonshire*, vol. 1, pp. 439-40.

73. Adrian Preston, 'Wolseley, the Khartoum Relief Expedition and the Defence of India, 1885-1900', *Journal of Imperial and Commonwealth History* 6/3 (1978), p. 256.

74. Hove, Wolseley Papers, SSL.9/1, ff. xxv, clxxviii and clxxxi; SSL.9 /2, ff. cccix-x, ccclxxxvi.

75. Preston, *In Relief of Gordon*, p. 42; Hove, Wolseley Papers, SSL.9/1, f. cdlxi.

76. Ibid., M1/12/27, f. x and SSL.9/2, ff. cclxxxiii-iv.

77. Letter dated 24 April 1884; Arthur, *Letters of Lord Wolseley*, p. 115.

78. Letter dated 24 July 1884; Lehmann, *All Sir Garnet*, p. 347.

79. Stephenson, *Battlefield*, p. 283.

80. National Maritime Museum, HMM/3-4; also T.F. Hammill, 'Passage of the Second Cataract and Cataract of Semneh by the Nile steamers "Nassif Kheir"

and "Gizeh" in September and October 1884' (London, Admiralty Foreign Intelligence Committee, No. 75, August 1885).

81. Sir William Butler, *The Campaign of the Cataracts: Being a Personal Narrative of the Great Nile Expedition of 1884-5* (London, Sampson Low, Marston, Searle & Rivington, 1887), p. 37.

82. Northbrook on 26 February 1885; *Hansard*, vol. 294, c. 1336.

83. Cecil, *Marquess of Salisbury*, vol. 3, p. 103.

84. Robinson, 'Imperial Problems', p. 153.

85. Cooke and Vincent, *The Governing Passion*, pp. 24-8.

86. Gwynn and Tuckwell, *Sir Charles Dilke*, vol. 2, pp. 60-61.

87. Palmer, *Memorials*, vol. 2, pp. 141-4.

88. Matthew, *Gladstone Diaries*, vol. 11, pp. 180-2.

89. Letter to Granville dated 15 July 1884: Fitzmaurice, *Life of Granville*, vol. 2, p. 390.

90. *Hansard* 291, c 1795; see also *Relief of General Gordon. 1884-85. Vote of Credit, £.300,000*, dated 4 August 1884.

91. Gwynn and Tuckwell, *Sir Charles Dilke*, vol. 2, pp. 43-4.

92. Matthew, *Gladstone Diaries*, vol. 11, p. 285.

93. Ibid., vol. 11, p. 288.

94. Stephenson, *Battlefield*, p. 40.

95. Telegram dated 11 August 1884; Col. Sir Charles Watson, 'The Campaign of Gordon's Steamers', *SNR* 12/2 (1929), p. 132.

96. Memorandum dated 4 August 1884; Butler, *Campaign of the Cataracts*, pp. 371-4.

97. Hove, Wolseley Papers, SSL.9/2, f. ccclxxxvii.

98. Telegram dated 29 August 1884; Stephenson, *Battlefield*, p. 40.

99. Stephenson, *Battlefield*, p. 39.

100. Colonel H.J. Crauford of the Grenadier Guards, quoted in Preston, 'Khartoum Relief Expedition', p. 257.

101. Kew, FO 78/3678 and 3679; see Appendix 1. Wolseley's instructions were drafted on 21 September 1884 and 'approved with amendments' by the cabinet as late as 8 October; Matthew, *Gladstone Diaries*, vol. 11, p. 221.

102. Preston, 'Khartoum Relief Expedition', p. 257.

103. Telegram dated 11 August 1884; Watson, 'Gordon's Steamers', p. 132.

104. Letter dated 13 September 1884; Arthur, *Letters of Lord Wolseley*, p. 119.

105. Hove, Wolseley Papers, SSL.9/1, f. x.

106. Matthew, *Gladstone Diaries*, vol. 11, p. 207.

107. These telegrams are Granville to Egerton, 23 April 1884, No. 36 in *Egypt No. 13 (1884)*, and Granville to Egerton, 17 May 1884, *Egypt No. 22 (1884)*.

108. Ramm, *Political Correspondence of Gladstone and Granville*, vol. 2, pp. 260-1.

109. Colomb, *Cooper Key*, pp. 469-70.

110. TCA, *Excursionist*, 8 September 1884, p. 3; see also ibid., 1 November 1884, p. 4.

111. Ibid., 2 February 1885, p. 3, and 2 November 1885, p. 3.
112. Ibid., 2 February 1885, p. 4.
113. Watson, 'Gordon's Steamers', p. 133.
114. TCA, *Excursionist*, 2 February 1885, p. 6.
115. BL, Gordon Papers, Add. Ms. 34479 (vol. 6), f. 82.
116. See Appendix 1.
117. Dated 26 September 1884; Kew, War Office Papers, WO 32/124/346.

Chapter 7

1. Inclosure in Wolseley to Baring, No. 117 in *Egypt No. 1 (1885)* .
2. BL, Gordon Papers, Add. Ms. 34478 (vol. 5), f. 81, and Add. Ms. 34479 (vol. 6), ff. 3 and 10.
3. Letter from Graham to Clarke, 12 October 1884; Vetch, *Sir Andrew Clarke*, p. 268.
4. Hake, *Journals of Major-Gen. Gordon*, pp. 442-5.
5. Wilson, 'Gordon's Staff-Officer', p. 330.
6. Original message, dated 28 June 1884, among Frank Power's papers; BL, Power Papers, Add. Ms. 58069, f. 122.
7. Baring to Granville, 17 September 1884, No. 129 in *Egypt No. 35 (1884)*.
8. Baring to Granville, 20 September 1884, No. 135 in ibid.; Matthew, *Gladstone Diaries*, vol. 11, pp. 210; Ramm, *Political Correspondence of Gladstone and Granville*, vol. 2, p. 260.
9. Muḥammad Nusshi, 'The Life of Gordon Pasha in Khartoum' (compiled in late 1885 by a committee of eight officers and officials who had witnessed the siege; translated by Naʿūm Shuqair of British military intelligence in 1891); NRO, INTEL 5/2/14, ff. 66-7.
10. Charles Chenevix Trench, 'Gordon's Staff Officer', *History Today* 25/3 (1975), p. 163. Kitchener's on-the-spot investigation is contained as Inclosure in Baring to Granville, 6 January 1885, No. 152 in *Egypt No. 1 (1885)* ; see also Archer, *War in Egypt and the Soudan*, vol. 3, p. 245-6.
11. Letter dated 2 Muharram 1302; Muḥammad Ibrāhīm Abū-Salīm (ed.), *al-Athār al-kāmila li'l-Imām al-Mahdī* ('The Collected Works of the Imām al-Mahdī') (7 vols.) (Khartoum: KUP, 1990-94), vol. 4, pp. 8-13; Appendix 2 has the full text of the letter.
12. BL, Gordon Papers, Add. Ms. 34478 (vol. 5), ff. 113-14 (Gordon's 'Appendix X').
13. BL, Gordon Papers (Moffitt Collection), Add. Ms. 51298, ff. 190-1.
14. BL, Gordon Papers, Add. Ms. 34479 (vol. 6), f. 35.
15. Ibid., Add. Ms. 34474 (vol. 1), ff. 6, 10-14, 18, 24, 32, 34-6, 49-51, 60 and 62.
16. Ibid., Add. Ms. 34475 (vol. 2), f. 20, Add. Ms. 34476 (vol. 3), f. 82, Add. Ms. 34477 (vol. 4), f. 15, and Add. Ms. 34479 (vol. 6), f. 89.

17. Hill, *Biographical Dictionary*, pp. 17, 279 and 297; also J.A. Reid, 'The Mahdi's Emirs', *Sudan Notes and Records* 20 (1937), pp. 308-12.

18. In Hake, *Journals of Major-Gen. Gordon*, pp. 217-18, the names were simply omitted.

19. Entry for 22 October 1884; BL, Gordon Papers, Add. Ms. 34478 (vol. 5), ff. 10-11.

20. Sir William Butler, *Charles George Gordon* (London: Macmillan, 1897), p. 231.

21. Entry for 23 September 1884; BL, Gordon Papers, Add. Ms. 34475 (vol. 2), f. 4.

22. Note dated 10 November 1884; Inclosure 2 in Wolseley to Hartington, No. 42 in *Egypt No. 9 (1885)* . See also Charles Gordon, *General Gordon's Last Journal* (London, Kegan Paul, Trench & Co., 1885), p. 1.

23. BL, Gordon Papers, Add. Ms. 34474 (vol. 1), f. 45.

24. Comments dated 21 March 1884; Cromer, *Political and Literary Essays*, vol. 1, pp. 101-2.

25. See entries for 15 September and 5 October 1884; BL, Gordon Papers, Add. Ms. 34474 (vol. 1), f. 35, and Add. Ms. 34476 (vol. 3), f. 32.

26. Letter dated 'Kartoum 16 April'; REM, Gordon Papers, framed double-sided original letter with seal, recto.

27. Letter dated '15.4.84 Kartoum'; ibid., verso.

28. BL, Gordon Papers, Add. Ms. 34474 (vol. 1), f. 45.

29. Ibid., ff. 16-17. See also ibid., Add. Ms. 34479 (vol. 6), ff. 14 and 16.

30. Hove, Wolseley Papers, SSL.9, f. cxcix.

31. Preston, *In Relief of Gordon*, p. 17.

32. Arthur, *Letters of Lord Wolseley*, p. 121.

33. BL, Gordon Papers, Add. Ms. 34476 (vol. 3), f. 31.

34. Arthur, *Letters of Lord Wolseley*, p. 124.

35. Entry dated 21 October 1884; BL, Gordon Papers, Add. Ms. 34478 (vol. 5), f. 4.

36. Traill, *England, Egypt, and the Sudan*, p. 89.

37. Entry dated 24 October 1884; BL, Gordon Papers, Add. Ms. 34478 (vol. 5), f. 21.

38. Preston, *In Relief of Gordon*, pp. 46-8.

39. Hove, Wolseley Papers, SSL.9, f. xxxii.

40. BL, Gordon Papers, Add. Ms. 34479 (vol. 6), f. 108.

41. *The Times*, 3 October 1884, p. 7.

42. Arthur, *Letters of Lord Wolseley*, p. 124.

43. *Leeds Mercury*, 4 October 1884, p. 6.

44. *Hansard*, vol. 293, c. 540.

45. Letter dated 15 January 1885; Hove, Wolseley Papers, W/P.14/1/i-ii.

46. *The Times*, 5 January 1885, p. 9.

47. Bahlman, *Sir Edward Walter Hamilton*, vol. 2, p. 763.

48. Hawkins and Powell, *Earl of Kimberley*, p. 351.

49. Gladstone's emphasis; Matthew, *Gladstone Diaries*, vol. 11, p. 271.

50. Matthew, *Gladstone Diaries*, vol. 11, p. 275.

51. Wylde, '83 to '87, vol. 2, p. 82.
52. F. Reginald Wingate, *Mahdiism and the Egyptian Sudan* (London: Macmillan, 1891), pp. 163-72.
53. Ibid., p. 170.
54. Maj. H.H. Kitchener, 'Notes on the Fall of Khartoum', Inclosure in Sir R. Thompson to Sir J. Pauncefoot, 11 September 1885, No. 42 in *Egypt No. 2 (1886) Further Correspondence Respecting the Affairs of Egypt.*
55. Bernard Allen, 'How Khartoum Fell', in *Journal of the Royal African Society*, 40/161 (1941), p. 329.
56. Rev. C.H. Robinson, 'Hausa Pilgrimages from the Western Sudan, Together with a Native Account of the Death of General Gordon', *The Geographical Journal* 2/5 (1893), pp. 451-4.
57. Preston, *In Relief of Gordon*, pp. 134-5.
58. Gwynn and Tuckwell, *Sir Charles Dilke*, vol. 2, p. 108.
59. Bahlman, *Sir Edward Walter Hamilton*, vol. 2, p. 788.
60. Matthew, *Gladstone Diaries*, vol. 11, p. 289.
61. J. Hirst Hollowell, *Did the Gladstone Government Abandon General Gordon? No: The Evidence of the Blue Books* (London, National Press Agency, 1885).
62. Charles Coe, *General Gordon In a New Light: The Cause of War and the Advocate of Peace* (Manchester, Tubbs, Brook & Chrystal, 1885), p. 15.
63. Strachey, *Eminent Victorians*, pp. 245-350.
64. Leslie Linder (ed.), *The Journal of Beatrix Potter: From 1881 to 1897* (London: Frederick Warne, 1974), p. 129.
65. Cromer, *Modern Egypt*, vol. 1, p. 583.
66. Boulger, *Life of Gordon*, p. 286.
67. Hove, Wolseley Papers, SSL.9, f. vii.
68. Ibid., f. cccx.
69. Wood, *Midshipman to Field Marshal*, vol. 2, pp. 172-3 and 180.
70. Buckle, *Letters of Queen Victoria*, vol. 3, p. 597.
71. Letter dated 17 February 1885; Charles Gordon, *Letters of General C.G. Gordon to His Sister M.A. Gordon* (London, Macmillan, 1888), pp. xvii-xviii.
72. Laffer, 'Gordon's Ghosts', pp. 62-8.
73. *The Times*, 6 February 1885, p. 9.
74. *The Morning Post*, 6 February 1885, p. 4.
75. *Reynold's Newspaper*, 22 February 1885.
76. National Union Publication No. 117, Manchester University, John Rylands Library, R142842.
77. Bahlman, *Sir Edward Walter Hamilton*, vol. 2, p. 789.
78. Hansard, vol. 286, cc. 760-1.
79. Gwynn and Tuckwell, *Sir Charles Dilke*, vol. 2, p. 110.
80. *Hansard*, vol. 294, c. 859; see also cc. 1052-1141 (23 February), 1193-1263 (24 February), 1425-1519 (26 February) and 1627-1726 (27 February).
81. Ibid., cc.1251-63.

82. Fabunmi, *Sudan in Anglo-Egyptian Relations*, p. 42.

83. *The Annual Register*, 1885, pp. 22-3.

84. Morley, *Life of Gladstone*, vol. 3, p. 176.

85. *Hansard*, vol. 294, c. 1597.

86. Cooke and Vincent, *The Governing Passion*, p. 35.

87. Robinson and Gallagher, *Africa and the Victorians*, pp. 141-51.

88. Gwynn and Tuckwell, *Sir Charles Dilke*, vol. 2, p. 111.

89. Entry for 8 March 1885; Hawkins and Powell, *Earl of Kimberley*, p. 352.

90. *The Times*, 14 March 1885, p. 4.

91. Richard Temple, 'The Mahdi and British India', *Contemporary Review* (March 1885), p. 314.

92. Gwynn and Tuckwell, *Sir Charles Dilke*, vol. 2, p. 110.

93. Matthew, *Gladstone Diaries*, vol. 11, pp. 291 fn.

94. Hartington to Wolseley, 9 February 1885, No. 17 in *Egypt No. 2 (1885) Correspondence Respecting British Military Operation in the Soudan*.

95. Vetch, *Sir Andrew Clarke*, pp. 269-71. see also J.B. Atlay, *Lord Haliburton: A Memoir of his Public Service* (Toronto, William Briggs, 1909), pp. 55-61.

96. *The Times*, 17 February 1885, p. 5.

97. *The Morning Post*, 7 February 1885, p. 3.

98. Matthew, *Gladstone Diaries*, vol. 11, pp. 293-4.

99. Holland, *Duke of Devonshire*, vol. 2, pp. 11-13.

100. Robinson, 'Imperial Problems', pp. 154-5.

101. Note dated 14 December 1884; Inclosure 4 in Wolseley to Hartington, No. 42 in *Egypt No. 9 (1885)*.

102. Wolseley to Hartington, dated 6 March 1885; Kew, War Office Papers, WO 32/127.

103. Mallet, *Earl of Northbrook*, p. 198.

104. Ramm, *Political Correspondence of Gladstone and Granville*, vol. 2, p. 348.

105. Quoted in Baring to Granville, 14 February 1885, No. 7 in *Egypt No. 3 (1885) Correspondence Respecting Prince Hassan's Mission to the Soudan*.

106. Buckle, *Letters of Queen Victoria*, vol. 3, pp. 622-3.

107. Gwynn and Tuckwell, *Sir Charles Dilke*, vol. 2, p. 114.

108. Bahlman, *Sir Edward Walter Hamilton*, vol. 2, p. 810.

109. Edward Spencer Beesley, *Retirement from the Soudan* (London, Positivist Society, 1885), p. 1.

110. Ibid., p. 2.

111. Matthew, *Gladstone Diaries*, vol. 11, p. 319.

112. Hawkins and Powell, *Earl of Kimberley*, p. 353.

113. Preston, *In Relief of Gordon*, pp. 166-7.

114. Gwynn and Tuckwell, *Sir Charles Dilke*, vol. 2, p. 117.

115. Buckle, *Letters of Queen Victoria*, vol. 3, p. 639.

116. Hove, Wolseley Papers, W/MEM/1/12.

117. Hartington to Wolseley, No. 40 in *Egypt No. 9 (1885)* .

Chapter 8

1. Letter dated; REM, Gordon Papers, 4801.39.1, ff. 3-4.
2. Helen Fenwick, *Civil Liberties and Human Rights* (Abingdon, Routledge-Cavendish, 2007), pp. 336-7.
3. Published on 10 March 1885 as *1884-85 (108)*. *Grant to the family of General Gordon. Estimate of the amount required in the year ending 31st March 1885, for a grant to the family of the late General Charles George Gordon*; see Laffer, 'Gordon's Ghosts', p. 58-9.
4. Note dated 19 March 1885; BL, Supplementary Gladstone Papers, Add. Ms. 56451, f. 176.
5. Hamilton's hand-written summary of correspondence between 18 March and 18 April 1885; BL, Gladstone Papers, Add. Ms. 44148, ff. 34-5.
6. Sir Henry Gordon to Edward Hamilton, 20 March 1886; ibid., f. 35.
7. Undated letter to Frank Power's mother, BL, Power Papers, Add. Ms. 58070, ff. 29-30.
8. BL, Supplementary Gladstone Papers, Add. Ms. 56451, f. 174; also BL, Gladstone Papers, Add. Ms. 44646, ff. 62-4.
9. Matthew, *Gladstone Diaries*, vol. 11, pp. 309-10.
10. Letter dated 22 March: Matthew, *Gladstone Diaries*, vol. 11, pp. 311.
11. Entry for 21 March 1885; Bahlman, *Sir Edward Walter Hamilton*, vol. 2, p. 818.
12. Entry for 22 March 1885; ibd., vol. 2, p 820.
13. Hamilton's summary; BL, Gladstone Papers, Add. Ms. 44148, f. 34.
14. Ibid., f. 35.
15. Hartington to Hamilton; ibid., ff. 30-2.
16. Matthew, *Gladstone Diaries*, vol. 11, p. 330.
17. A. Egmont Hake, *The Story of Chinese Gordon* (London: Remington, 1884).
18. Correspondence with Lord Cranborne, son of Lord Salisbury; Hatfield House, Salisbury Papers, S (4) 2/84.
19. Blunt, *Gordon At Khartoum*, p. 439.
20. WSRO, Blunt Papers, Box 25.
21. University College London (UCL), Special Collections, Kegan Paul Publication Accounts, Ledger 169.
22. Contract dated 7 May 1885; UCL, Special Collections, Contracts 142 (1874-1909); see 'Literary and Other Notes', *John Bull* (3,364/1885), p. 303.
23. Letter dated 7 July 1885; Stanley Lane-Poole, *Watson Pasha* (London, John Murray, 1919), p. 167.
24. Entry for 6 December 1884; BL, Gordon Papers, Add. Ms. 34479 (vol. 6), f. 98.
25. Ibid., Add. Ms. 34471 (vol. 1), f. 42.
26. Entry for 18 November 1884; ibid., Add. Ms. 34479 (vol. 6), f. 58.
27. Ibid., Add. Ms. 34479 (vol. 6), f. 4.
28. Ibid., f. 91.
29. Ibid., Add. Ms. 34474 (vol. 1), f. 22.
30. Ibid., Add. Ms. 34475 (vol. 2), f. 41. See also Robert Hunter, *Egypt Under the*

Khedives, 1805-1879: From Household Government to Modern Bureaucracy (Pittsburgh, University of Pittsburgh Press, 1984), p. 173.

31. BL, Gordon Papers, Add. Ms. 34475 (vol. 2), f. 32.

32. Cromer, *Modern Egypt*, vol. 1, p. 432.

33. Letter from Colonel Louis Gordon (son of Sir Henry) in Blunt, *Gordon at Khartoum*, p. 538.

34. Ibid., p. 475.

35. Alice Gascoyne-Cecil, *A Memory, 1887-1947* (London, n.p., 1950), p. 10.

36. Hatfield, Salisbury Papers, S (4) 1/37 and 2/84.

37. Captain Richard Middleton (Chief Agent from 1885-1902) to Cranborne; ibid., S (4) 1/19.

38. Letter dated 10 September 1885; ibid., S (4) 1/20.

39. Letter dated 17 October 1885; ibid., S (4) 1/25.

40. *Glasgow Herald*, 3 October 1885, p. 4.

41. *The Hull Packet and East Riding Times*, 13 November 1884.

42. *Country Gentleman*, 27 June 1885.

43. *Birmingham Daily Post*, 25 June 1885.

44. *Daily News*, 25 June 1885.

45. *Graphic*, 27 June 1885, and *The Times*, 25 June 1885, p. 8.

46. *Trewman's Exeter Flying Post*, 1 July 1885.

47. *Daily News*, 25 June 1885.

48. *Western Mail*, 25 June 1885, and *Aberdeen Weekly Journal*, 26 June 1885.

49. BL, Gordon Papers, Add. Ms. 34479 (vol. 6), f. 27; *Belfast News-Letter*, 25 June 1885.

50. *Glasgow Herald*, 25 June 1885; see Hake, *Journals of Major-Gen. Gordon*, p. xli.

51. Jeffrey Richards, *Imperialism and Music* (Manchester, MUP, 2001), p. 331. See also Andrew Thompson, *The Empire Strikes Back? The Impact of Imperialism on Britain from the Mid-Nineteenth Century* (London, Longman, 2005), pp. 50-1.

52. Bernard Porter, *Absent-Minded Imperialists: Empire, Society, and Culture in Britain* (Oxford: OUP, 2004), pp. 152 and 375 (Note 105); also N.G. Travers, *Too Late! (In Memoriam of General Gordon, the Hero of Khartoum)* (London, Hopwood & Crew, 1885).

53. William Muskerry and John Jourdain, *Khartoum! or, the Star of the Desert* (London, Samuel French, 1885).

54. Porter, *Absent-Minded Imperialists*, pp. 54, 336 (Note 92) and 337 (Note 111).

55. Richards, *Imperialism and Music*, pp. 60-61. Jerrold Moore, *Edward Elgar: A Creative Life* (Oxford, OUP, 1984), pp. 119-120 and 246-7, shows that Elgar had asked Jaeger not to add pressure by declaring any major work to be imminent.

56. Drage, *Cyril*, pp. 375-85, 478-82 and 498-9.

57. Anon., *Khartoum and Thither: A Poem* (Manchester, Heywood & Sons, 1885).

58. H.T. Rhoades in Anon. (ed.), *Epitaphs on C.G. Gordon* (London, William Rice, 1885), p. 19.

59. Longford, *Pilgrimage of Passion*, p. 184; also Lucy McDiarmid, 'Lady Gregory, Wilfrid Blunt, and London Table Talk', *Irish University Review* 34/1 (2004), pp. 67-80.

60. 'The Wind and the Whirlwind (1883)'; Wilfrid Blunt, *The Poetical Works of Wilfrid Scawen Blunt: A Complete Edition* (2 vols.) (London, Macmillan, 1914), pp. 221-35.

61. Letter dated 21 October 1882; WSRO, Blunt Papers, Box 24.

62. Blunt, *Gordon At Khartoum*, pp. 372-4.

63. John Holmes, *Dante Gabriel Rossetti and the Late Victorian Sonnet Sequence: Sexuality, Belief and the Self* (Aldershot, Ashgate, 2005), pp. 146-54.

64. *National Review*, 5 (1885), pp. 484-9.

65. 'Protest on Behalf of Boer Independence', quoted in Ann Colley, *Robert Louis Stevenson and the Colonial Imagination* (Aldershot, Ashgate, 2004), pp. 142-3.

66. Bradford Booth and Ernest Mehew (eds.), *The Letters of Robert Louis Stevenson* (6 vols.) (New Haven, Yale University Press, 1995), vol. 5, pp. 80-1.

67. Ibid., vol. 5, 81.

68. Ibid., vol. 6, pp. 250-1 fn.

69. Laity, *British Peace Movement*, p. 101.

70. Ibid., p. 102.

71. Fiona MacCarthy, *William Morris: A Life for Our Time* (London, Faber & Faber, 1994), p. 494.

72. Letter to his daughter, May Morris, dated 20 February 1885; Norman Kelvin (ed.), *The Collected Letters of William Morris* (5 vols.) (Princeton, Princeton University Press, 1987), vol. IIb (1885-8), p. 388.

73. Nicholas Salmon, *The William Morris Chronology* (Bristol, Thoemmes Press, 1996), pp. 143-4.

74. Edward Thompson, *William Morris: Romantic to Revolutionary* (London, Lawrence & Wishart, 1955), pp. 386.

75. Kelvin, *Letters of William Morris*, vol. IIb, p. 397.

76. *Pall Mall Gazette*, 11 February 1885, p. 7.

77. E. Belfort Bax, *Manifesto of the Socialist League on the Soudan War*, p. 3; International Institute of Social History, Amsterdam, Socialist League Archives, 177 and 3441.

78. Kelvin, *Letters of William Morris*, vol. IIb, p. 410.

79. Besant, *Gordon Judged*, p. 16.

80. Churchill, *The River War*, vol. 1, p 90.

81. Cynthia Behrman, 'The After-Life of General Gordon', *Albion: A Quarterly Journal Concerned with British Studies* 3/2 (1971), pp. 47-9.

82. An alliance between the Conservatives (316 seats) and the Liberal Unionists (77) achieved a comfortable parliamentary majority over the Liberals (reduced to 192) and the Irish Nationalists (85).

83. Mowat, 'From Liberalism to Imperialism', pp. 119-20.

84. G.N. Sanderson, *England, Europe and the Upper Nile, 1882-1899: A Study in the Partition of Africa* (Edinburgh, EUP, 1965), pp. 203-10.

85. Terje Tvedt, *The River Nile in the Age of the British: Political Ecology and the Quest for Economic Power* (London: I.B. Tauris, 2004), pp. 26-7.

86. ʿAbd-al-Wahāb Aḥmad ʿAbd-al-Raḥman, *Tūshka: Dirāsa tārīkhīa li-ḥamlat ʿAbd-al-Raḥman al-Nujūmi ʿala Miṣr* (Tūshka: An Historical Study of the Campaign of ʿAbd-al-Raḥman al-Nujūmi to Egypt') (Khartoum: KUP, 1989).

87. Speaking in the House of Commons on 5 February 1897, during a debate over a £800,000 allocation for the successful British advance on Dongola; *Hansard*, Series 4, vol. 45 (19 January-9 February 1897), c. 1446.

88. Letter dated 29 June 1894; Daly, *The Sirdar*, p. 66.

89. Ceulemans, 'Les Tentatives de Léopold II pour Engager le Colonel Charles Gordon', pp. 251-74; see also Shibeika, *British Policy*, p. 349, on Leopold's visit to London in October 1895 to press the point in person.

90. Robinson and Gallagher, *Africa and the Victorians*, p. 475.

91. Wylde, *'83 to '87*, vol. 2, p. 266.

92. Cromer, *Modern Egypt*, vol. 2, p. 80.

93. Lord Cromer's 'Report on the Conditions of Egypt (1891)', quoted in Omar, *The Soudan Question*, pp. 38-9.

94. Letter dated 13 February 1885; Inclosure 3 in No. 43, *Egypt No. 9 (1885)* .

95. Peter Holt, *The Source-Materials of the Sudanese Mahdīa* (Oxford: Clarendon Press, 1958), pp. 109-11. See also Daly, *The Sirdar*, p. 83.

96. Slatin, *Fire and Sword in the Sudan*, p. 630.

97. Ohrwalder, *Ten Years' Captivity*, pp. 449-50.

98. *The Times*, 26 October 1892, p. 11.

99. *The Graphic*, 22 Oct 1892, p. 502.

100. *Morning Post*, 2 December 1892, p. 4.

101. Major Reginald Wingate, 'General Report on the Egyptian Soudan, March 1895, Compiled from Statements made by Slatin Pasha', quoted in Daly, *The Sirdar*, p. 75.

102. 'Slatin Pasha's Story'; *The Times*, 3 February 1896, p. 10.

103. Baring to Rosebery, Kew, Cromer Papers, FO 633/6.

104. Cromer, *Modern Egypt*, vol. 2, p. 81.

105. Churchill, *River War*, vol. 2, p. 363.

106. Earl of Cromer, *Abbas II* (London, Macmillan, 1915).

107. Tvedt, *The River Nile in the Age of the British*, p. 335, Note 104.

108. Cromer, *Political Essays*, vol. 1, pp. 112-14.

109. Shibeika, *British Policy*, pp. 351-2; also Sanderson, 'Contributions from African Sources', pp. 84-8.

110. Cromer, *Political Essays*, vol. 2, pp. 313-14.

111. Magnus, *Kitchener*, p. 109.

112. Peter Holt, *A Calendar of the Correspondence of the Khalifa Abdullahi and Mahmoud Ahmed, A.H. 1315/1897-8 A.D.* (Khartoum, Ministry of the Interior, 1955).

113. Sanderson, 'Contributions from African Sources', pp. 74-5.
114. Secret memorandum from Salisbury to Cromer, 3 June 1898; Kew, Foreign Office Papers, FO 78/5050.
115. *Matthew, Gladstone Diaries, vol. 11, p. 165.*
116. Cromer, *Political Essays*, vol. 2, pp. 219-20.
117. Traill, *England, Egypt, and the Sudan*, pp. 231-2.

Appendix 1

Wolseley's instructions, 21 September 1884

Before you leave Cairo Her Majesty's Government think it desirable that you should receive general instructions as to the course which you are to pursue in connection with the affairs of the Soudan. The primary object of the expedition up the Valley of the Nile is to bring away General Gordon and Colonel Stewart from Khartoum. When that object has been secured no further offensive operations of any kind are to be undertaken.

Although you are not precluded from advancing as far as Khartoum, should you consider such a step essential to insure the safe retreat of General Gordon and Colonel Stewart, you should bear in mind that Her Majesty's Government is desirous to limit the sphere of your military operations as much as possible. They rely on you, therefore, not to advance further southwards than is absolutely necessary in order to attain the primary object of the expedition. You will endeavour to place yourself in communication with General Gordon and Colonel Stewart as soon as possible.

Supreme political and civilian power will be conferred upon you in respect of the affairs of the Nile valley south of Aswan. General Gordon and Colonel Stewart are placed under your orders.

In respect of all political matters, you will communicate with Her Majesty's Government, and receive their instructions through the Consul-General [Baring] at Cairo. You are aware that the policy of Her Majesty's Government is that Egyptian rule in the Soudan should cease. It is desirable that you should receive general orders as to two points which necessarily arise in connection with the method of carrying this policy into execution.

These are:

1. The steps to be taken to insure the safe retreat of the Egyptian troops and civil employés;

2. The policy to be adopted in respect to the future government of the Soudan, and especially of Khartoum.

The negotiations with the tribes for endeavouring to secure the safe retreat of the garrisons at Kassala may most conveniently be treated from Suakin and Massowah. You need not, therefore, take any steps in connection with this branch of the subject.

The position of the garrisons in Darfour, Bahr-el-Gazelle and Equatorial provinces renders it impossible that you should take any action which would facilitate their retreat without extending your operations far beyond the sphere which Her Majesty's Government is ready to sanction. As regards the Senaar garrison, Her Majesty's Government is not prepared to sanction the dispatch of an expedition of British troops up the Blue Nile in order to secure its retreat. From the last telegrams received from General Gordon, there is reason to hope that he has already taken steps to withdraw the Egyptian portion of the Senaar garrison.

You will use your best endeavours to insure the safe retreat of the Egyptian troops which constitute the Khartoum garrison, and of such of the civilian employés of Khartoum, together with their families, as may wish to return to Egypt.

As regards the future government of the Soudan, and especially of Khartoum, Her Majesty's Government would be glad to see [establish] a Government at Khartoum which, as far as all matters connected with the internal administration of the country are concerned, would be wholly independent of Egypt. The Egyptian Government would be prepared to pay a reasonable subsidy to any Chief or number of Chiefs who would be sufficiently powerful to maintain orders along the Valley of the Nile from Wady Halfa to Khartoum, and who would agree to the following condition:

1. To remain at peace with Egypt, and to repress any raids on Egyptian territory;

2. To encourage trade with Egypt;

3. To prevent and discourage by all possible means, any expedition for the sale of and capture of slaves.

You are authorised to conclude any arrangements which fulfil these general conditions. The main difficulty will consist in the selection of an individual, or of a number of individuals, having sufficient authority to maintain order. You will, of course, bear in mind that any ruler established south of Wady Halfa will have to rely solely on his own strength in order to maintain his position. I have already mentioned that under certain conditions the Egyptian government would be prepared to pay a moderate subsidy in order to secure tranquillity and fairly good government in the Valley of the Nile.

Beyond the adoption of this measure neither Her Majesty's Government nor the Egyptian Government are ready to assume any responsibility whatsoever for the government of the Nile Valley south of Wady Halfa.

Appendix 2

The Mahdī to Gordon on the capture of the ʿAbbās, 22 October 1884

Translation by ʿUthmān al-Nuṣairi

In the name of God, the merciful and compassionate. Praise be to Allah, the overall noble ruler, and blessings be upon our lord Mohammed and his descendents! What follows is from the devotee who holds fast to Allah and seeks His refuge, Muḥammad al-Mahdī, son of ʿAbdallah, addressed to Gordon Pasha of Khartoum, may Allah guide him to the right path! Amen.

Now to business. You should know that your small steamer [coll. Ar. *wabūr*, from Fr. *vapeur*, 'steamer'], the ʿAbbās, which you sent to carry your news to Egypt via Dongola and on board which were your deputy, Stewart Pasha, the French and English Consuls and their other companions, has fallen into our hands, with permission from Allah. Those among them who believed in my calling as the Mahdī and surrendered to me survived and were spared. Those who did not – including your deputy, the Consuls and the others – perished. Allah took their souls straight to Hell – what a wretched end! The steamer and its cargo are now become spoils for the faithful.

We have now read all the correspondence and documentation, in Arabic, English – as well as those in code [coll. Ar. *jafrawīa*, from Fr. *chiffre*, 'code'], for the cypher was cracked by those of us whose hearts were blessed with faith and illuminated with intelligence. The letters you sent to the Mudīr of Dongola, in addition to those addressed to Egypt and Europe, have all been seized and their contents made known to us. Initially, I resolved to return the whole collection to you as they are of no further use to me; however, I have decided instead to cite a representative sample as proof of what has happened – in the hope that Allah will guide you to Islam and submission, so that you and your subordinates will be safe and will win the eternal grace of Allah.

So: among these documents I have the following:

- A coded letter, dated 1 Dhū al-Ḥijja 1301 [21 September 1884; this must be an error], addressed to Muṣṭafa Yāwir, Mudīr of Dongola, in reply to his letter of 30 August 1882 by the Frankish [European] calendar, in which you promoted him to the rank of general. Attached is a telegram to the Khedive of Egypt endorsing the promotion;
- An inventory of your grain supply, stamped with the seal of its supervisor, ʿUthmān Mūsa: 3,374¾ ardabs of sorghum;
- An inventory of ammunition, stamped with the seal of its supervisor, Muḥammad Mūsa, and dated 25 Shawwāl 1301 [17 August 1884]: 580,395 rounds;
- A telegram written to the Khedive of Egypt, Nūbār Pasha and the English Consul-General in Egypt [Baring] from 19 individuals whose seals it bears, among them the Chief of the Appeal Council, Ḥassan ʿAbd-al-Moneim, and others who express the wish to replace the Sudanese railway line planned by the Egyptian government with river boats, military posts and telegraph lines between the Nile cataracts
- A letter, found on the body of the French Consul, written by you to him on 18 Ramadān 1301 [12 July 1884], about the distribution of 100 francs to the poor;
- Your letter, dated Dhū al-Qaʿda 1301 [22 August-20 September 1884] and addressed to Nūbār Pasha, the English Consul-General and the overseer of the Egyptian treasury, informing them about the fate of the £50,000 sent by Egypt and seized as booty by the Anṣār of the Faith;
- Notification of a loan from Khartoum merchants, at 1% interest, to be paid to their representatives in Cairo;
- Your letter, dated Dhū al-Qaʿda 1301 [22 August-20 September 1884], to the head of the Council of Nuzār [tribal chieftains], with an attachment listing 16 applicants to be granted the rank of nāzir;
- Your letter dated 21 Shawwāl 1302 [13 August 1884], to the Khedive of Egypt, confirming promotions and decorations awarded to 11 named officers, among them al-Nūr Bakr Muḥammad, garrison commander at Sinnār, who is made a general;*
- Your telegram, dated Dhū al-Qaʿda 1301 [22 August-20 September 1884], to

---

* Al-Nūr Muḥammad, a Sinnār native, was a career soldier in the Egyptian army. He lost both his legs in the siege.

the Khedive, endorsing the promotions of Ibrāhīm Fawzī, Mūsa Shawqī and Muḥammad Nusshi to the rank of general;

- Letters in English describing the siege of Khartoum, the loss of your steamers, the number of your troops, your stock of artillery and other guns, your military deployments, your defeats, your requests for a rescue expedition – even one consisting of just one division;
- Letters describing the conversion of your agent Cuzzi to Islam, as well as the letters you have received from my commanders and administrators with their sound advice;
- A list of the Europeans still in Khartoum: three Englishmen, two Austrians, one Frenchman, four Italians and 40 Greeks;
- An inventory of rifles, ammunitions, artillery and other equipment, stamped with the seal of Faraj al-Zein, your troop commandant: two Krupps guns with 284 shells; 21 mountain guns with 2,303 shells; two mortars with 315 rounds, five different artillery pieces with 565 rockets; two mitrailleuses with no ammunition; eight rocket-tubes with 599 rockets; 7,460 Remington rifles with 150,233 bullets; 1,205 other rifles; 246 double-barrelled guns; 127 old-fashioned muskets; and 19 pistols;
- A list of your own *jihādīa* [lit. 'holy warriors', an elite rifle corps]: two generals, two colonels, five junior officers and 2,370 soldiers, along with Bashi-bazouk units, the Shaiqīa and the Khidairīa, making a total of 4,797 men in 26 units;
- Statements about the arsenal and the steamers, one after another;
- The letters of Sālih al-Malik [*sic*], the former Sanjak who surrendered to the Mahdīa. One of these was dated 4 Rajab 1301 [30 April 1884]; in another, he described his deeds and asked to be paid his dues;
- The telegram signed by 43 officers, heads of government departments, judges, muftis and *ʿulamā*ʾ, dated 9 Dhū al-Qaʿda 1301 [30 August 1884], in which they begged the Khedive for the assistance of the Egyptian government. Attached to that was your own compass, sent to the Mudīr of Dongola so that he could forward it;
- Your coded telegrams, one dated 15 Shawwāl 1301 [7 August 1884] and addressed to the Khedive, in which you state that on your arrival at Khartoum you realized that evacuating the troops to Egypt was impossible because of the uprising and the disruption of the route. That, you say, was why you asked for a rescue expedition, which did not come, even when the *mudīrīa* of Berber was under threat. You add that you were one of only seven men to come to Khartoum after the destruction of Hicks' army. You request to have telegrams sent to you in Arabic so that the people of Khartoum may know things clearly: coded messages have been a useless waste of time. Your frequent promises to the people of Khartoum – that a rescue expedition was

on its way, or Syrian [*sic*] troops, or that your deputy, Stewart, and his companions (whom Allah has annihilated) were on their way to [Muṣṭafā] Yāwar of Dongola – have only made you look like a liar;

- A second telegram of the same date, addressed to the head of the Council of Nuzār and the English Consul-General in Egypt;

- Another, dated 5 Dhū al-Qaʿda 1301 [26 August 1884] and sent to the Khedive, in which you promise to send troops to strike Sheikh al-ʿUbeiḍ: the troops made their sortie and were annihilated by Allah;

- An undated letter to the Khedive, in which you ask variously for English troops to be sent, for al-Zubeir Pasha to be appointed at the head of an expedition of Egyptian forces or for Sudan to be placed under the authority of the [Ottoman] Sultan at the cost of £200,000. None of these options were implemented and those soldiers already in Sudan are being killed;

- Your statement declaring that Muḥammad ʿAlī Pasha is the only reliable officer in Sudan and that you rely on him as your deputy. But Allah annihilated this Muḥammad ʿAlī of yours;

- A telegram dated Dhū al-Qaʿda 1301 [22 August-20 September 1884] to the Khedive, Nūbār Pasha and the English Consul-General, in which you reveal that you are expecting the requested expedition by the Merowe route;

- A telegram sent to the same officials on the same date, in which you describe your skirmishes against the Anṣār; also that you have supplies to last you for five months;

- A telegram dated 3 Dhū al-Qaʿda 1301 [24 August 1884] to the same officials, in which you claim that Sheikh al-ʿUbeiḍ had been killed and repeat the mistaken report that I had arrived in the vicinity of Khartoum;

- Your letter to the head of the Council of Nuzār and the English Consul-General, dated 15 Shawwāl 1301 [7 August 1884], in which you report that you have despatched three steamers to assess the situation at Sinnār and that you will be sending troops by boat to retake Berber – and that you will send Stewart and the Consuls (whom Allah annihilated) with them;

- A telegram of the same date to the same recipients, in which you promise to send 2,000 soldiers to retake Berber and warning them that if the expedition does not come to reinforce them the town will be captured as before, when the Nile falls;

- A telegram to the Khedive and Nūbār Pasha dated 17 Dhū al-Qaʿda 1301 [7 September 1884], in which you state that, while you had hoped to relieve the Sinnār garrison, it had not been possible. You also report the discomfort of the townspeople and garrisons of both Khartoum and Sinnār because of the non-appearance of the rescue expedition;

- One dated 8 Dhū al-Qaʿda 1301 [29 August 1884] to the Khedive, Nūbār Pasha and the English Consul-General, which refers to the despatch of Stewart and his companions aboard the small steamer. You say you have repeatedly written to request an expedition, as well as a re-evaluation of the predicament of the Sudanese, but have received no response at all;

- Your telegram of 15 Shawwāl 1301 [7 August 1884], in which you state that the Khedive's firman to the tribal chiefs, dignitaries and people of Sudan – declaring that the troops were to be evacuated from the country and that it was to be left under the leadership of its own people – could not be made public because of events;
- Two seals engraved with my name, which are clearly forgeries.

In conclusion, all your news is known to me: everything that you hide in your innermost thoughts and all that you rely upon for your sense of power and invincibility, which was not given you by God. It was no good using codes or different languages in your correspondence, because nothing escapes the eye of Allah. As to your expecting reinforcements, reliance for succour on anything other than Allah will bring you nothing but destruction: it is the biggest peril of this life and the afterlife. That is because, by my declaration as the Mahdī, Allah has banished corruption and suppressed the deviant and the obstinate. God has guided the reasonable to the path of integrity. As for me, I take as my only points of reference Allah and his Prophet.

You have no doubt been informed of what happened to your brothers at Suakin who also hoped be rescued: Allah scattered and exterminated them.

I am now on the bank of the river, not far from Omdurman, and by God's will I am coming in your direction. If you become a Muslim and surrender to God's order and that of his Messenger and if you believe in me as the Mahdī, send me a message, after laying down your arms and giving up all thought of fighting, so that I may send you someone to give you safe conduct. In this way, you will win the advantages and blessings of this life and the next. If, however, you do not, you will have to face war from Allah and his Messenger!

Allah is capable of destroying you, as he has destroyed those stronger and more numerous than you before. Your property and families will then be loot and spoils for the faithful. You will then regret your choice – and once war breaks out regret is useless. There is no power or strength except through Allah – and peace lies upon those who follow the right path.

Bibliography

Abbreviations

BJMES: *British Journal of Middle Eastern Studies*
BL: British Library
CR: *Contemporary Review*
EUP: Edinburgh University Press
HJ: *The Historical Journal*
HMSO: Her Majesty's Stationery Office
JAH: *Journal of African History*
JICH: *Journal of Imperial and Commonwealth History*
JRAS: *Journal of the Royal African Society*
KUP : Khartoum University Press
MUP: Manchester University Press
NC: *The Nineteenth Century*
OUP: Oxford University Press
PUP: Princeton University Press
SAD: Sudan Archive, University of Durham
SNR: *Sudan Notes and Records*
SOAS: School of Oriental and African Studies
SS: *Sudan Studies*
UBP : University of Bergen Press
UCP: University of California Press
UPP: University of Pittsburgh Press
YUP: Yale University Press

Primary Sources

BOOKS AND ARTICLES
Abū-Salīm, Muḥammad Ibrāhīm, (ed.) *al-Athār al-kāmila li'l-Imām al-Mahdī* ('The Collected Works of the Imām al-Mahdī'). 7 vols. Khartoum: KUP, 1990-94.

194

Adye, Sir John, *Recollections of a Military Life*. New York: Macmillan & Co., 1895.

Allen, Charles H. *The Life of "Chinese" Gordon, R.E., C.B.* London: HMSO, 1884.

Anonymous. *The Annual Register, 1885*

—— (ed.) *Epitaphs on C.G. Gordon*. London: William Rice, 1885.

—— 'From Suakin to Berber', *Science* 5/12 (1885): 254-6.

—— *Khartoum and Thither: A Poem*. Manchester: Heywood & Sons, 1885.

—— *Life of Gordon*. London: Walter Scott, n.d.

—— *Mr. John M. Cook's Visit to the Soudan, in Connection with the Expedition of 1884-85*. London: n.p., 1885.

—— [Sir Henry Gordon] 'The Position of General Gordon: A Conversation', *CR* 45/866 (1884).

Archer, Thomas. *War in Egypt and the Soudan: An Episode in the History of the British Empire*. 4 vols. London: Blackie & Son, 1886.

Arthur, Sir George. (ed.) *The Letters of Lord and Lady Wolseley*. London: Heinemann, 1922.

Bahlman, Dudley. (ed.) *The Diary of Sir Edward Walter Hamilton, 1880-1885*. 2 vols. Oxford: Clarendon Press, 1972.

Baker, Sir Samuel White. 'Egypt's Proper Frontier, *NC* 89 (July 1884).

—— 'The Soudan and its Future', *CR* 45/65 (1884).

Bax, E. Belfort and Morris, William. 'Manifesto of the Socialist League on the Soudan War', *Labour Monthly* 34/7 (1952): 303-6.

Beesley, Edward Spencer. *Retirement from the Soudan*. London: Positivist Society, 1885.

Besant, Annie W. *Gordon Judged out of his Own Mouth*. London: Freethought Publishing Co., 1885.

Birkbeck Hill, George. (ed.) *Colonel Gordon in Central Africa, 1874-79, from Letters and Documents*. London: T. de la Rue & co., 1881.

Blunt, Wilfrid Scawen. *Gordon At Khartoum: Being a Personal Narrative of Events*. London: Stephen Swift & Co., 1911.

—— *Secret History of the English Occupation of Egypt: A Personal Narrative of Events*. New York: Knopf, 1922.

Boulger, Demetrius. *Life of Gordon*. 2 vols. London: T. Fisher Unwin, 1896.

Bowen, John. 'The Conflict of East and West in Egypt. III: The Sûdan and the Mahdi', *Political Science Quarterly* 1/4 (1886): 636-77.

Buckle, George E. (ed.) *The Letters of Queen Victoria: Second Series, 1879-1885*. 3 vols. London: John Murray, 1928.

Burnett, Charles J. *What is it it to be: Order or Chaos: Out of our Egyptian and North-Eastern Central African Crisis . . . ?* London: n.p., 1884.

Butler, Sir William. *The Campaign of the Cataracts: Being a Personal Narrative of the Great Nile Expedition of 1884-5*. London: Sampson Low, Marston, Searle & Rivington, 1887.

—— *Charles George Gordon*. London: Macmillan, 1897.

—— *Sir William Butler: An Autobiography*. London: Constable, 1913.

Chaillé Long, Charles. *The Three Prophets: Chinese Gordon, Mohammed-Ahmed (El Maahdi), Arabi Pasha*. New York: D. Appleton & Co., 1884.

Childers, Lt.-Col. Spencer. *The Life and Correspondence of the Right Honourable Hugh C.E. Childers, 1827-1896*. 2 vols. London: John Murray, 1901.

Churchill, Winston. *The River War: An Historical Account of the Reconquest of the Soudan*. 2 vols. London: Longman, Green & Co., 1899.

Coe, Charles C. *General Gordon in a New Light: The Cause of War and the Advocate of Peace*. London: Simpkin, Marshall & Co., 1885.

Colomb, Vice-Admiral Philip H. *Memoirs of Admiral the Right Honble. Sir Astley Cooper Key*. London: Methuen & Co., 1898.

Cromer, Earl [Sir Evelyn Baring]. *Abbas II*. London: Macmillan, 1915.

—— *Modern Egypt*. 2 vols. London: Macmillan, 1908.

—— *Political and Literary Essays, 1908-1913*. 3 vols. London: Macmillan, 1913-16.

Daly, Martin. (ed.) *The Road to Shaykan: Letters of General William Hicks Pasha, Written During the Sennar and Kordofan Campaigns, 1883*. Durham: University of Durham, 1983.

Felkin, Dr Robert. 'The Egyptian Soudan', *The Scottish Geographical Magazine* 1/6 (June 1885): 235-6.

Fitzmaurice, Lord Edmond. *The Life of Granville George Leveson Gower: Second Earl Granville, K.G., 1815-1891*. 2 vols. London: Longmans, Green & Co., 1905.

Galloway, William. *The Battle of Tofrek: Fought Near Suakin, March 22nd, 1885*. London: W.H. Allen, 1887.

Gascoyne-Cecil, Alice. *A Memory, 1887-1947*. London: n.p., 1950.

Gladstone, William. 'Aggression on Egypt and Freedom in the East', *NC* 2 (1877): 149-66.

—— *The Bulgarian Horrors and the Question of the East*. London: John Murray, 1876.

—— 'England's Mission', *NC* 4 (1878): 560-84.

—— *Political Speeches in Scotland, March and April 1880*. 2 vols. Edinburgh: Andrew Elliot, 1880.

Gordon, Charles G. *General Gordon's Last Journal*. London: Kegan Paul, Trench & Co., 1885.

—— *Letters of General C.G. Gordon to His Sister M.A. Gordon*. London: Macmillan, 1888.

Graham, Lt.-Gen. Sir Gerald. *Last Words with Gordon*. London: Chapman & Hall, 1887.

Grant, James. 'Route March, with Camels, from Berber to Korosko in 1863', *Proceedings of the Royal Geographical Society* 6/6 (1884): 326-35.

Gwynn, Stephen. *The Life of the Rt. Hon. Sir Charles W. Dilke, Bart., M.P.* (ed. Gertrude Tuckwell). 2 vols. London: John Murray, 1917.

Haggard, Andrew. *Under Crescent and Star*. London: William Blackwood, 1895.

Hake, A. Egmont. *The Journals of Major-General C.G. Gordon, C.B., at Kartoum*. London: Kegan, Paul, Trench & Co., 1885.

—— *The Story of Chinese Gordon*. London: Remington, 1884.

Hammill, Captain Tynte F. *Passage of the Second Cataract and Cataract of Semneh by the Nile Steamers "Nassif Khaeir" and "Gizeh" in September and October 1884.* London: Admiralty Foreign Intelligence Committee, No. 75 (August 1885).

Hawkins, Angus and Powell, John. (eds.) *The Journal of John Wodehouse, First Earl of Kimberley, for 1862-1902.* London: Royal Historical Society, 1997.

Henley, W.E. and Wyndham, George Blunt (eds.). *The Poetical Works of Wilfrid Scawen Blunt: A Complete Edition.* 2 vols. London: Macmillan, 1914.

Holland, Bernard. *The Life of Spencer Compton, Eight Duke of Devonshire* [Lord Hartington]. 2 vols. London: Longmans, Green & Co., 1911.

Hollowell, J. Hirst. *Did the Gladstone Government Abandon General Gordon? No: The Evidence of the Blue Books.* London: National Press Agency, 1885.

Holt, Peter. *A Calendar of the Correspondence of the Khalifa Abdullahi and Mahmoud Ahmed, A.H. 1315/1897-8 A.D.* Khartoum: Ministry of the Interior, 1955.

de Kusel, Baron Samuel Selig. *An Englishman's Recollections of Egypt 1863-1887.* London: John Lane, 1915.

Lang, Andrew. *Life, Letters, and Diaries of Sir Stafford Northcote, First Earl of Iddesleigh.* Edinburgh: William Blackwood & Sons, 1891.

Linder, Leslie. (ed.) *The Journal of Beatrix Potter: From 1881 to 1897.* London: Frederick Warne, 1974.

Loring, Maj.-Gen. William. *A Confederate Soldier in Egypt.* New York: Dodd, Mead & Co., 1884.

Mallet, Bernard. *Thomas George, Earl of Northbrook, G.C.S.I.: A Memoir.* London: Longmans, Green & Co., 1908.

von Malortie, Baron Karl. *Here There and Everywhere: Being the Second Part of "'Twixt Old Times and New".* London: Ward & Downey, Ltd., 1895.

Matthew, Colin. (ed.) *The Gladstone Diaries: With Cabinet Minutes and Prime Ministerial Correspondence.* 14 vols. Oxford: Clarendon Press, 1986.

Muskerry, William and Jourdain, John. *Khartoum! or, the Star of the Desert.* London: Samuel French, 1885.

Ohrwalder, Fr Joseph. *Ten Years' Captivity in the Mahdi's Camp, 1882-1892* (ed. F.R. Wingate). London: Sampson Low Marston & Co., 1892.

Palmer, Roundell [Lord Selborne]. *Memorials: Part II. Personal and Political 1865-1895.* 2 vols. London: Macmillan & Co., 1898.

Patterson, Henry. *The Imâm Mahdi; or The Moslem Millennium, from the Koran and Authentic Traditions.* London: Hamilton, Adams & Co., 1884.

Pimblett, W. Melville. *Story of the Soudan War: From the Rise of the Revolt July, 1881, to the Fall of Khartoum and death of Gordon, Jan., 1885.* London: Remington & Co., 1885.

Ponsonby, Arthur. *Henry Ponsonby: Queen Victoria's Private Secretary: His Life from His Letters.* London: Macmillan: 1942.

Power, Frank. *Letters from Khartoum: Written During the Siege.* London: Sampson, Low, Marston, Searle & Rivington, 1885.

Preston, Adrian. (ed.) *In Relief of Gordon: Lord Wolseley's Campaign Journal of the Khartoum Relief Expedition 1884-1885*. London: Hutchinson, 1967.

Ramm, Agatha. (ed.) *The Political Correspondence of Mr. Gladstone and Lord Granville, 1876-1886*. 2 vols. Oxford: Clarendon Press, 1962.

Robinson, Rev. C.H. 'Hausa Pilgrimages from the Western Sudan, Together with a Native Account of the Death of General Gordon', *The Geographical Journal* 2/5 (1893): 451-4.

Slatin, Rudolf. *Fire and Sword in the Sudan: A Personal Narrative of Fighting and Serving the Dervishes, 1879-1895* (ed. F.R. Wingate). London: Edward Arnold, 1896.

Stanley, Henry Morton. *The Congo and the Founding of its Free State: A Story of Work and Exploration*. 2 vols. London: Sampson Low, Marston, Searle & Rivington, 1886.

—— *In Darkest Africa: Or the Quest, Rescue and Retreat of Emin, Governor of Equatoria*. 2 vols. London: Sampson Low, 1890.

Stephenson, Lt.-Gen. Sir Frederick. *At Home and on the Battlefield: Letters from the Crimea, China and Egypt, 1854-1888*. London: John Murray, 1915.

Stone, Col. Charles P. 'The Route from Suakin to Berber', *Science* 5/114 (1885): 290.

Stronach, George and Halkett, George. *The Egyptian Red Book*. Edinburgh: William Blackwood & Sons, 1885.

Temple, Richard. 'The Mahdi and British India', *CR* (March 1885): 306-14.

Travers, N.G. *Too Late! (In Memoriam of General Gordon, the Hero of Khartoum*. London: Hopwood & Crew, 1885.

Vetch, Col. Robert. *Life of Lieut.-General the Hon. Sir Andrew Clarke, G.C.M.G, C.B., C.I.E.* London: John Murray, 1905.

—— *Life, Letters, and Diaries of Lieut.-General Sir Gerald Graham, V.C., C.B., R.E.: With Portraits, Plans and His Principal Despatches*. Edinburgh: William Blackwood & Sons, 1901.

Villiers, Frederic. 'My Friend Corporal Tonbar', *The Canadian Magazine* 15 (1900): 38-43.

Walling, Robert. (ed.) *The Diaries of John Bright*. London: Cassell, 1930.

Wilson, Col. Sir Charles. 'Gordon's Staff-Officer at Khartum', *Blackwood's Edinburgh Magazine* 161/977 (March 1897): 317-30.

Wolseley, Field Marshal Viscount Garnet. *The Story of a Soldier's Life*. 2 vols. London: Archibald Constable & Co., 1903.

—— *The Use of Railroads in War: A Lecture Delivered at Aldershot, on the 20th January, 1873* London: Edwin S. Boot, 1873

Wood, Sir Evelyn. *From Midshipman to Field Marshal*. 2 vols. London: Methuen, 1906.

Wylde, Augustus B. *'83 to '87 in the Soudan : With an Account of Sir William Hewett's Mission to King John of Abyssinia*. 2 vols. London: Remington & Co., 1888.

GOVERNMENT PAPERS

Egypt No. 1 (1883) Further Correspondence Respecting the Affairs of Egypt

Egypt No. 2 (1883) Correspondence Respecting Reorganization in Egypt

Egypt No. 5 (1883) Further Correspondence Respecting the Affairs in Egypt

Egypt No. 6 (1883) Further Correspondence Respecting Reorganization in Egypt

Egypt No. 11 (1883) Report on the Soudan by Lieutenant-Colonel Stewart

Egypt No. 13 (1883) Correspondence Respecting the Affairs of Egypt

Egypt No. 22 (1883) Further Correspondence Respecting the Affairs of Egypt

Egypt No. 1 (1884) Further Correspondence Respecting the Affairs of Egypt

Egypt No. 2 (1884) Correspondence Respecting General Gordon's Mission to Egypt

Egypt No. 6 (1884) Despatch from Her Britannic Majesty's Agent and Consul-General in Egypt, Inclosing Further Instructions to General Gordon

Egypt No. 8 (1884) Further Correspondence Respecting the Affairs of the Soudan

Egypt No. 12 (1884) Further Correspondence Respecting the Affairs of Egypt

Egypt No. 13 (1884) Further Correspondence Respecting the Affairs of Egypt

Egypt No. 22 (1884) Further Correspondence Respecting the Affairs of Egypt

Relief of General Gordon. 1884-85. Vote of Credit, £.300,000

Egypt No. 34 (1884) Further Correspondence Respecting the Affairs of Egypt

Egypt No. 35 (1884) Further Correspondence Respecting the Affairs of Egypt

Egypt No. 1 (1885) Further Correspondence Respecting the Affairs of Egypt

Egypt No. 2 (1885) Correspondence Respecting British Military Operations in the Soudan

Egypt No. 3 (1885) Correspondence Respecting Prince Hassan's Mission to the Soudan

Egypt No. 9 (1885) Further Correspondence Respecting British Military Operations in the Soudan

1884-85 (108) Grant to the family of General Gordon. Estimate of the amount required in the year ending 31st March 1885, for a grant to the family of the late General Charles George Gordon

1884-85 (298). Supplementary Estimate for Civil Services, 1885-86 (Monument in Memory of General C.G. Gordon)

Egypt No. 2 (1886) Further Correspondence Respecting the Affairs of Egypt

The Monthly Army List for January, 1884. London: War Office, 1883.

The Monthly Army List for January, 1885. London: War Office, 31 December 1884.

The Monthly Army List for October, 1884. London: War Office, 1884.<

HANSARD

1883: Vol. 276 (15 Feb – 9 March); Vol. 277 (10 March – 10 April); Vol. 278 (11 April – 4 May); Vol. 279 (7 May – 7 June); Vol. 280 (8 – 29 June); Vol. 281 (2 – 19 July); Vol. 282 (20 July – 9 August); Vol. 283 (10 – 25 August)

[Parliament was prorogued until 12 November 1883, then until 19 December, then until 5 February 1884.]

1884: Vol. 284 (5 – 25 February); Vol. 285 (26 February – 15 March); Vol. 286 (17

March – 7 April); Vol. 287 (8 April – 9 May); Vol. 288 (12 May – 10 June); Vol. 289 (11 June – 3 July); Vol. 290 (4 – 21 July); Vol. 291 (22 July – 5 August); Vol. 292 (6 – 14 August)

[Parliament was prorogued until 15 September 1884, then until 23 October.]

Vol. 293 (23 October – 17 November)

[Parliament was adjourned from 24 November to 2 December 1884, then from 6 December to 19 February 1885.]

1885: Vol. 294 (19 February – 3 March 1885); Vol. 295 (4 – 19 March)

NEWSPAPERS AND PERIODICALS
Aberdeen Weekly Journal, Belfast News-Letter, Belford's Magzine, Berrow's Worcester Journal, Birmingham Daily Post, Birmingham Gazette, Bristol Mercury, Country Gentleman, Daily News, Daily Post, Daily Telegraph, Derby Mercury, Exeter Flying Post, Freeman's Journal & Daily Commercial Advertiser, Glasgow Herald, Graphic, Hull Packet and East Riding Times, Ipswich Journal, Irish Times, John Bull, Leeds Mercury, Liberté, Liverpool Mercury, Lloyd's Weekly Newspaper, Manchester Guardian, Monthly Packet, Morning Advertiser, Morning Post, New York Times, Pall Mall Gazette, Punch, Quebec Morning Chronicle, Reynold's Newspaper, Saturday Review, Spectator, Standard, Strand Magazine, Sydney Herald, The Times, Trewman's Exeter Flying Post, Vanity Fair, Western Mail, Yorkshire Herald, Yorkshire Post

MANUSCRIPTS
British Library (Add. Mss.), London
11601.H.13: *Poems 1885-99*
34474-9: Gordon Papers: Khartoum journals and correspondence
43573: Ripon Papers: Correspondence with Northbrook, Gordon et al. (1880-4)
43875 and 43923: Dilke Papers: Correspondence re. Gordon Relief Expedition
44131, 441478, 44267, 44629 and 44646: Gladstone Papers: Correspondence and
    official documents (1884-5)
51298-300: Gordon Papers (Moffitt Collection)
52388: Gordon Papers (Bell Collection): Correspondence
55074: Macmillan Archive: Seeley correspondence
56451-2: Supplementary Gladstone Papers: 1884-5 cabinet minutes, notes, corre-
    spondence and telegrams; copy of Gordon's will
58069 and 58070: Power Papers: Correspondence

National Records Office (Dār al-Wathāʿiq al-Qawmīa), Khartoum
CAIRINT 1/3/8: Khedive Ismail's firman to Gordon (16 February 1874)

CAIRINT 1/3/15: 'Insurrection of the False Prophet 1881-83' (report by Captain
    JJ Leverson, 1883-4)
INTEL 1/15/74: Gordon's pamphlet, *Account of the Actions of Zubeir Pasha*
INTEL 5/2/12-14: Nusshi report/Bordeini commentary on fall of Khartoum

Hatfield House (Salisbury Papers)
S (4) 1/19, 20, 25, 26, 37; 2/84: Correspondence between Hake and Cranborne

Hove Public Library (Wolseley Papers)
M1/12/27: Notes on Gordon relief expedition
NRA.1047: Miscellaneous Wolseley correspondence
SSL/9/1-2: Wolseley's notes for (unpublished) third and fourth volumes of his
    autobiography, *The Story of a Soldier's Life*
W/MEM/1: Miscellaneous Wolseley memoranda
W/P.13: 'Special General Order, Dongola, 30th November, 1884'
W/P.14: Letters from Wolseley to his wife
W/PLB.1: Correspondence with King Leopold of Belgium re. Gordon
[No shelfmark]: Coded letter from Wolseley to Gordon

International Institute of Social History, Amsterdam
Socialist League Archives, 177 and 3441: E. Belfort Bax, *Manifesto of the Socialist
    League on the Soudan War*

National Archives, Kew, London
CAB 37/12: Cabinet Papers: Gordon Relief Expedition
FO 30/129/146: Foreign Office Papers: Granville-Cross correspondence
FO 633/4: Cromer Papers: Correspondence with Northbrook
FO 633/6-7: Cromer Papers: Correspondence re. Egypt/Sudan
FO 633/53-4: Cromer Papers: Correspondence relating to Gordon's mission
FO 78/3442: Foreign Office Papers: Malet correspondence re. Egypt/Sudan
FO 78/3620: Foreign Office Papers: Dufferin correspondence re. Egypt/Sudan
FO 78/3680-4: Foreign Office Papers: Baring correspondence (1884)
FO 78/5050: Foreign Office Papers: Nile expedition
PRO 30/29: Granville Papers: Correspondence re. Egypt/Sudan
WO 32/124: War Office Papers: Correspondence relating to the Nile and Suakin
    expeditions, the proposed Suakin-Berber railway and various military
    matters

National Maritime Museum, London
HMM/3-4: Report by Captain Tynte Hammill, RN: 'Passage of the Second Cataract
    and Cataract of Semneh by the Nile steamers "Nassif Kheir" and "Gizeh" in
    September and October 1884'

Norfolk County Library, Norwich (Baggallay Papers)
MC 84/398/532.x.4: Memoranda on Suakin-Berber railway (1884)

Royal Engineers' Museum, Chatham (Gordon Papers)
CHARE 4801.156: Gordon telegram dated 8 April 1884
CHARE.4801.39.1: Wolseley letter
CHARE.4801.45: Gordon letter to Watson, dated 6 March 1884
CHARE.7208.01: Gordon letter to cousin Amy, dated 4 March 1884
Frame: Gordon letters dated 'Kartoum 16 April' (recto) and '15.4.84 Kartoum'
    (verso)
'Gordon Letters' file
'Lady Watson's Scrapbook'

Thomas Cook Archive, Peterborough
Cook's Excursionist and Home and Tourist Advertiser (1883-5)
Ledger 16: The Sudan Campaign 1884

University of Birmingham Library (Chamberlain Papers)
5/7/30: Gladstone correspondence with Bright (1883)

University College London (Special Collections)
Contracts 142 (1874-1909) (G): Kegan Paul contract with Sir Henry Gordon
Kegan Paul Publication Accounts, Ledger 169: Financial details relating to publi-
    cation of
Hake's *Khartoum Journals*

University of Durham (Sudan Archive)
230/1-17: Wingate Papers: Materials relating to publication of Ohrwalder's *Ten
    Years Captivity in the Mahdi's Camp*
630/5-8: Brocklehurst Papers: Correspondence with and concerning Gordon
896/3-7: Stewart Papers: Correspondence and journal

University of Manchester (John Rylands Library)
R142842: National Union of Conservative and Constitutional Associations
    pamphlet:
'Publication No. 117: Gordon and the Government'

University of Reading (Special Collections)
Pamphlet Books T002 and T004: Political pamphlets relating to Sudan by Beesley,
    Coe and Hirst Hollowell

West Sussex Record Office, Chichester
Boxes 24, 25 and 65: Blunt Papers: Correspondence with Gladstone, Hake, Gordon, etc.

Secondary sources

BOOKS AND ARTICLES

ʿAbbās, Ibrāhīm Muḥammad ʿAlī. 'The British Debate on the Containment of the Sudanese Mahdist Revolution, November 1883-February 1885', *Adab* 2-3 (1975): 1-43.

ʿAbd-al-Rahman, ʿAbd-al-Wahāb Aḥmad. *Tūshka: Dirāsa tārīkhīa li-ḥamlat ʿAbd-al-Raḥman al-Nujūmi ʿala Miṣr* ('Tūshka: An Historical Study of the Campaign of ʿAbd-al-Raḥman al-Nujūmi to Egypt'). Khartoum: KUP, 1989.

Allen, Bernard. 'How Khartoum Fell'. *JRAS* 40/161 (1941): 329.

Ascherson, Neal. *The King Incorporated: Leopold II in the Age of Trusts*. London: Allen & Unwin, 1963.

Atlay, J.B. *Lord Haliburton: A Memoir of his Public Service*. Toronto: William Briggs, 1909.

Auchterlonie, Paul. 'From the Eastern Question to the Death of General Gordon: Representations of the Middle East in the Victorian Periodical Press, 1876-1885', *BJMES* 28/1 (2001): 5-24.

Balfour Browne, John. *Essays, Critical and Political*. 2 vols. London: Longmans, Green & Co., 1907.

Behrman, Cynthia. 'The After-Life of General Gordon', *Albion: A Quarterly Journal Concerned with British Studies* 3/2 (1971): 47-61.

Biagini, Eugenio. 'Exporting "Western and Beneficient Institutions": Gladstone and Empire, 1880-1885', *Gladstone Centenary Essays* (eds. David Bebbington and Roger Swift). Liverpool: LUP, 2000.

Booth, Bradford A. and Mehew, Ernest. (eds.) *The Letters of Robert Louis Stevenson*. 6 vols. New Haven: YUP, 1995.

Bray, Jean. *The Mysterious Captain Brocklehurst: General Gordon's Unknown Aide*. Cheltenham: Reardon, 2006.

Brooke, John and Sorensen, Mary. (eds.) *W.E. Gladstone, Vol. IV: Autobiographical Memoranda 1868-1894*. London: HMSO, 1981.

Callwell, Col. C.E. *Small Wars: A Tactical Textbook for Imperial Soldiers*. London: Greenhill Books, 1990.

Cecil, Lady Gewndoline. *Life of Robert, Marquis of Salisbury*. 4 vols. London: Hodder & Stoughton, 1921.

Ceulemans, R.P.P. 'Les Tentatives de Léopold II pour Engager le Colonel Charles Gordon au Service de l'Association Internationale Africaine, 1880' ('Leopold II's Attempts to Recruit Colonel Charles Gordon in the Service of the International African Association, 1880'), *Zaïre* 12 (1958): 251-74.

Chenevix Trench, Charles. *Charley Gordon: An Eminent Victorian Reassessed.* London: Allen Lane, 1978.

—— 'Gordon's Staff Officer', *History Today* 25/3 (1975): 153-63.

Churchill, Lt.-Col. Seton. *General Gordon: A Christian Hero.* London: James Nisbet & Co., Ltd., 1904.

Cole, Juan. *Colonialism and Revolution in the Middle East: Social and Cultural Origins of Egypt's ʿArābi Movement.* Princeton: PUP, 1993.

Colley, Ann. *Robert Louis Stevenson and the Colonial Imagination.* Aldershot: Ashgate, 2004.

Cook, Edward. *The Life of Florence Nightingale.* 2 vols. London: Macmillan & Co., 1913.

Cooke, A.B. and Vincent, John. *The Governing Passion: Cabinet Government and Party Politics in Britain, 1885-86.* Brighton: The Harvester Press, 1974.

Cotton, James S. and Payne, Edward J. *Colonies and Dependencies.* London: Macmillan & Co., 1883.

Cumpston, I.M. 'The Discussion of Imperial Problems in the British Parliament', *Transactions of the Royal Historical Society* 13 (1963): 29-48.

Daly, Martin. *The Sirdar: Sir Reginalf Wingate and the British Empire in the Middle East.* Philadelphia: American Philosophical Society, 1997.

Darwin, John. *The Empire Project: The Rise and Fall of the British World System, 1830-1970.* Cambridge: CUP, 2009.

Drage, Geoffrey. *Cyril: A Romantic Novel.* London: W.H. Allen & Co., Ltd., 1889.

Fabunmi, Lawrence A. M *The Sudan in Anglo-Egyptian Relations: A Case Study in Power Politics, 1800-1956.* London: Longmans, 1967.

Faught, C. Brad. *Gordon: Victorian Hero.* Washington: Potomac Books Inc., 2008.

Featherstone, Donald. *Khartoum 1885: General Gordon's Last Stand.* Oxford: Osprey, 1993.

Fenwick, Helen. *Civil Liberties and Human Rights.* Abingdon: Routledge-Cavendish, 2007.

Flint, John. *Cecil Rhodes.* London: Hutchinson, 1974.

Henderson Robb, Janet. *The Primrose League, 1883-1906.* New York: Columbia University Press, 1942.

Hill, Richard. *A Biographical Dictionary of the Sudan.* Oxford: Clarendon Press, 1967.

—— 'Review of Gerald Sparrow's Gordon: Mandarin and Pasha', *Victorian Studies* (1963): 210-12.

—— 'The Suakin-Berber Railway', *SNR* 20/1 (1937): 107-24.

Hilmy, Prince Ibrahim. *The Literature of Egypt and the Soudan.* 2 vols. London: Trübner & Co., 1885.

Holmes, John. *Dante Gabriel Rossetti and the Late Victorian Sonnet Sequence: Sexuality, Belief and the Self.* Aldershot: Ashgate, 2005.

Holt, Peter. *The Source-Materials of Sudanese Mahdīa.* Oxford: Clarendon Press, 1958.

Hopkins, A.G. 'The Victorians and Africa: A Reconsideration of the Occupation of Egypt, 1882', *JAH* 27/2 (1986): 363-91.

Hoppen, Theodore. *The Mid-Victorian Generation 1846-1886*. Oxford: Clarendon Press, 1998.

Hunter, Robert. *Egypt Under the Khedives, 1805-1879: From Household Government to Modern Bureaucracy*. Pittsburgh: UPP, 1984.

Issawi, Charles. (ed.) *The Economic History of the Middle East 1800-1914*. Chicago: UCP, 1966.

Jackson, Henry. *Black Ivory and White, or The Story of El Zubeir Pasha, Slaver and Sultan, as Told by Himself*. Oxford: B.H. Blackwell, 1913.

Kelvin, Norman. (ed.) *The Collected Letters of William Morris*. 5 vols. Princeton: PUP, 1987.

Keown-Boyd, Henry. *Soldiers of the Nile: A Biographical History of the British Officers of the Egyptian Army*. Thornbury: Thornbury Publications, 1996.

Laity, Paul. *The British Peace Movement, 1870-1914*. Oxford: Clarendon Press, 2001.

Lane-Poole, Stanley. *Watson Pasha*. London: John Murray, 1919.

Lehmann, Joseph. *All Sir Garnet: A Life of Field Marshal Wolseley*. London: Jonathan Cape, 1964.

Longford, Elizabeth. *A Pilgrimage of Passion: The Life of Wilfrid Scawen Blunt*. London: Weidenfeld & Nicolson, 1979.

Luwel, Marcel. *Sir Francis de Winton: Administrateur Général du Congo, 1884-1886*. Tervuren: Musée Royal de l'Afrique Centrale, 1964.

MacCarthy, Fiona. *William Morris: A Life for Our Time*. London: Faber & Faber, 1994.

McDiarmid, Lucy. 'Lady Gregory, Wilfrid Blunt, and London Table Talk'. *Irish University Review* 34/1 (2004): 67-80.

Magnus, Philip. *Kitchener: Portrait of an Imperialist*. London: John Murray, 1958.

Moore, Jerrold. *Edward Elgar: A Creative Life*. Oxford: OUP, 1984.

Moore-Harell, Alice. *Egypt's Africa Empire: Samuel Baker, Charles Gordon and the Creation of Equatoria*. Brighton: Sussex Academic Press, 2010.

Morley, John. *The Life of William Ewart Gladstone*. 3 vols. London: Macmillan, 1903.

Mowat, R.C. 'From Liberalism to Imperialism: The Case of Egypt 1875-1887', *HJ* 16/1 (1973): 109-24.

Newsinger, John. 'Liberal Imperialism and the Occupation of Egypt in 1882', *Race & Class* 49/3 (2008): 54-75.

Nicoll, Fergus. *An Index to the Complete Works of al-Imām al-Mahdi*. London: Nusairi Publishing, 2009.

—— *A New Bibliography of the Mahdīa*. Khartoum: Gasim Data Centre, 2010.

—— *The Sword of the Prophet: The Mahdi of Sudan and the Death of General Gordon*. Stroud: Sutton Publishing, 2004.

—— 'Three Empires on the Nile', *The Kenana Handbook of Sudan* (ed. Peter G. Hopkins). London: Kegan Paul, 2007.

—— '3000 = Mahdi; 3260 = Gordon: Breaking Cypher O', *SS* 35 (2005): 2-17.

Nightingale, Robert. *The Personnel of the British Foreign Office and Diplomatic Service, 1851-1929*. London: The Fabian Society, 1930.

Omar, Abd-al-Moneim Muḥammad. *The Soudan Question: Based on British Documents*. Cairo: Misr Press, 1952.

Owen, Roger. 'The Brismes Annual Lecture 2004: Biography and Empire: Lord Cromer (1841-1917) Then and Now', *BJMES* 32/1 (2005).

—— 'The Influence of Lord Cromer's Indian Experience on British Policy in Egypt 1883-1907', *St Antony's Papers* 17 (1965).

—— *Lord Cromer: Victorian Imperialist, Edwardian Proconsul*. Oxford: OUP, 2004.

Porter, Bernard. *The Absent-Minded Imperialists: Empire, Society, and Culture in Britain*. Oxford: OUP, 2004.

Preston, Adrian. 'Wolseley, the Khartoum Relief Expedition and the Defence of India, 1885-1900', *JICH* 6/3 (1978): 254-80.

Raugh, Harold. *The Victorians At War, 1815-1914: An Encyclopedia of British Military History*. New York: ABC-CLIO Ltd., 2004.

Reid, J.A. 'The Mahdi's Emirs', *SNR* 20 (1937): 308-12.

Richards, Jeffrey. *Imperialism and Music*. Manchester: MUP, 2001.

Robinson, Rev. C.H. 'Hausa Pilgrimages from the Western Sudan, Together with a Native Account of the Death of General Gordon'. *The Geographical Journal* 2/5 (1893): 451-4.

Robinson, Ronald E. 'Imperial Problems in British Politics, 1880-1895', *The Cambridge History of the British Empire* (eds.: J. Holland Rose, A. P. Newton and E. A. Benians). 9 vols. Cambridge: CUP, 1929-61.

—— and Gallagher, John (with Denny, Alice) (eds.) *Africa and the Victorians: The Official Mind of Imperialism*. London: Macmillan, 1961.

Rundle Charles, Elizabeth. *Three Martyrs of the Nineteenth Century: Studies from the Lives of Livingstone, Gordon, and Patteson*. London: Society for Promoting Christian Knowledge, 1885.

Russell, Bertrand. *Freedom and Organization (1814-1914)*. London: Allen & Unwin, 1934.

Salmon, Nicholas. *The William Morris Chronology*. Bristol: Thoemmes Press, 1996.

Sanderson, G.N. 'Contributions from African Sources to the History of European Competition in the Upper Valley of the Nile', *JAH* 3/1 (1962): 69-90.

—— *England, Europe and the Upper Nile, 1882-1899: A Study in the Partition of Africa*. Edinburgh: EUP, 1965.

al-Sayyid, Afaf Lutfi. *Egypt and Cromer: A Study in Anglo-Egyptian Relations*. London: John Murray, 1968.

Seeley, Prof. Sir John. *The Expansion of England: Two Courses of Lectures*. London: Macmillan, 1883.

Shannon, Richard. *Gladstone: Heroic Minister 1865-1898*. London: Allen Lane, 1999.

Shibeika, Makkī. *British Policy in the Sudan 1882-1902*. London: Geoffrey Cumberledge, 1952.

Stengers, Par J. 'Une Facette de la Question du Haut-Nil: Le Mirage Soudanais' ('An Aspect of the Upper Nile Question: The Sudanese Mirage'), *JAH* 10/4 (1969): 599-622.

Strachey, Lytton. *Eminent Victorians*. London: Chatto & Windus, 1918.

Theobald, Alan B. *The Mahdīya: A History of the Anglo-Egyptian Sudan, 1881-1899*. London: Longmans, 1951.

Thompson, Andrew. *The Empire Strikes Back? The Impact of Imperialism on Britain from the Mid-Nineteenth Century*. London: Longman, 2005.

Thompson, Edward. *William Morris: Romantic to Revolutionary*. London: Lawrence & Wishart, 1955.

Traill, Henry. *England, Egypt, and the Sudan*. London: Archibald Constable & Co., Ltd., 1900.

—— *Lord Cromer: A Biography*. London: Bliss, Sands & Co., 1897.

Tvedt, Terje. *The River Nile and its Economic, Political, Social and Cultural Role: An Annotated Bibliography*. Bergen: UBP, 2000.

—— *The River Nile in the Age of the British: Political Ecology and the Quest for Economic Power*. London: I.B. Tauris, 2004.

Wallace, Donald Mackenzie. *Egypt and the Egyptian Question*. London: Macmillan, 1883.

Watson, Col. Sir Charles M. 'The Campaign of Gordon's Steamers', *Sudan Notes and Records* 12/2 (1929): 119-41.

Watson, William. *The Collected Poems of William Watson*. London: John Lane, 1899.

Welsby, Derek. *Sudan's First Railway: The Gordon Relief Expedition and the Dongola Campaign*. London: Sudan Archaeological Research Society, 2011.

Wilson, Robert. *The Life and Times of Queen Victoria*. 4 vols. London: Cassell, 1901.

Wingate, F. Reginald. *Mahdiism and the Egyptian Soudan*. London: Macmillan, 1891.

THESES AND LECTURES

Laffer, Stephanie. 'Gordon's Ghosts: British Major-General Charles George Gordon and his Legacies'. Tallahassee: Florida State University PhD thesis, 2010.

Little, Tony. 'Gladstone, Granville and Ireland, 1885-6'. Lecture given at Gladstone Conference, Hawarden Castle, 2010.

Willy, Todd Gray. 'The Agitation in Parliament and England over Charles George "Chinese" Gordon and his Mission to the Sudan: January 1884 to February 1885'. Iowa City: University of Iowa PhD thesis, 1962.

Index